MACROMEDIA® FLASH™ MX
COMPLETE DESIGN PROFESSIONAL

D1305104

MACROMEDIA® FLASH™ MX
COMPLETE
DESIGN PROFESSIONAL

JAMES LINDSAY • PIYUSH PATEL • JIM SHUMAN

THOMSON
COURSE TECHNOLOGY

Macromedia® Flash™ MX Complete—Design Professional
By James Lindsay, Piyush Patel, and Jim Shuman

Managing Editor:
Nicole Jones Pinard

Senior Product Manager:
Rebecca Berardy

Product Manager:
Christina Kling Garrett

Editorial Assistant:
Elizabeth Harris

Production Editor:
Melissa Panagos

Development Editor:
Barbara Waxer

Composition House:
GEX Publishing Services

QA Manuscript Reviewers:
Chris Carvalho, Shawn Day,
John Freitas, Christian Kunciw,

Danielle Shaw, Marianne Snow,
and Susan Whalen

Text Designer:
Ann Small

Illustrator:
Philip Brooker

Cover Design:
Philip Brooker

For permission to use material from this text or product, contact us by
Tel (800) 730-2214
Fax (800) 730-2215
www.thomsonrights.com

ISBN 0-619-01766-X

Design Professional Series Vision

The Design Professional Series is your guide to today's hottest multimedia applications. These comprehensive books teach the skills behind the application, showing you how to apply smart design principles to multimedia products, such as dynamic graphics, animation, Web sites, software authoring tools, and video.

A team of design professionals including multimedia instructors, students, authors, and editors worked together to create this series. We recognized the unique learning environment of the digital media or multimedia classroom and have created a series that:

- Gives you comprehensive step-by-step instructions
- Offers in-depth explanation of the "why" behind a skill
- Includes creative projects for additional practice
- Explains concepts clearly using full-color visuals

It was our goal to create a book that speaks directly to the multimedia and design community—one of the most rapidly growing computer fields today. This series was designed to appeal to the creative spirit. We would like to thank Philip Brooker for developing the inspirational artwork found on each unit opener and book cover. We would also like to give special thanks to Ann Small of A Small Design Studio for developing a sophisticated and instructive book design.

—The Design Professional Series

Author Vision

Writing a textbook on an animation program is quite challenging. How do you take such a feature-rich program like Macromedia Flash MX and put it in a context that helps students learn? Our goal is to provide a comprehensive, yet manageable, introduction to Macromedia Flash MX—just enough conceptual information to provide the needed context, and then move right into working with the application. Our thought is that you'll get so caught up in the hands-on activities and compelling projects that you'll be pleasantly surprised at the level of Macromedia Flash MX skills and knowledge you've acquired at the end of each unit.

What a joy it has been to be a part of such a creative and energetic team. The new Design Professional Series is a great format for teaching and learning Macromedia Flash MX, and the Design Professional Series team took the ball and ran with it. We would like to thank Nicole Pinard, who provided the vision for the project, and everyone at Course Technology for their professional guidance.

A special thanks to Barbara Waxer for her editorial expertise and encouragement. We would like to thank the reviewers—Tyler Feikema, the University of Health Sciences; Brenda Jacobsen, Idaho State University; and David Rhugnanan, Miami Dade Community College. The reviewing team at Macromedia—Angela Drury, Bentley Wolfe, and Jason Wylie—also added their technical expertise to the book, for which we are grateful.

—The Authors

I want to give a heartfelt thanks to my wife, Barbara, for her patience and support.

—Jim Shuman

I would like to thank my wife, Lisa, and son, Nicholas, for their support. You inspire me to be the man I am. Lastly I would like to thank my Multi-Media & Digital Communications' family, Tanya, Kyle, and Brad for their support, expertise, and freeing up time to let me finish this project.

—Piyush Patel

I would like to dedicate this book to Laurie and Philip, who keep my life as animated as a Flash Web site.

—James Lindsay

SERIES & AUTHOR VISION

v

Introduction

Welcome to *Macromedia® Flash™ MX Complete—Design Professional*. This book offers creative projects, concise instructions, and complete coverage of basic to advanced Macromedia Flash MX skills, helping you to create and publish Flash animation. Use this book both in the classroom and as your own reference guide.

This text is organized into eleven units. In these units, you will learn many skills to create interesting, graphics-rich movies that include sound, animation, and interactivity. In addition, you will learn how to publish your Flash movies.

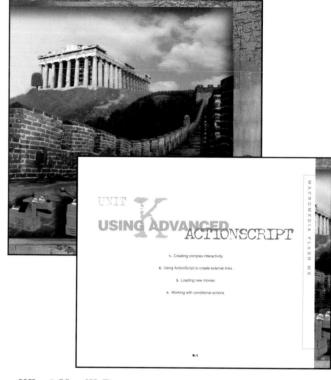

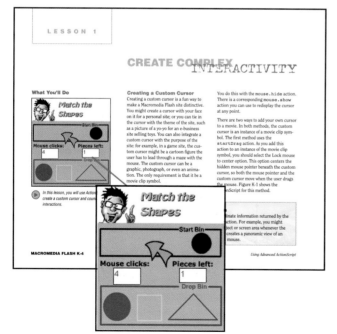

What You'll Do

A What You'll Do figure begins every lesson. This figure gives you an at-a-glance look at the skills covered in the unit and shows you the completed data file for that lesson. Before you start the lesson, you will know—both on a technical and artistic level—what you will be creating.

Comprehensive Conceptual Lessons

Before jumping into instructions, in-depth conceptual information tells you "why" skills are applied. This book provides the "how" and "why" through the use of professional examples. Also included in the text are helpful tips and sidebars to help you work more efficiently and creatively.

Step-by-Step Instructions

This book combines in-depth conceptual information with concise steps to help you learn Macromedia Flash MX. Each set of steps guides you through a lesson where you will apply tasks to a Macromedia Flash MX data file. Step references to large colorful images and quick step summaries round out the lessons.

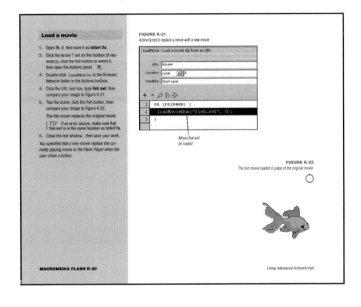

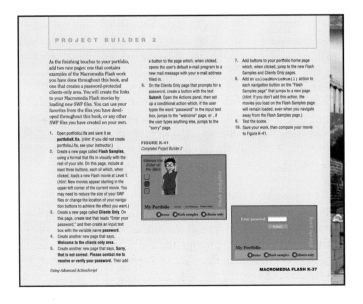

Projects

This book contains a variety of end-of-unit material for additional practice and reinforcement. The Skills Review contains hands-on practice exercises that mirror the progressive nature of the lesson material. The unit concludes with four projects: two Project Builders, one Design Project, and one Group Project. The Project Builders require you to apply the skills you've learned in the unit to build a Web site and portfolio. Design Projects explore design principles by sending you to the Web to view Macromedia Flash animation. Group Projects encourage group activity as students use the resources of a team to create a project.

A series of QuickTime movies are included on the Instructor's Resource CD-ROM. These movies will guide students through a capstone project—one project that incorporates the skills of the book.

What Instructor Resources are Available with this Book?

The Instructor's Resource CD-ROM is Course Technology's way of putting the resources and information needed to teach and learn effectively into your hands. All the resources are available for both Macintosh and Windows operating systems, and many of the resources can be downloaded from *www.course.com*.

Instructor's Manual

Available as an electronic file, the Instructor's Manual is quality-assurance tested and includes unit overviews and detailed lecture topics with teaching tips for each unit. The Instructor's Manual is available on the Instructor's Resource CD-ROM, or you can download it from *www.course.com*.

Syllabus

Prepare and customize your course easily using this sample course outline (available on the Instructor's Resource CD-ROM).

PowerPoint Presentations

Each unit has a corresponding PowerPoint presentation that you can use in lecture, distribute to your students, or customize to suit your course.

Figure Files

Figure Files contain all the figures from the book in bitmap format. Use the figure files to create transparency masters or in a PowerPoint presentation.

Data Files for Students

To complete most of the units in this book, your students will need Data Files. Put them on a file server for students to copy. The Data Files are available on the Instructor's Resource CD-ROM, the Review Pack, and can also be downloaded from *www.course.com*. Instruct students to use the Data Files List at the end of this book. This list gives instructions on copying and organizing files.

Solutions to Exercises

Solution Files are Data Files completed with comprehensive sample answers. Use these files to evaluate your students' work. Or, distribute them electronically or in hard copy so students can verify their work. Sample solutions to all lessons and end-of-unit material are provided.

Test Bank and Test Engine

ExamView is a powerful testing software package that allows instructors to create and administer printed, computer (LAN-based), and Internet exams. ExamView includes hundreds of questions that correspond to the topics covered in this text, enabling students to generate detailed study guides that include page references for further review. The computer-based and Internet testing components allow students to take exams at their computers, and also save the instructor time by grading each exam automatically.

Additional Activities for Students

We have included a capstone project, which asks your students to use the skills of the book to build one project. The project is delivered to your students through a series of QuickTime movies found only on *www.course.com* or on the Instructor's Resource CD-ROM.

We have included **Macromedia Fundamentals** interactive training tutorials to help students learn the basics of each of the applications in Macromedia Studio MX.

BRIEF CONTENTS

ix

UNIT C   WORKING WITH SYMBOLS AND INTERACTIVITY

CONTENTS

UNIT E CREATING SPECIAL EFFECTS

CONTENTS

UNIT H   BUILDING COMPLEX ANIMATIONS

CONTENTS

CONTENTS

UNIT J   ADDING SOUNDS

CONTENTS

UNIT K   **USING ADVANCED ACTIONSCRIPT**

Intended Audience

This text is designed for the beginner or intermediate student who wants to learn how to use Macromedia Flash MX. The book is designed to provide basic and in-depth material that not only educates, but encourages the student to explore the nuances of this exciting program.

Approach

The text allows you to work at your own pace through step-by-step tutorials. A concept is presented and the process is explained, followed by the actual steps. To learn the most from the use of the text, you should adopt the following habits:

- Proceed slowly: Accuracy and comprehension is more important than speed.
- Understand what is happening with each step before you continue to the next step.
- After finishing a process, ask yourself: Can I do the process on my own? If the answer is no, review the steps.

Icons, Buttons, and Pointers

Symbols for icons, buttons, and pointers are shown at the end of the step each time they are used.

Fonts

Data and Solution Files contain a variety of commonly used fonts, but there is no guarantee that these fonts will be available on your computer. Each font is identified in cases where fonts other than Arial or Times New Roman are used. If any of the fonts in use are not available on your computer, you can make a substitution, realizing that the results may vary from those in the book.

Grading Tips

Many students have Web-ready accounts to which they can post their completed assignments. The instructor can access the student accounts using a browser and view the image online.

Creating a Portfolio

One method for students to submit and keep a copy of all of their work is to create a portfolio of their projects that they link to a simple Web page and that can be saved on a CD-ROM.

Windows and Macintosh

Macromedia Flash MX works virtually the same on Windows and Macintosh operating systems. In those cases where there is a difference, the abbreviations (Win) and (Mac) are used.

Windows System Requirements

Macromedia Flash MX runs under Windows 98 SE, Windows ME, Windows NT 4.0, Windows 2000, and Windows XP. For Windows operating systems, Macromedia Flash MX requires an Intel 200 MHz or equivalent processor, 64 MB of RAM (128 recommended), 85 MB of disk space, a 16-bit color monitor capable of displaying a resolution at 1024×768, and a CD-ROM drive.

Macintosh System Requirements

Macromedia Flash MX runs under Mac OS 9.1 (or later) and Mac OS X version 10.1 (or later). For Macintosh operating systems, Macromedia Flash MX requires a Power Macintosh, 64 MB of RAM (128 MB recommended), 85 MB of disk space, a 16-bit color monitor capable of displaying a resolution at 1024×768, and a CD-ROM drive.

Data Files

To complete the lessons and end-of-unit material in this book, you need to obtain the necessary Data Files. Please refer to the directions on the inside back cover for various methods to obtain these files. Once obtained, select where to store the files, such as the hard drive, a network server, or a zip drive. The instructions in the lessons will refer to "the drive and folder where your Data Files are stored" when referring to the Data Files for the book.

Projects

Several projects are presented at the end of each unit that allow students to apply the skills they have learned in the unit. Two projects, Ultimate Tours and the Portfolio, build from unit to unit. You will need to contact your instructor if you plan to work on these without having completed the previous unit's project.

Dreamweaver MX

Unit F discusses transferring Macromedia Flash files from your computer to a Web server on the Internet so that the files can be used in a Web site. Macromedia Dreamweaver MX is a Web site development tool and has a feature that allows you to transfer Macromedia Flash files to a Web server. You will need to have access to the Macromedia Dreamweaver MX program to complete some of the steps in Unit F. If you do not have Macromedia Dreamweaver MX, steps are also given to create a remote site and use FTP to transfer files.

UNIT A

GETTING STARTED WITH MACROMEDIA FLASH

1. Understand the Macromedia Flash environment.

2. Open a document and play a movie.

3. Create and save a movie.

4. Work with layers and the timeline.

5. Plan a Web site.

6. Distribute a Macromedia Flash movie.

UNIT A
GETTING STARTED WITH MACROMEDIA FLASH

Introduction

Macromedia Flash is a program that allows you to create compelling interactive experiences, primarily by using animation. Yet, while it is known as a tool for creating complex animations for the Web, Macromedia Flash also has excellent drawing tools and tools for creating interactive controls, such as navigation buttons and menus. In addition, you can use its publishing capabilities to create Web sites and Web-based applications.

In only a few short years, Macromedia Flash has become the standard for both professional and casual Web developers. The reason that Macromedia Flash has become so popular is that the program is optimized for the Web. Web developers try to provide high-impact experiences for the user, to make sites come alive and turn them from static text and pictures to dynamic, interactive experiences. The problem has been that incorporating high-quality graphics and motion into a Web site can dramatically increase the download time and frustrate viewers as they wait for an image to appear or for an animation to play. Macromedia Flash directly addresses this problem by allowing developers to use vector images, which reduce the size of graphic files. Vector images appeal to developers for two reasons. First, they are scalable, which means they can be resized and reshaped without distortion. For example, you could easily have an object, such as an airplane, become smaller as it moves across the screen without having to create the plane in different sizes. Second, Macromedia Flash provides for streaming content over the Internet. Instead of waiting for the entire contents of a Web page to load, the viewer sees a continuous display of images. For example, if your Web site has a Macromedia Flash movie that is played when the viewer first visits your Web site, the viewer does not have to wait for the entire movie to be downloaded before it starts. Streaming allows the movie to start playing when the Web site is opened, and it continues as frames of the movie are delivered to the viewer's computer.

Tools You'll Use

Toolbox

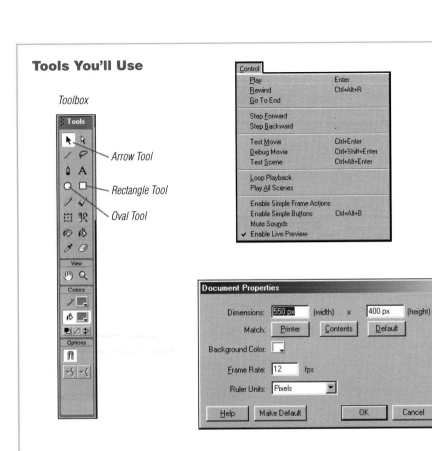

Arrow Tool

Rectangle Tool

Oval Tool

Window

New Window	Ctrl+Alt+N
Toolbars	▶
✓ Tools	Ctrl+F2
✓ Timeline	Ctrl+Alt+T
✓ Properties	Ctrl+F3
Answers	Alt+F1
Align	Ctrl+K
Color Mixer	Shift+F9
Color Swatches	Ctrl+F9
Info	Ctrl+I
Scene	Shift+F2
Transform	Ctrl+T
Actions	F9
Debugger	Shift+F4
Movie Explorer	Alt+F3
Reference	Shift+F1
Output	F2
Accessibility	Alt+F2
Components	Ctrl+F7
Component Parameters	Alt+F7
Library	F11
Common Libraries	▶
Sitespring	
Panel Sets	▶
Save Panel Layout...	
Close All Panels	
Cascade	
Tile	
✓ 1 Untitled-7	

Document Properties

Dimensions: [550 px] (width) x [400 px] (height)

Match: [Printer] [Contents] [Default]

Background Color: [ ]

Frame Rate: [12] fps

Ruler Units: [Pixels ▼]

[Help] [Make Default] [OK] [Cancel]

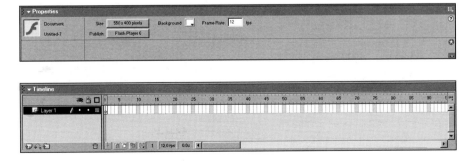

Controller

UNDERSTAND THE MACROMEDIA FLASH ENVIRONMENT

What You'll Do

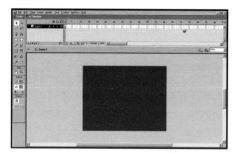

 In this lesson, you will learn about the development environment in Macromedia Flash and how to change Macromedia Flash settings to customize your workspace.

Organizing the Macromedia Flash Development Environment

As a developer, one of the most important things to do is to organize your workspace—that is, to decide what to have displayed on the screen and how to arrange the various tools and windows. Because **Macromedia Flash** is such a powerful program with many tools, your workspace may become cluttered. Fortunately, it is easy to customize the workspace to display only the tools needed at any particular time.

The development environment in Macromedia Flash operates according to a movie metaphor: you create scenes on a stage; these scenes run in frames on a timeline. As you work in Macromedia Flash, you create a movie by arranging objects (such as graphics and text) on the stage, and animate the objects using the

timeline. You can play the movie on the stage, as you are working on it, by using the movie controls (start, stop, rewind, and so on). In addition, you can test the movie in a browser. When the movie is ready for distribution, you can export it as a Macromedia Flash Player movie, which viewers can access using a Macromedia Flash Player. A Macromedia Flash Player is a program that is installed on the viewer's computer to allow Macromedia Flash movies to be played in Web browsers or as stand-alone applications. Millions of people have installed the Macromedia Flash Player (a free download from the Macromedia Web site), allowing them to view and interact with Macromedia Flash movies and Web applications. Macromedia Flash movies can also be saved as executable files, called projectors, which can be viewed without the need for the Macromedia Flash Player.

When you start Macromedia Flash, three basic parts of the development environment are displayed: the stage, the timeline, and the workspace. In addition, you can choose to have other parts of the program displayed. You use the toolbox to create and edit graphics, and you use panels to control the characteristics and change the attributes of selected objects. A description of the Macromedia Flash development environment follows.

Stage

The stage contains all of the objects that are part of the movie that will be seen by your viewers. It shows how the objects behave within the movie and how they interact with each other. You can resize the stage and change the background color applied to it. You can draw objects on or import objects to the stage, and then edit and animate them.

Timeline

The timeline is used to organize and control the movie's contents by specifying when each object appears on the stage. The timeline is critical to the creation of movies, because a movie is merely a series of still images that appear over time. The images are contained within frames, which are units of the timeline. Frames in a Macromedia Flash movie are similar to frames in a motion picture. When a Macromedia Flash movie is played, a playhead moves from frame to frame in the timeline, causing the contents of each frame to appear on the stage in a linear sequence.

The timeline indicates where you are at any time within the movie and allows you to insert, delete, select, and move frames. It shows the animation in your movie and the layers that contain objects. Layers help to organize the objects on the stage. You can draw and edit objects on one layer without affecting objects on other layers. Layers are a way to stack objects so they can overlap and give a 3-D appearance on the stage.

Toolbox

The toolbox contains a set of tools used to draw and edit graphics and text. It is divided into four sections.

Tools—Includes draw, paint, text, and selection tools, which are used to create lines, shapes, illustrations, and text. The selection tools are used to select objects so that they can be modified in a number of ways.

View—Includes the Zoom Tool and the Hand Tool, which are used to zoom in on and out of parts of the stage and to pan the stage window, respectively.

Colors—Includes tools and icons used to change the stroke (border of an object) and fill (area inside an object) colors.

Options—Includes options for selected tools, such as allowing you to choose the size of the brush when using the Brush Tool.

Panels

Panels are used to view, organize, and modify objects and features in a movie. For example, the Properties panel (also called the Property Inspector) is used to change the properties of an object, such as the fill color of a circle. The Properties panel is context sensitive so that if you are working with text it displays the appropriate options, such as font and font size.

Although several panels are available, you may choose to display them only when they are needed. This keeps your workspace from becoming too cluttered. The toolbox and panels are floating elements, meaning that you can move them around the workspace. This allows you to dock (link) panels together as a way of organizing them in the workspace. You can also make room in the workspace by collapsing panels so only their title bars are displayed.

Regardless of how you decide to customize your development environment, the stage and the menu bar are always displayed. Usually, you display the timeline, toolbox, and one or more panels. Figure A-1 shows the Macromedia Flash default development environment with the stage, timeline, toolbox, and panels displayed.

When you start a new Macromedia Flash document (movie), you can set the document properties, such as the size of the window (stage) the movie will play in, the background color, and the speed of the movie in frames per second. You can change these settings using the Document command on the Modify menu. To increase the size of the stage so that the objects on the stage can be more easily edited, you can change the magnification setting using commands on the View menu.

FIGURE A-1

Macromedia Flash default development environment

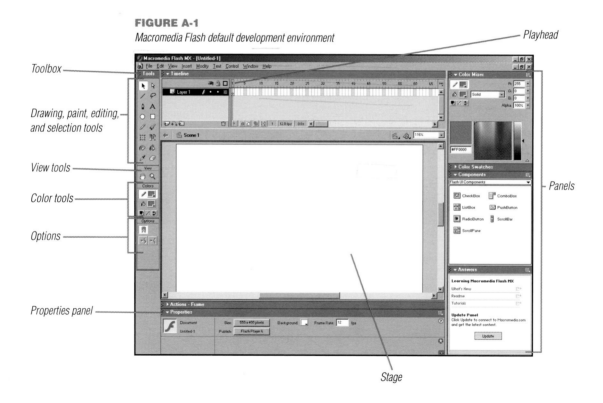

Toolbox

Drawing, paint, editing, and selection tools

View tools

Color tools

Options

Properties panel

Playhead

Panels

Stage

FIGURE A-2
Document Properties dialog box

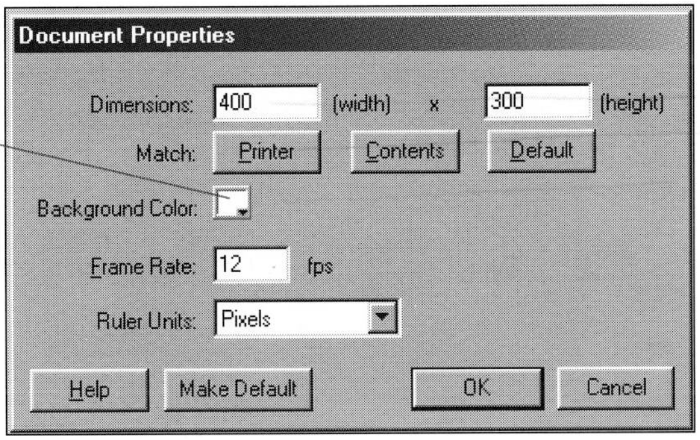

Click Background color swatch to change background color

Document Properties
Dimensions: `400` (width) x `300` (height)
Match: [Printer] [Contents] [Default]
Background Color: [ ]
Frame Rate: `12` fps
Ruler Units: [Pixels ▾]
[Help] [Make Default]   [OK] [Cancel]

1. Click the Start button on the taskbar, point to All Programs, point to the Macromedia folder, then click the Macromedia Flash MX program icon (Win). 🪁

   TIP If you are starting Macromedia Flash on a Macintosh, double-click the hard drive icon, double-click the Applications folder, double-click the Macromedia Flash MX folder, and then double-click the Macromedia Flash MX program icon. 🪁

2. Click the Maximize button in the movie title bar, if necessary.

3. Click Window on the menu bar, then verify that Properties is checked.

4. Click the Document properties button in the Property inspector to display the Document Properties dialog box. `550 x 400 pixels`

5. Double-click the width text box (if necessary), type **400**, double-click the height text box, then type **300**.

6. Click the Background Color swatch, shown in Figure A-2, then click the blue color swatch on the left column of the color palette. ■

(continued)

7. Accept the remaining default values, then click OK to close the Document Properties dialog box.

8. Drag the scroll bars at the bottom and the right of the screen to center the stage.

9. Click View on the menu bar, point to Magnification, then click 100%.

10. Click 100% in the View magnification box at the top of the stage, as shown in Figure A-3, type **90**, and then press [Enter] (Win) or [return] (Mac).

11. Click File on the menu bar, click Save As, then save your file as **devenvironment.fla**.

You started the Macromedia Flash program, set the document properties and background color, then named the movie.

FIGURE A-3
View magnification box

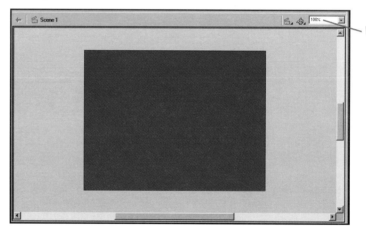

View magnification box

FIGURE A-4

The Properties panel

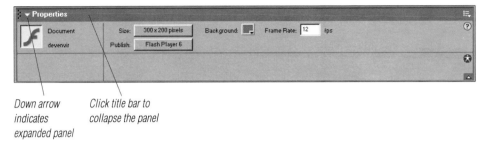

*Down arrow
indicates
expanded panel*

*Click title bar to
collapse the panel*

Change panel display

1. Click Window on the menu bar, point to Panel Sets, then click Default Layout.

2. Click the Property inspector title bar to collapse the panel, as shown in Figure A-4 (Win).

   Only the title bar displays.

3. Click the Property inspector title bar to expand the panel (Win).

4. Right-click (Win) the Property inspector title bar, then click Close Panel, or click the circled X in the upper-left corner (Mac) to close the panel and remove it from the workspace.

5. Click Window on the menu bar, then click Close All Panels.

   Instead of removing the panels from the workspace, the Close All Panels option collapses all panels so that only their title bars are displayed (Win), or the panels close (Mac).

6. Right-click (Win) the title bar of each panel, then click Close Panel to close each panel.

7. Click Window on the menu bar, then click Properties.

   The Property inspector displays fully.

8. Click File on the menu bar, then click Close.

You customized the development environment by displaying panels, using the default panel layout, and collapsing and closing panels.

Understanding your workspace

Organizing the Macromedia Flash development environment is like organizing your desktop. You may work more efficiently if you have many of the most commonly used items in view and ready to use. Alternately, you may work better if your workspace is relatively uncluttered, giving you more free "desk space." Fortunately, Macromedia Flash makes it easy for you to decide which items to display and how they are arranged while you work. You should become familiar with quickly opening and closing the various windows and panels in Macromedia Flash, and experimenting with different layouts and screen resolutions to find the environment that works best for you.

OPEN A DOCUMENT AND PLAY A MOVIE

What You'll Do

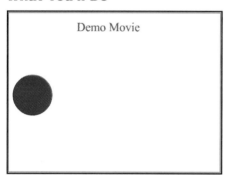

Demo Movie

 In this lesson, you will open a Macromedia Flash document (movie) and then preview, test, and save the movie.

Opening a Movie in Macromedia Flash

Macromedia Flash gives movies a .fla file extension. For example, if you have created a movie and saved it with the name mymovie, the file name will be mymovie.fla. Files with the .fla file extension can only be opened using Macromedia Flash. After they are opened, you can edit and resave them. Another file format for Macromedia Flash movies is the Macromedia Flash Player (.swf) format. These files are created from Macromedia Flash movies using the Publish command, which allows them to be played in a browser without the Macromedia Flash program. However, the viewer would need to have the Macromedia Flash Player installed on his or her computer. Because .swf files cannot be edited in the Macromedia Flash program, you should preview movies on the stage and test them before you publish them. Be sure to keep the original .fla file so that you can make changes at a later date.

Previewing a Movie

After opening a Macromedia Flash movie, you can preview it within the development environment in several ways. When you preview a movie, you play the frames by directing the playhead to move through the timeline, and you watch it on the stage.

Control menu commands (and keyboard shortcuts)

Figure A-5 shows the Control menu commands, which resemble common VCR-type options:

- Play ([Enter] (Win) or [return] (Mac)) begins playing the movie, frame by frame, from the location of the playhead and continuing until the end of the movie. For example, if the playhead is on Frame 5 and the last frame is Frame 40, choosing the Play command will play Frames 5–40 of the movie.

Play / Stop [return]

QUICKTIP

When a movie starts, the Play command changes to a Stop command. You can also stop the movie by pressing [Enter] (Win) or [return] (Mac).

- Rewind ([Ctrl][Alt][R] (Win)) or [alt] [command][R] (Mac) moves the playhead to Frame 1.
- Step Forward (.) moves the playhead forward one frame at a time.
- Step Backward (,) moves the playhead backward one frame at a time.

You can turn on the Loop Playback setting to allow the movie to continue playing repeatedly. A check mark next to the Loop Playback command on the Control menu indicates that the feature is turned on. To turn off this feature, click the command.

Controller

You can also preview a movie using the Controller, shown in Figure A-6. To display the Controller, click the Controller option on the Toolbar command of the Window menu (Win), or click the Controller command on the Window menu (Mac).

QUICKTIP

The decision of which controls to use (the Control menu, keyboard shortcuts, or the Controller) is a matter of personal preference.

Testing a Movie

When you preview a movie, some interactive functions, such as buttons, that are used to jump from one part of the movie to another, do not work unless the movie is played using a Macromedia Flash Player. You can use the Test Movie command on the Control menu to test the movie using the Macromedia Flash Player.

FIGURE A-5
Control menu commands

VCR-type commands

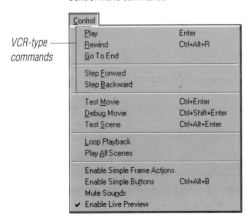

FIGURE A-6
Controller toolbar

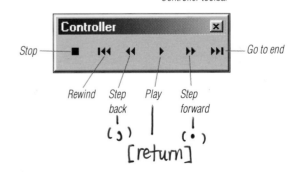

Stop — Go to end

Rewind   Step   Play   Step
         back   forward

[return]

Open and play a movie using the Control menu and the Controller

1. Open fla_1.fla from the drive and folder where your data files are stored for Unit A, then save it as **demomovie.fla**.

2. Click Control on the menu bar, click Play, then notice how the playhead moves across the timeline, as shown in Figure A-7.

3. Click Control on the menu bar, then click Rewind.

4. Press [Enter] (Win) or [return] (Mac) to play the movie, then press [Enter] (Win) or [return] (Mac) again to stop the movie before it ends.

5. Click Window on the menu bar, point to Toolbars (Win), then click Controller.

6. Use all of the Controller buttons to preview the movie, then close the Controller.

7. Click Control on the menu bar, click Loop Playback to turn it on, then play the movie.

   The movie plays continuously.

8. After viewing the movie looping, click Control on the menu bar, then click Loop Playback to turn it off.

9. Save your work.

You opened a Macromedia Flash movie and previewed it in the development environment, using various controls.

FIGURE A-7
Playhead moving across timeline

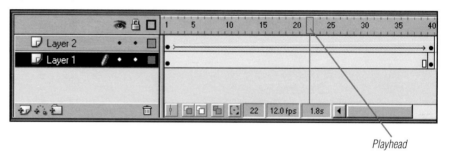

Playhead

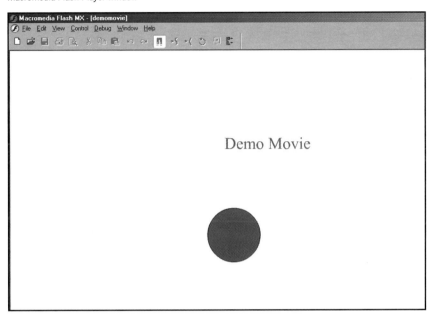

Test a movie

1. Click Control on the menu bar, then click Test Movie to view the movie in the Macromedia Flash Player window, as shown in Figure A-8.

2. Click Control on the menu bar, noting the respective commands.

3. Click File on the menu bar, then click Close to close the Macromedia Flash Player window.

   TIP   When you test a movie, Macromedia Flash automatically runs the movie in Macromedia Flash Player, which creates a file that has a .swf extension in the folder where your movie is stored.

4. Close demomovie.fla.

You tested a movie in the Macromedia Flash Player window.

Using the Macromedia Flash Player

In order to view a Macromedia Flash movie on the Web, your computer needs to have the Macromedia Flash Player installed. An important feature of multimedia players, such as Macromedia Flash Player, is that they can decompress a file that has been compressed to give it a small file size that can be more quickly delivered over the Internet. In addition to Macromedia, companies such as Apple, Microsoft, and RealNetworks create players that allow applications, developed with their and other company's products, to be viewed on the Web. The multimedia players are distributed free and can be downloaded from the company's Web site. The Macromedia Flash Player is created by Macromedia and is available at *www.macromedia.com/downloads*.

CREATE AND SAVE A MOVIE

What You'll Do

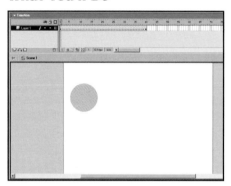

In this lesson, you will create a Macromedia Flash movie that will include a simple animation, and then save the movie.

Creating a Macromedia Flash Movie

Macromedia Flash movies are created by placing objects (graphics, text, sounds, photos, and so on) on the stage, editing these objects (for example, changing their brightness), animating the objects, and adding interactivity with buttons and menus. You can create graphic objects in Macromedia Flash using the drawing tools, or you can develop them in another program, such as Macromedia Fireworks or Adobe Photoshop, and then import them into a Macromedia Flash movie. In addition, you can acquire clip art and stock photographs and import them into a movie. When objects are placed on the stage, they are automatically placed in a layer and in the currently selected frame of the timeline.

Figure A-9 shows a movie that has an oval object created in Macromedia Flash. Notice that the playhead is on Frame 1 of the movie. The objects placed on the stage appear in Frame 1 and appear on the stage when the playback head is on Frame 1. The dot in Frame 1 on the timeline indicates that this frame is a keyframe. A keyframe is always the first frame of every animation and is also a frame you can add that allows you to define a change in an animation.

The oval object in Figure A-9 was created using the Oval Tool. To create an oval or a rectangle, you select the desired tool and then drag the pointer over an area on the stage. If you want to draw a perfect circle or square, press and hold [Shift] when the tool is selected, and then drag the shape. If you make a mistake, you can click Edit on the menu bar, and then click Undo. In order to edit an object, you must first select it. You can use the Arrow Tool to select an entire object or group of objects. You drag the Arrow Tool pointer around the entire object to make a marquee selection. An object that has been selected displays a dot pattern.

Creating an Animation

Figure A-10 shows another movie that has 40 frames, as specified in the timeline. <u>The arrow</u> in the timeline indicates a motion animation. In this case, the object will move from left to right across the stage. The movement of the object is caused by having the object in different places on the stage in different frames of the movie. A basic motion animation requires two keyframes. The first keyframe sets the starting position of the object, and the second keyframe sets the ending position of the object. The number of frames between the two keyframes determines the length of the animation. For example, if the starting keyframe is Frame 1 and the ending keyframe is Frame 40, the object will be animated for 40 frames. Once the two keyframes are set, Macromedia Flash automatically fills in the frames between them, with a process called motion tweening.

Adding an Effect to an Object

In addition to animating the location of an object (or objects), you can also animate an object's appearance; for example, <u>its shape, color, brightness, or transparency.</u> The color of the circle on the left of the stage in Figure A-10 has been lightened using the Brightness effect on the Property inspector. When the movie is played, the color of the circle will start out light and then become darker as it moves to the right.

FIGURE A-9

Oval object in Frame 1

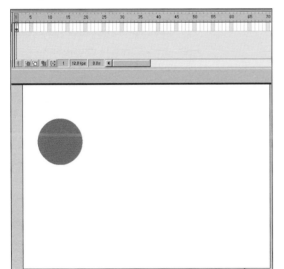

FIGURE A-10

Motion animation

Arrow indicates motion animation

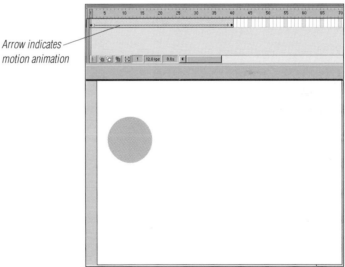

perfect circle —> hold [shift] when the tool is selected
or square

Create objects using drawing tools

1. Click File on the menu bar, click New, then save the movie as **tween.fla**.

2. Click the Oval Tool on the toolbox.

3. Click the Fill Color Tool on the toolbox, then, if necessary, click the red color swatch in the left column of the color palette.

4. Press and hold [Shift], then drag the Oval Tool on the stage to draw the circle shown in Figure A-11.

5. Click the Arrow Tool on the toolbox, then drag a marquee selection around the object to select it, as shown in Figure A-12.

   The object appears covered with a dot pattern.

6. Save your work.

You created an object using the Oval Tool and then selected the object using the Arrow Tool.

Create basic animation

1. Click Insert on the menu bar, then click Create Motion Tween.

   A blue border surrounds the object.

2. Click Frame 40 on Layer 1 of the timeline.

3. Click Insert on the menu bar, then click Keyframe.

   A second keyframe is defined in Frame 40, and Frames 1–40 appear shaded.

   (continued)

FIGURE A-11
Drawing a circle

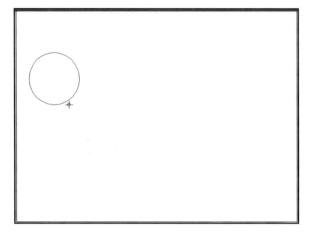

FIGURE A-12
Creating a marquee selection

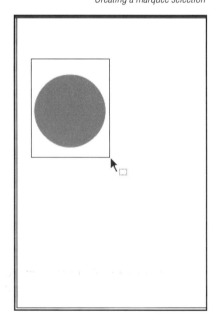

FIGURE A-13

The circle on the right side of the stage

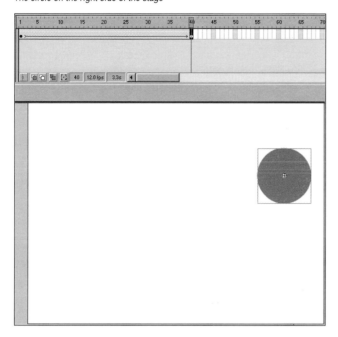

4. Drag the circle to the right side of the stage, as shown in Figure A-13.

   The movement of the circle on the stage corresponds to the new location of the circle as defined in the keyframe in Frame 40.

5. Play the movie.

   The playhead moves through the timeline in Frames 1–40, and the circle moves across the stage.

6. Save your work.

You created a basic motion tween animation by inserting a keyframe and changing the location of an object.

Change the brightness of an object

1. Click Window on the menu bar, then verify that the Properties command is checked.

2. Click Frame 1 on Layer 1, then click the circle.

3. Click the Color Styles list arrow in the Property inspector, then click Brightness.

4. Click the Brightness Amount list arrow, then drag the slider to 70%.

   TIP   You can also double-click the Brightness Amount box and type a percentage.

5. Click anywhere in the workspace to close the slider.

6. Play the movie, save your work.

   The circle becomes brighter as it moves across the stage.

You used the Property inspector to change the brightness of the object in one of the keyframes.

Using options and shortcuts

There is often more than one way to complete a particular function when using Macromedia Flash. For example, if you want to change the font for text you have typed, you can use Text menu options or the Property inspector. In addition, Macromedia Flash provides context menus that are relevant to the current selection. For example, if you point to a graphic and right-click (Win) or [control] click (Mac), a menu appears with graphic-related commands, such as rotate and skew. Shortcut keys are also available for many of the most common commands, such as [Ctrl][Z] (Win) or [command][Z] (Mac) for Undo.

WORK WITH LAYERS AND THE TIMELINE

What You'll Do

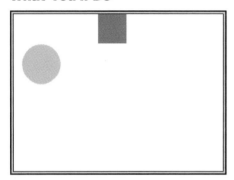

 In this lesson, you will add another layer, allowing you to create additional animation, and you will use the timeline to help organize your movie.

Understanding the Timeline

The timeline organizes and controls a movie's contents over time. By learning how to read the information provided in the timeline, you can determine and change what will be happening in a movie, frame by frame. You can determine which objects are animated, what types of animations are being used, when the various objects will appear in a movie, which objects will appear on top of others, and how fast the movie will play. Features of the timeline are shown in Figure A-14 and explained in this lesson.

Using Layers

Each new Macromedia Flash movie contains one layer, named Layer 1. **Layers** are like transparent sheets of acetate that are stacked on top of each other, as shown in Figure A-15. Each layer can contain one or more objects. You can add layers using the Layer command on the Insert menu or by clicking the Insert Layer icon on the timeline. When you add a new layer, Macromedia Flash stacks it on top of the other layer(s) in the timeline. The stacking order of the layers in the timeline is important because objects on the stage will appear in the same stacking order. For example, if you had two overlapping layers, and the top layer had a drawing of a tree and the bottom layer had a drawing of a house, the tree would appear as though it were in front of the house. You can change the stacking order of layers simply by dragging them up or down in the list of layers. You can name layers, hide them so their contents do not appear on the stage, and lock them so that they cannot be edited.

Using Frames

The timeline is made up of individual units called **frames**. The content of each layer is displayed in frames as the playhead moves over them while the movie plays. Frames are numbered in increments of five for easy reference, and colors and symbols are used to indicate the type of frame (for example, keyframe or motion animation). The upper-right corner of the timeline contains a pop-up menu. This menu provides different views of the timeline, showing more frames or showing thumbnails of the objects on a layer, for example. The status bar at the bottom of the timeline indicates the current frame (the frame that the playhead is currently on), the frame rate (frames per second), and the elapsed time from Frame 1 to the current frame.

Using the Playhead
The playhead indicates which frame is playing. You can manually move the playhead

by dragging it left or right. This makes it easier to locate a frame that you may want to edit. Dragging the playhead also allows you to do a quick check of the movie without having to play it.

Understanding Scenes
When you create a new movie, Scene 1 also appears in the timeline. A scene is a section of the timeline designated for a specific part of the movie. For example, a movie created for a Web site could be divided into a number of scenes: an introduction, a home page,

and content pages. Scenes are a way to organize long movies. Without them, scrolling through the timeline to work on different parts of the movie could become a very frustrating and inefficient way to work. You can insert new scenes by using the Insert menu. Scenes can be given descriptive names, which will help you find them easily if you need to edit a particular scene. You can click the Scene command on the Modify menu to change the play order of scenes in your movie. The number of scenes is limited only by the computer's memory.

FIGURE A-14
Elements of the timeline

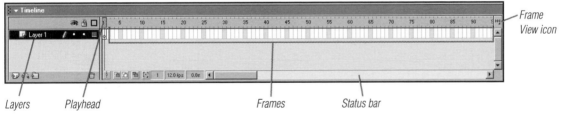

Layers   Playhead   Frames   Status bar   Frame View icon

FIGURE A-15
The concept of layers

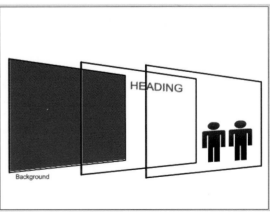

Working with the Timeline

Figure A-16 shows the timeline of a movie created in Lesson 2 with a second object, a square at the top of the stage. By studying the timeline, you can learn several things about this movie. First, the second object is placed on its own layer, Layer 2. Second, the layer has a motion animation (indicated by the arrow and blue background in the frames). Third, the animation runs from Frame 1 to Frame 40. Fourth, if the objects intersect, the square will be on top of the circle, because the layer it is placed on is above the layer that the circle is placed on. Fifth, the frame rate is set to 12, which means that the movie will play 12 frames per second. Sixth, the playhead is at Frame 1, which causes the contents for both layers of Frame 1 to be displayed on the stage.

QUICKTIP

You can adjust the size of the timeline by positioning the mouse over the bottom edge, and then dragging the border up or down.

FIGURE A-16

The timeline of a movie with a second object

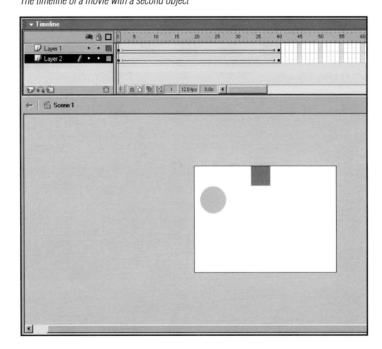

FIGURE A-17
Drawing a square

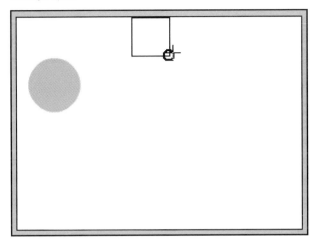

FIGURE A-18
Positioning the square at the bottom of the stage

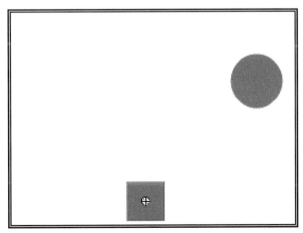

Add a layer

1. Save tween.fla as **layers.fla**.
2. Click Frame 1 on Layer 1.
3. Click View on the menu bar, point to Magnification, then click 50%.
4. Click Insert on the menu bar, then click Layer.

   A new layer—Layer 2—appears at the top of the timeline.
5. Save your work.

You added a layer to the timeline.

Create a second animation

1. Click the Rectangle Tool on the toolbox, press and hold [Shift], then draw a square resembling the dimensions shown in Figure A-17. ▢
2. Click the Arrow Tool on the toolbox, then drag a marquee around the square. ▸
3. Click Insert on the menu bar, then click Create Motion Tween.
4. Click Frame 40 on Layer 2, then insert a keyframe.
5. Drag the square to the bottom of the stage, as shown in Figure A-18, then play the movie.

   The square appears on top when the two objects intersect.
6. Save your work.

You drew an object and used it to create a second animation.

Work with layers and view features in the timeline

1. Click Layer 2 on the timeline, then drag it below Layer 1.

   Layer 2 is now the bottom layer.

2. Play the movie and notice how the square appears beneath the circle when they intersect.

3. Click the Frame View icon on the end of the timeline to display the menu shown in Figure A-19.

4. Click Tiny to display more frames.

5. Click the Frame View icon, click Preview, then note the object thumbnails that appear on the timeline.

6. Click the Frame View icon, then click Normal.

7. Save your work.

You changed the order of the layers and changed the display of frames on the timeline.

FIGURE A-19
Changing the view of the timeline

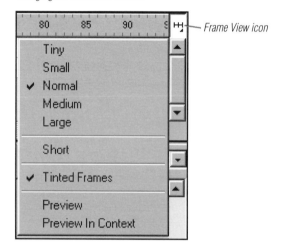

Frame View icon

FIGURE A-20
Changing the frame rate

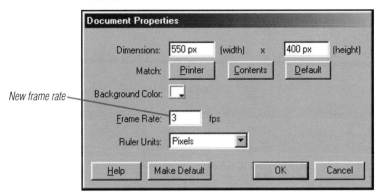

New frame rate

1. Double-click the Frame Rate box on the bottom of the timeline. `12.0 fps`

2. Double-click the Frame Rate text box, type **3**, then compare your Document Properties dialog box to Figure A-20. `12.0 fps`

3. Click OK.

4. Play the movie and notice how slowly the movie plays.

5. Repeat Steps 1 and 2, but change the frame rate to 18 and then to 12.

6. Click Frame 1 on the timeline.

7. Drag the playhead left and right to display specific frames.

8. Save your work, then close layers.fla.

You changed the frame rate of the movie.

Getting Help
Macromedia Flash provides a comprehensive Help feature that can be very useful when first learning the program. You can access Help by clicking commands on the Help menu. The Help feature includes the Macromedia Flash manual, which is organized by topic and can be accessed through the index or by using a keyword search. In addition, the Help menu contains samples and tutorials that cover basic Macromedia Flash features.

PLAN A WEB SITE

What You'll Do

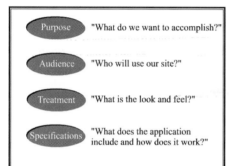

Purpose   "What do we want to accomplish?"

Audience   "Who will use our site?"

Treatment   "What is the look and feel?"

Specifications   "What does the application include and how does it work?"

 In this lesson, you will learn how to plan a Macromedia Flash application. You will also learn about the guidelines for screen design and the interactive design of Web pages.

Planning an Application

Macromedia Flash can be used to develop animations (movies) that are part of a product, such as a game or educational tutorial, delivered on CD-ROM or DVD. You can use Macromedia Flash to create enhancements to Web pages, such as animated logos and interactive navigation buttons. You can also use Macromedia Flash to create entire Web sites. No matter what the application, the first step is planning. Often, the temptation is to jump right into the program and start developing movies. The problem is that this invariably results in a more time-consuming process at best; and wasted effort, resources, and money at worst. The larger in scope and the more complex the project

is, the more critical the planning process. Planning an entire Web site should involve the following steps:

Step 1: Stating the Purpose (Goals). "What, specifically, do we want to accomplish?"

Determining the goals of a site is a critical step in planning, because goals guide the development process, keep the team members on track, and provide a way to evaluate the site both during and after its development.

Step 2: Identifying the Target Audience. "Who will use the Web site?"

Understanding the potential viewers helps in developing a site that can address their needs. For example, children respond to exploration and surprise, so having a dog wag its tail when the mouse pointer rolls over it might appeal to this audience.

Step 3: Determining the Treatment. "What is the look and feel?"

The treatment is how the Web site will be presented to the user, including the tone, approach, and emphasis.

Tone. Will the site be humorous, serious, light, heavy, formal, or informal? The tone of a site can often be used to make a statement projecting a progressive, high-tech, well-funded corporate image, for instance.

Approach. How much direction will be provided to the user? An interactive game site might focus on exploration, while an informational site might provide lots of direction, such as menus.

Emphasis. How much emphasis will be placed on the various multimedia elements? For example, a company may want to develop an informational site that shows the features of their new product line, including animated demonstrations of how each product works. The budget might not allow for the expense of creating the animations, so the emphasis would shift to still pictures with text descriptions.

Step 4: Developing the Specifications and Storyboard. "What precisely does the application include and how does it work?"

The specifications state what will be included in each screen, including the arrangement of each element and the functionality of each object (for example, what happens when you click the button

labeled Skip Intro). Specifications should include the following:

Playback System. The choice of what configuration to target for playback is critical, especially Internet connection speed, browser versions, screen resolution, and plug-ins.

Elements to Include. The specifications should include details about the various elements that are to be included in the site. What are the dimensions for the animations, and what is the frame rate? What are the sizes of the various objects such as photos, buttons, and so on? What fonts, font sizes, and type styles will be used?

Functionality. The specifications should include the way the program reacts to an action by the user, such as a mouse click. For example, clicking on a door (object) might cause the door to open (an animation), a doorbell to ring (sound), an "exit the program" message to appear (text), or an entirely new screen to be displayed.

User Interface. The user interface involves designing the appearance of objects (how each object is arranged on the screen) and the interactivity (how the user navigates through the site).

A storyboard is a representation of what each screen will look like and how the screens are linked. The purpose of the storyboard is to provide an overview of the project, provide a guide (road map) for the developer, illustrate the links among

screens, and illustrate the functionality of the objects. Figure A-21 shows a storyboard. The exact content (such as a specific photo) does not have to be decided upon, but it is important to show where text, graphics, photos, buttons, and other elements, will be placed. Thus, the storyboard includes placeholders for the various elements. An important feature of the storyboard is the navigation scheme. The Web site designer decides how the various screens will be linked and represents this in the storyboard. In this way, problems with the navigation scheme can be identified before the development begins.

Using Screen Design Guidelines

The following screen design guidelines are used by Web developers. The implementation of these guidelines is affected by the goals of the site, the intended audience, and the content.

Balance—Balance in screen design refers to the distribution of optical weight in the layout. Optical weight is the ability of an object to attract the viewer's eye, as determined by the object's size, shape, color, and so on. In general, a balanced design is more appealing to a viewer.

FIGURE A-21
Sample storyboard

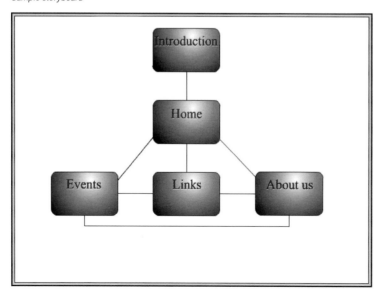

Unity—Intra-screen unity has to do with how the various screen objects relate and how they all fit in. Unity helps them reinforce each other. Inter-screen unity refers to the design that viewers encounter as they navigate from one screen to another, and it provides consistency throughout the site.

Movement—Movement refers to the way the viewer's eye moves through the objects on the screen. Techniques in an animation, such as movement, can be used to draw the viewer to a location on the screen.

Using Interactive Design Guidelines

In addition to screen design guidelines, interactive guidelines determine the interactivity of the site. The following guidelines are not absolute rules but are affected by the goals of the site, the intended audience, and the content:

- Make it simple, easy to understand, and easy to use. Make the site intuitive so that viewers do not have to spend time learning what the site is all about and what they need to do.
- Build in consistency in the navigation scheme. Help the users know where they are in the site and help them avoid getting lost.
- Provide feedback. Users need to know when an action, such as clicking a button, has been completed. Changing its color or shape, or adding a sound can indicate this.
- Give the user control. Allow the user to skip long introductions; provide controls for starting, stopping, and rewinding animations, video, and audio; and provide controls for adjusting audio.

DISTRIBUTE A MACROMEDIA FLASH MOVIE

What You'll Do

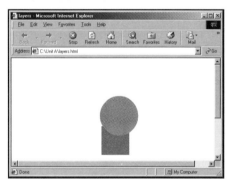

In this lesson you will prepare a movie for distribution in various formats.

Distributing Movies

When you develop Macromedia Flash movies, the application saves them in a file format (.fla) that only users who have the Macromedia Flash program installed on their computers can view. Usually, Macromedia Flash movies are viewed on the Web as part of a Web site or directly from a viewer's computer using the Macromedia Flash Player. In order to view your Macromedia Flash movies on the Web, you must change the movie to a Macromedia Shockwave (.swf) file format and generate the HTML code that references the Macromedia Shockwave file. You can accomplish both of these tasks by using the publish feature of Macromedia Flash.

The process for publishing a Macromedia Flash movie is to create and save a movie and then click the Publish command on the File menu. You can also specify various settings such as dimensions for the window that the movie plays within in the browser, before publishing the movie. Publishing a movie creates two files: an HTML file and a Macromedia Shockwave file. Both of these files retain the same name as the Flash movie file, but with different file extensions:

- .html—the HTML document
- .swf—the Macromedia Shockwave file

You can change these names as you would any files on your computer. The HTML document contains the code that the browser interprets to display the movie on the Web. The code also specifies the Macromedia Shockwave movie that the browser will play. Sample HTML code referencing a Macromedia Shockwave movie is shown in Figure A-22.

Macromedia Flash provides several other ways to distribute your movies that may or may not involve delivery on the Web. You can create a stand-alone movie called a **projector** Projector files, such as Windows .exe files, maintain the movie's interactivity. Alternately, you can create self-running movies, such as Quicktime .mov files, that are not interactive.

You can play projector and non-interactive files directly from a computer, or you can incorporate them into an application, such as a game, that is delivered from a download on a CD or DVD.

FIGURE A-22

Sample HTML code

```
<HTML>
<HEAD>
<meta http-equiv=Content-Type content="text/html;  charset=ISO-8859-1">
<TITLE>layers</TITLE>
</HEAD>
<BODY bgcolor="#FFFFFF">
<!-- URL's used in the movie-->
<!-- text used in the movie-->
<OBJECT classid="clsid:D27CDB6E-AE6D-11cf-96B8-444553540000"
 codebase="http://download.macromedia.com/pub/shockwave/cabs/flash/swflash.cab#version=6,0,0,0"
 WIDTH="550" HEIGHT="400" id="layers" ALIGN="">
 <PARAM NAME=movie VALUE="layers.swf"> <PARAM NAME=quality VALUE=high> <PARAM NAME=bgcolor
VALUE=#FFFFFF> <EMBED src="layers.swf" quality=high bgcolor=#FFFFFF  WIDTH="550" HEIGHT="400" NAME="layers"
ALIGN=""
 TYPE="application/x-shockwave-flash" PLUGINSPAGE="http://www.macromedia.com/go/getflashplayer"></EMBED>
</OBJECT>
</BODY>
</HTML>
```

Code specifying the Macromedia Shockwave movie that the browser will play

.swf extension indicates a Macromedia Shockwave file

Publish a movie for distribution on the Web

1. Open layers.fla.

2. Click File on the menu bar, then click Publish.

3. Open the file management tool that is on your operating system, then navigate to the drive and folder where you save your work for this unit.

4. Notice the three files that begin with "layers", as shown in Figure A-23.

   Layers.fla, the Flash movie; layers.swf, the Macromedia Shockwave file; and layers.htm, the HTML document, appear in the window.

5. Open your browser.

6. Open layers.htm, then notice that the movie plays in the browser.

7. Close the browser.

You used the Publish command to create an HTML document and a Macromedia Shockwave file, then displayed the HTML document in a Web browser.

FIGURE A-23

The three layers files after publishing the movie

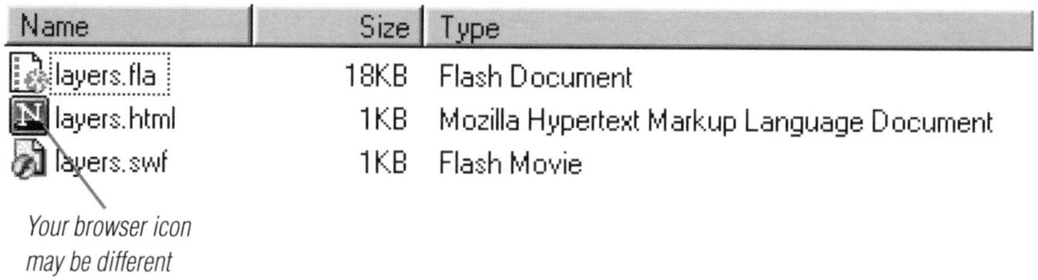

Name	Size	Type
layers.fla	18KB	Flash Document
layers.html	1KB	Mozilla Hypertext Markup Language Document
layers.swf	1KB	Flash Movie

Your browser icon may be different

FIGURE A-24

The Flash Player window playing the Macromedia Shockwave movie

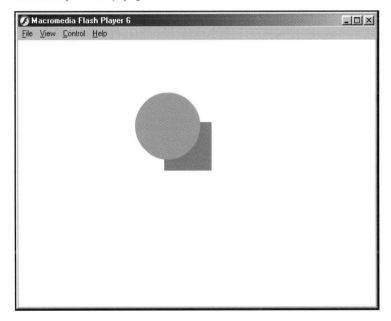

1. Click File on the menu bar, then click Publish Settings.

2. Click the Windows Projector (.exe) (Win) or Macintosh Projector (Mac) option, then deselect other file formats, if necessary.

3. Click Publish, then click OK.

4. Open the file management tool that is on your operating system, then navigate to the drive and folder where you save your work for this unit.

5. Double-click layers.exe (Win), or layers Projector (Mac), then notice that the application plays in the Macromedia Flash Player window, as shown in Figure A-24.

6. Close the Macromedia Flash Player window.

7. Close layers.fla in Macromedia Flash.

You created and displayed a stand-alone projector file.

Start Macromedia Flash, open a movie, and set the movie properties and magnification.

1. Start Macromedia Flash, open fla_2.fla, and then save it as **skillsdemoA.fla**.
2. Display the Document Properties dialog box.
3. Change the movie window dimensions to width: 550 px and height: 400 px.
4. Change the background color to yellow. (*Hint*: Select the yellow color swatch in the left column of the color palette.)
5. Close the Document Properties dialog box.
6. Change the magnification to 50% using the View menu.
7. Change the magnification to 75% using the View magnification box.
8. If necessary, use the scroll bars at the bottom and the right of the screen to center the stage in the workspace.

Display, close, and collapse panels.

1. Set panels to their default layout. (*Hint*: Use the Panel Sets command on the Window menu.)
2. Collapse all panels.
3. Close each panel to remove them from the screen.
4. Display the Property inspector.
5. Close and open the Toolbox.

Play and test a movie.

1. Use the controls in the Control menu to play and rewind the movie.
2. Use the Controller to rewind, play, stop, and start the movie.
3. Turn Loop Playback on, play the movie, and then stop it.
4. Test the movie in the Macromedia Flash Player window, and then close the window.

Create an object, create a basic animation, and apply an effect.

1. Rewind the movie, insert a layer, and then draw a red circle in the lower-right corner of the stage, approximately the same size as the green ball. (*Hint*: Use the scroll bar on the timeline to view the new layer, if necessary.)
2. Select the circle, and then add Create Motion Tween animation to it.
3. Animate the circle so that it moves across the screen from right to left beginning in Frame 1 and ending in Frame 65. (*Hint*: Add a keyframe in the ending frame.)
4. Use the Arrow Tool to select the circle, then change brightness from 0% to -100%.
5. Play the movie, then rewind it.

Add a layer, change the frame rate, and change the view of the timeline.

1. Add a layer, select Frame 1, and then create a second circle approximately the same size as the previously created circle in the lower-left corner of the stage.
2. Animate the circle so that it moves across the screen from left to right beginning in Frame 1 and ending in Frame 65.
3. Use the Arrow Tool to select the circle, then change brightness from 0% to 100%.
4. Play the movie.
5. Use the timeline to change the frame rate to 8 frames per second.

6. Change the view of the timeline to display more frames.
7. Change the view of the timeline to display a preview of the object thumbnails.
8. Change the view of the timeline to display the Normal view.
9. Use the playhead to display each frame.
10. Save the movie, and then compare your movie to Figure A-25.

Publish a movie.

1. Click File on the menu bar, then click Publish.
2. Open your browser, then open skillsdemoA.htm.
3. View the movie, then close your browser.

Create a projector.

1. Display the Publish Setting dialog box.
2. Select the appropriate projector setting for your operating systems and remove all of the other settings.
3. Publish the movie.
4. Open the file management tool that is on your operating system, navigate to the drive and folder where you save your work for this unit, then open skillsdemoA.fla.
5. View the movie, then close the Macromedia Flash Player window.
6. Close the movie in Macromedia Flash.

FIGURE A-25
Completed Skills Review

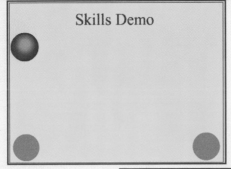

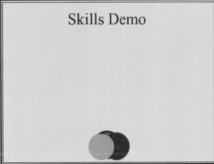

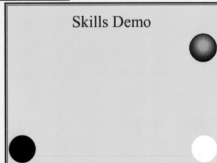

A friend cannot decide whether to sign up for a class in Macromedia Flash or Dreamweaver. You help her decide by showing her what you already know about Macromedia Flash. Since you think she'd love a class in Macromedia Flash, you decide to show her how easy it is to create a simple animation involving two objects that move diagonally across the screen.

1. Open a new movie, and then save it as **demonstration.fla**.
2. Create a simple shape or design, and place it in the upper-left corner of the stage.
3. Animate the object using the Create Motion Tween command.
4. Insert a keyframe in Frame 50.
5. Move the object to the lower-right corner of the stage.
6. Insert a new layer, and then select Frame 1.
7. Create another object in the upper-right corner of the stage.
8. Animate the object using the Create Motion Tween command.
9. Insert a keyframe in Frame 50.
10. Move the object to the lower-left corner of the stage.
11. Play the movie, and then click Frame 1.
12. Change the brightness for both objects to 80%.
13. Preview the movie and test it.
14. Save the movie, and then compare your movie to Figure A-26.

FIGURE A-26
Completed Project Builder 1

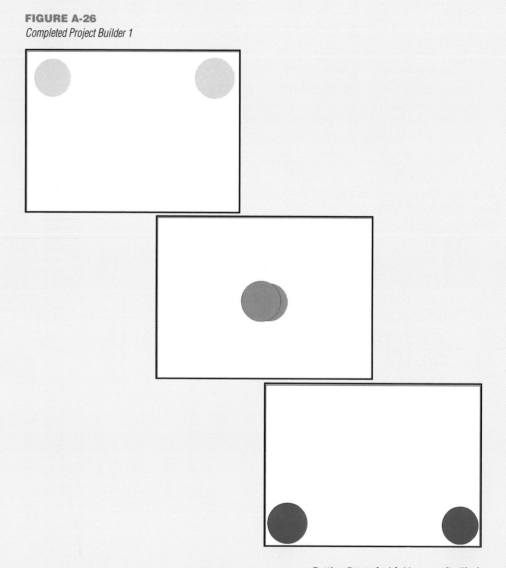

You've been asked to develop a simple movie about recycling for a day care center. For this project, you will add two animations to an existing movie. You will show three objects that appear on the screen at different times, and then move to a recycle bin at different times. You can use any objects you can draw easily.

1. Open fla_3.fla, then save it as **recycle.fla**.
2. Play the movie and study the timeline to familiarize yourself with the movie's current settings.
3. Insert a new layer, insert a keyframe in Frame 10 of the new layer, then draw a small object in the upper-left corner of the stage.
4. Create a motion animation that moves the object to the recycle bin.
5. Insert a new layer, insert a keyframe in Frame 20, draw a small object in the upper center of the stage, then create a motion animation that moves the object to the recycle bin.
6. Insert a new layer, insert a keyframe in Frame 30, draw a small object in the upper-right corner of the stage, then create a motion animation that moves the object to the recycle bin.
7. Play the movie.
8. Save the movie, then compare your movie to Figure A-27.

FIGURE A-27
Completed Project Builder 2

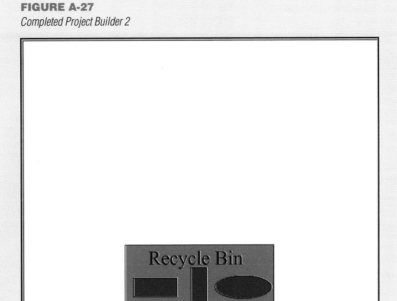

Figure A-28 shows the home page of a Web site. Study the figure and answer the following questions. For each question, indicate how you determined your answer.

1. Connect to the Internet, and go to *www.course.com*. Navigate to the page for this book, click the Student Online Companion, then click the link for this unit.
2. Open a document in a word processor or open a new Macromedia Flash movie, save the file as **dpuUnitA**, then answer the following questions. (*Hint*: Use the Text Tool in Macromedia Flash.)
   - Whose Web site is this?
   - What is the goal(s) of the site?
   - Who is the target audience?
   - What treatment (look and feel) is used?
   - What are the design layout guidelines being used (balance, movement, etc.)?
   - How can animation enhance this page?
   - Do you think this is an effective design for the company, its products, and its target audience? Why, or why not?
   - What suggestions would you make to improve on the design, and why?

FIGURE A-28
Design Project

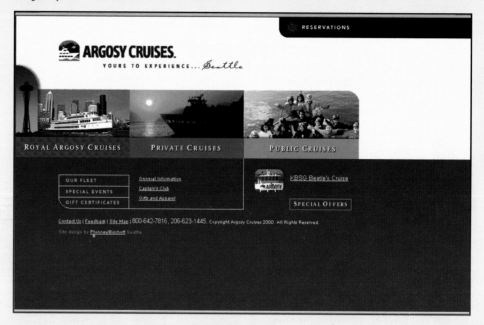

Your group can assign elements of the project to individual members, or work collectively to create the finished product.

There are numerous companies in the business of developing Web sites for others. Many of these companies use Macromedia Flash as one of their primary development tools. These companies promote themselves through their own Web sites and usually provide online portfolios with samples of their work. Use your favorite search engine (use keywords such as Macromedia Flash developers and Macromedia Flash animators) to locate three of these companies, and generate the following information for each one. A sample is shown in Figure A-29. Each member of your group will work independently on the following research project, and then you will meet to compare your results and choose the three companies that you feel are the best.

1. Company name:
2. Contact information (address, phone, and so on):
3. Web site URL:
4. Company mission:
5. Services provided:
6. Sample list of clients:

7. Describe three ways they seem to have used Macromedia Flash in their own sites. Were these effective? Why, or why not?
8. Describe three applications of Macromedia Flash that they include in their portfolios (or showcases or samples). Were these effective? Why, or why not?

9. Would you want to work for this company? Why, or why not?
10. Would you recommend this company to another company that was looking to enhance its Web site? Why, or why not?

FIGURE A-29
Group Project

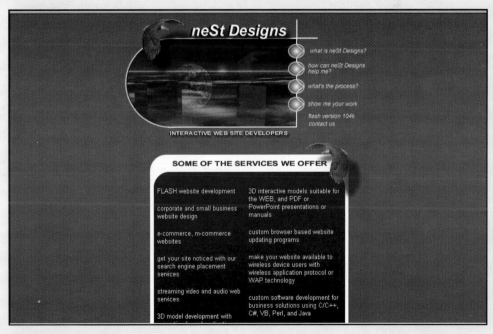

UNIT B

DRAWING IN MACROMEDIA FLASH

1. Use the Macromedia Flash drawing tools.

2. Edit drawings.

3. Work with objects.

4. Work with text.

5. Work with layers.

UNIT B
DRAWING IN MACROMEDIA FLASH

Introduction

One of the most compelling features of Macromedia Flash is its ability to create and manipulate vector graphics. Computers can display graphics in either a bitmap or a vector format. The difference between these formats is in how they describe an image. Bitmap graphics represent the image as an array of dots, called pixels, which are arranged within a grid. Each pixel in an image has an exact position on the screen and a precise color. To make a change in a bitmap, you modify the pixels. When you enlarge a bitmap graphic, the number of pixels remains the same, resulting in jagged edges that decrease the quality of the image. Vector graphics represent the image using lines and curves, which you can resize without losing image quality. Also, because vector images are generally smaller than bitmap images, they are particularly useful for a Web site. However, vector graphics are not as effective as bitmap graphic for representing photo-realistic images.

As you learned in Unit A, images created using Macromedia Flash drawing tools have a stroke, a fill, or both. In addition, the stroke of an object can be segmented into smaller lines. You can modify the size, shape, rotation, and color of each stroke, fill, and segment.

Tools You'll Use

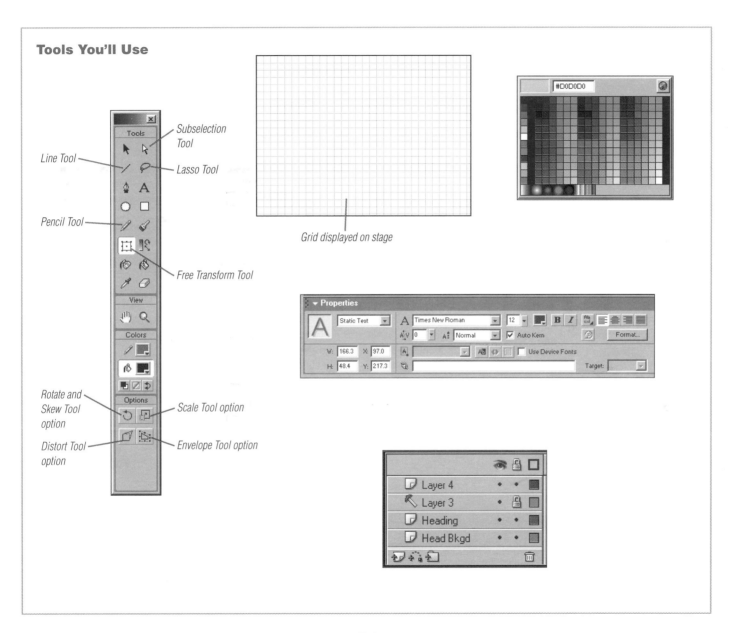

Subselection Tool

Line Tool

Lasso Tool

Pencil Tool

Free Transform Tool

Grid displayed on stage

#D0D0D0

Rotate and Skew Tool option

Scale Tool option

Distort Tool option

Envelope Tool option

Static Text — Times New Roman — 12

Properties

A

W: 166.3 X: 97.0

H: 48.4 Y: 217.3

Auto Kern

Use Device Fonts

Format...

Target:

Layer 4

Layer 3

Heading

Head Bkgd

USE THE MACROMEDIA FLASH DRAWING TOOLS

What You'll Do

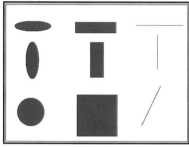

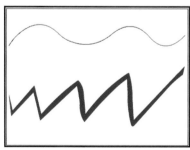

In this lesson, you will use several drawing tools to create various vector graphics.

Using Macromedia Flash Drawing and Editing Tools

When you point to a tool on the toolbox, its name appears next to the tool and a description of its function is displayed on the Status bar at the bottom of the screen. Figure B-1 identifies the tools described below. Several of the tools have options that modify their use.

Arrow—Used to select an object or parts of an object, such as the stroke or fill; and to reshape objects. The options available for the Arrow Tool are Snap to Objects (aligns objects), Smooth (smoothes lines), and Straighten (straightens lines).

Subselection—Used to select, drag, and reshape an object. Vector graphics are composed of lines and curves (each of which is a segment) connected by **anchor points**. Selecting an object with this tool displays the anchor points and allows you to use them to edit the object.

Line—Used to draw straight lines. You can draw vertical, horizontal, and 45° diagonal lines by pressing and holding [Shift] while drawing the line.

Lasso—Used to select objects or parts of objects. The Polygon Mode Tool option allows you to draw straight lines when selecting an object.

Pen—Used to draw lines and curves by creating a series of dots, known as <u>anchor points</u>, that are automatically connected.

Text—Used to create and edit text.

Oval—Used to draw oval shapes. Press and hold [Shift] to draw a perfect circle.

Rectangle—Used to draw rectangular shapes. Press and hold [Shift] to draw a perfect square. The Round Rectangle Radius Tool option allows you to round the corners of a rectangle.

Pencil—Used to draw freehand lines and shapes. The options available for the Pencil Tool are Straighten (draws straight lines), Smooth (draws smooth curved lines), and Ink (draws freehand with no modification).

Brush—Used to draw (paint) with brush-like strokes. Options allow you to set the size and shape of the brush, and to determine the area to be painted, such as inside or behind an object.

Free Transform—Used to transform objects by rotating, scaling, skewing, and distorting them.

Fill Transform—Used to transform a gradient fill by adjusting the size, direction, or center of the fill.

Ink Bottle—Used to apply line colors and thickness to the stroke of an object.

Paint Bucket—Used to fill enclosed areas of a drawing with color. Options allow you to fill areas that have gaps and to make adjustments in a gradient fill.

Eyedropper—Used to copy stroke, fill, and text attributes from one object to another.

Eraser—Used to erase lines and fills. Options allow you to choose what part of the object to erase, as well as the size and shape of the eraser.

The Oval, Rectangle, Pencil, Brush, Line, and Pen Tools are used to create vector objects.

Displaying Gridlines and Rulers

Gridlines and rulers can be used to position objects on the stage. The Grid and Ruler commands, found on the View menu, are used to turn on and off these features. You can modify the grid size and color, and you can specify the units for the rulers.

FIGURE B-1
Macromedia Flash tools

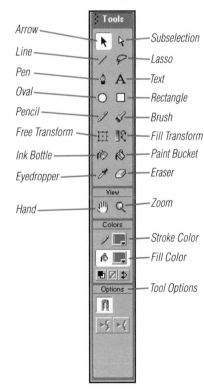

Arrow · Subselection
Line · Lasso
Pen · Text
Oval · Rectangle
Pencil · Brush
Free Transform · Fill Transform
Ink Bottle · Paint Bucket
Eyedropper · Eraser
Hand · Zoom
Stroke Color
Fill Color
Tool Options

Show gridlines and check settings

1. Open a new movie, then save it as **tools.fla**.

2. Verify that the movie size is 550 × 400 pixels.

   TIP   In addition to clicking the Document properties button to access document properties, you can also click Modify on the menu bar and then click Document.

3. Click the Stroke Color Tool on the toolbox, then click the black color swatch in the left column of the color palette (if necessary).

4. Click the Fill Color Tool on the toolbox, then click the blue color swatch in the left column of the color palette (if necessary).

5. Click View on the menu bar, point to Grid, then click Show Grid to display the gridlines.

   A gray grid appears on the stage.

6. Click Window on the menu bar, point to Toolbars, then click Main and Status if they do not have check marks next to them (Win).

7. Point to several tools on the toolbar, then read about their functions on the Status bar (Win), as shown in Figure B-2.

8. Save your work.

You displayed the grid and viewed tool descriptions on the Status bar.

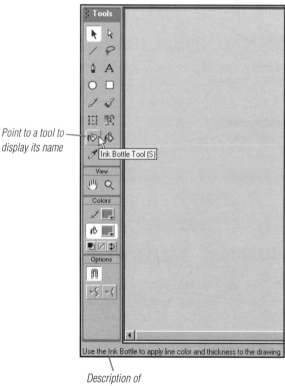

FIGURE B-2
Tool description on the Status bar

Point to a tool to display its name

Ink Bottle Tool (S)

Use the Ink Bottle to apply line color and thickness to the drawing

Description of the tool

FIGURE B-3
Objects created with drawing tools

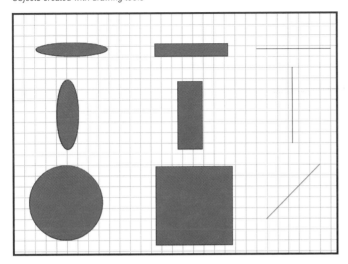

FIGURE B-4
Positioning the Pen Tool on the stage

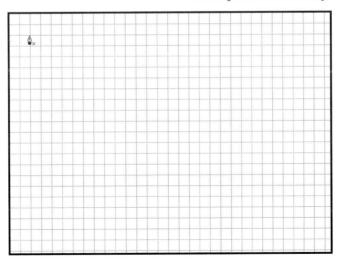

Use the Oval, Rectangle, and Line Tools

1. Click the Oval Tool on the toolbox, then using Figure B-3 as a guide, draw the three oval shapes. ⬭

   TIP   Use the grid to approximate shape sizes.

2. Repeat Step 1 using the Rectangle Tool. ☐

3. Repeat Step 1 using the Line Tool. ╱

   TIP   To undo an action, click the Undo command on the Edit menu.

4. Save your work.

You used the Oval, Rectangle, and Line Tools to draw objects on the stage.

Use the Pen Tool

1. Click Insert on the menu bar, then click Layer.

   A new layer—Layer 2—appears above Layer 1.

   TIP   Macromedia Flash numbers new layers sequentially, even if you delete previously created layers.

2. Insert a keyframe in Frame 5 on Layer 2.

   Since the objects were drawn in Frame 1, they are no longer visible when you insert a keyframe in Frame 5.

3. Click View on the menu bar, point to Magnification, click 200%, then center the upper-left corner of the stage in the workspace.

4. Click the Pen Tool on the toolbox, position it in the upper-left quadrant of the stage as shown in Figure B-4, then click to set an anchor point. ✒

   (continued)

5. Using Figure B-5 as a guide, click the remaining anchor points to complete drawing an arrow.

   TIP To close an object, be sure to re-click the first anchor point as your last action.

6. Save your work.

You added a layer, inserted a keyframe, and then used the Pen Tool to draw an arrow.

Use the Pencil and Brush Tools

1. Click View on the menu bar, point to Magnification, then click 100%.

2. Insert a new layer, Layer 3, then insert a keyframe in Frame 10.

3. Click the Pencil Tool on the toolbox. 🖉

4. Click the Pencil Mode Tool in the Options section of the toolbox, then click the Smooth Tool option, as shown in Figure B-6. 🖉

   TIP A small arrow in the corner of an icon indicates that you can access additional icons. ◢

(continued)

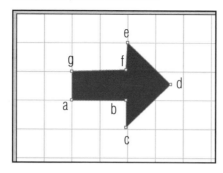

Click Pencil Mode Tool to display remaining options

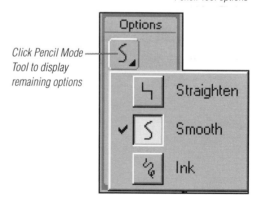

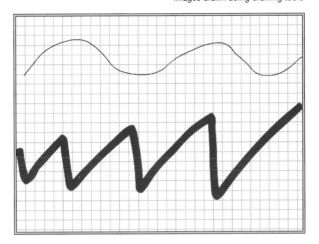

FIGURE B-7

Images drawn using drawing tools

FIGURE B-8

Changing the brush size

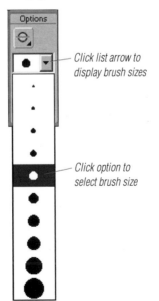

Click list arrow to
display brush sizes

Click option to
select brush size

5. Draw the top image shown in Figure B-7.

   TIP Collapse the Property inspector, if
   necessary.

6. Click the Brush Tool on the toolbox.

7. Click the Brush Size list arrow in the Options
   section of the toolbox, then click the 5th
   option from the top, as shown in Figure B-8.

8. Repeat Step 4, drawing the bottom image.

9. Save your work.

*You selected the Smooth option for the Pencil Tool
and drew an object; you selected a brush size for
the Brush Tool and drew an object.*

Modify an object using tool options

1. Click the Arrow Tool on the toolbox, then
   drag a marquee around the top object to
   select it.

   Options for the Arrow Tool appear in the
   Options section of the toolbox.

2. Click the Smooth Tool option in the
   Options section of the toolbox at least
   three times.

   The line becomes smoother.

3. Select the bottom object, then click the
   Straighten Tool option in the Options section
   of the toolbox at least three times.

   The segments of the line become straighter.

4. Save your work.

You smoothed and straightened objects.

EDIT DRAWINGS

What You'll Do

▶ *In this lesson, you will use several techniques to select objects, change the color of strokes and fills, and create a gradient fill.*

Selecting Objects

Before you can edit a drawing, you must first select the objects on which you want to work. Objects are made up of a stroke(s) and a fill. Strokes can have several segments. For example, a rectangle will have four stroke segments, one for each side of the object. These can be selected separately or as a whole. Macromedia Flash highlights objects that have been selected, as shown in Figure B-9. When the stroke of an object is selected, a colored line appears. When the fill of an object is selected, a dot pattern appears; and when objects are grouped, a bounding box appears.

Using the Arrow Tool

You can use the Arrow Tool to select part or all of an object, and to select multiple objects. To select only the fill, click just the fill; to select only the stroke, click just the stroke. To select both the fill and the stroke, double-click the object or draw a marquee around it. To select part of an object, drag a marquee that defines the area you wish to select, as shown in Figure B-10. To select multiple objects or combinations of strokes and fills, press and hold [Shift], then click each item. To deselect an item(s), click a blank area of the stage.

Using the Lasso Tool

The Lasso Tool provides more flexibility when selecting an area on the stage. You can use the tool in a freehand manner to select any size and shape of area. Alternately, you can use the Polygon Mode Tool option to draw straight lines and connect them.

Working With Colors

Macromedia Flash allows you to change the color of the stroke and fill of an object. Figure B-11 shows the Colors section of the toolbox. To change a color, you click the Stroke Color Tool or the Fill Color Tool, and then select a color swatch on the color palette.

You can set the desired colors before drawing an object, or you can change a color of a previously drawn object. You can use the Ink Bottle Tool to change the stroke color, and you can use the Paint Bucket Tool to change the fill color. You can also use the Property inspector to change the stroke and fill colors.

Working With Gradients

A gradient is a color fill that makes a gradual transition from one color to another. Gradients can be very useful for creating a 3-D effect, drawing attention to an object, and generally enhancing the appearance of an object. You can apply a gradient fill by using the Paint Bucket Tool. The position of the Paint Bucket Tool over the object is important because it determines the direction of the gradient fill.

FIGURE B-10
Selecting part of an object

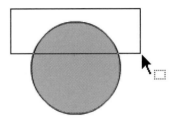

FIGURE B-9
Objects or parts of objects are highlighted when selected

Unselected	*Stroke selected*	*Fill selected*	*Stroke and Fill selected*	*Group selected*

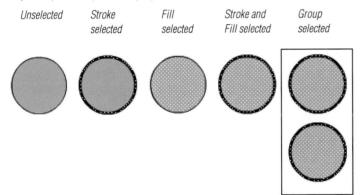

FIGURE B-11
The Colors section of the toolbox

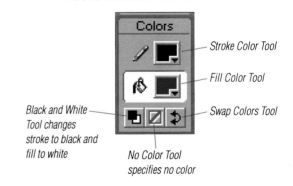

Stroke Color Tool

Fill Color Tool

Swap Colors Tool

Black and White Tool changes stroke to black and fill to white

No Color Tool specifies no color

Select a drawing using the mouse and the Lasso Tool

1. Click Frame 1 on the timeline.

   TIP The actions you perform on the stage will produce very different results depending on whether you click a frame on the timeline or on a layer.

2. Click the Arrow Tool on the toolbox (if necessary), then drag the marquee around the perfect circle to select the entire object (both the stroke and the fill). ▶

3. Click anywhere on the stage to deselect the object.

4. Click inside the circle to select the fill only, then click outside the circle to deselect it.

5. Click the stroke of the circle to select it, as shown in Figure B-12, then deselect it.

6. Double-click the circle to select it, press and hold [Shift], double-click the square to select both objects, then deselect both objects.

7. Click the right border of the square to select it, as shown in Figure B-13, then deselect it.

8. Click the Lasso Tool on the toolbox, then encircle the objects, as shown in Figure B-14. ⌐

   TIP The encircled objects are selected when you release the mouse.

9. Save your work.

You used the Arrow Tool to select the stroke and fill of an object, and you used the Lasso Tool to select a group of objects.

FIGURE B-12
Using the Arrow Tool to select the stroke of the circle

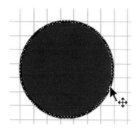

FIGURE B-13
Using the Arrow Tool to select a segment of the stroke of the square

FIGURE B-14
Using the Lasso Tool to select several objects

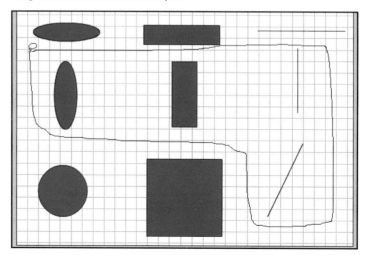

Drawing in Macromedia Flash

FIGURE B-15
Circles drawn with the Oval Tool

FIGURE B-16
Changing the stroke color

1. Click Layer 3, insert a new layer—Layer 4—then insert a keyframe in Frame 15.

2. Click View on the menu bar, point to Grid, then click Show Grid to remove the gridlines.

3. Click the Oval Tool on the toolbox, then draw circles similar to those shown in Figure B-15. ◯

4. Click the Fill Color Tool on the toolbox, then click the yellow color swatch in the left column of the color palette. 👆🖳

5. Click the Paint Bucket Tool on the toolbox, then click the fill of the right circle. 👆

6. Click the Stroke Color Tool on the toolbox, then click the yellow color swatch in the left column of the color palette. ╱🔲

7. Click the Ink Bottle Tool on the toolbox, then click the stroke of the left circle, as shown in Figure B-16. ⌲

8. Save your work.

You changed the fill and stroke colors of an object.

Create a gradient

1. Click the Fill Color Tool on the toolbox, then click the red gradient color swatch in the bottom row of the color palette, as shown in Figure B-17.

2. Click the Paint Bucket Tool on the toolbox, then click the yellow circle.

3. Continue to click different parts of the circle, then click the right side, as shown in Figure B-18.

4. Click the Fill Transform Tool, then click the gradient-filled circle.

(continued)

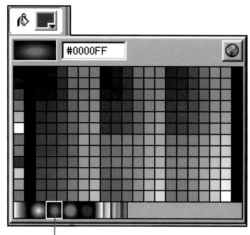

Click red gradient color swatch to select it

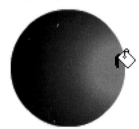

5. Drag each of the four handles, shown in Figure B-19, to determine their effects on the gradient, then click the stage to deselect the circle.

6. Click the Fill Color Tool, then click the blue color swatch in the left column of the color palette. 🖋️ 🔲

7. Save your work.

You applied a gradient fill and you used the Fill Transform Tool to alter the gradient.

FIGURE B-19
Fill Transform handles

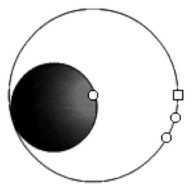

WORK WITH OBJECTS

What You'll Do

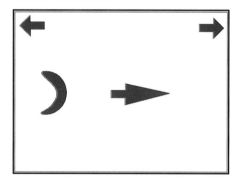

 In this lesson, you will copy, move, and transform (resize, rotate, and reshape) objects.

Copying and Moving Objects

To copy one or more objects, select them, then click the Copy command on the Edit menu. Macromedia Flash places a copy of the object on the clipboard. To paste the object, click the Paste command on the Edit menu. You can copy an object to another layer by selecting the layer prior to pasting the object.

You can move an object by selecting it and dragging it to a new location. You can precisely position an object by selecting it and then pressing the arrow keys, which move the selection up, down, left, and right in small increments.

Transforming Objects

You can use the Free Transform Tool to resize, rotate, skew, and reshape objects. After selecting an object, you can click the Free Transform Tool to display eight square-shaped handles used to transform the object, and a circle-shaped transformation point located at the center of the object. The transformation point is the point around which the object can be rotated. You can also change its location. The Free Transform Tool has four options: Rotate and Skew, Scale, Distort, and Envelope. These tool options restrict the transformations that can be completed; you can select only one option at a time.

Resizing an Object

You can enlarge or reduce the size of an object using the Scale Tool option of the Free Transform Tool. The process is to select the object and click the Free Transform Tool, then click the Scale Tool option in the Options section of the toolbox. Eight handles appear around the selected object. You can drag the corner handles to resize the object without changing its proportions. That is, if the object starts out as a square, dragging a corner handle will change the size of the object, but it will still be a square. On the other hand, if you drag one of the middle handles, the object will be reshaped as taller, shorter, wider, or narrower.

Rotating and Skewing an Object

You can use the Rotate and Skew Tool option of the Free Transform Tool to rotate an object and to skew it. Select the object, click the Free Transform Tool, then click the Rotate and Skew Tool option in the Options section of the toolbox. Eight square-shaped handles appear around the object. You can drag the corner handles to rotate the object, or you can drag the middle handles to skew the object, as shown in Figure B-20. The Transform panel can be used to rotate and skew an object in a more precise way; select the object, display the Transform dialog box, enter the desired rotation of skew in degrees, then press [Enter] (Win) or [return] (Mac).

Distorting an Object

You can use the Distort and Envelope Tool options to reshape an object by dragging its handles. The Envelope Tool option provides more than eight handles to allow for more precise distortions.

Reshaping a Segment of an Object

You can use the Subselection Tool to reshape a segment of an object. Click an edge of the object to display handles that can be dragged to reshape the object.

You can use the Arrow Tool to reshape objects. When you point to the edge of an object, the pointer displays an arc symbol. Using the Arc pointer, you can drag the edge of the object you want to reshape, as

shown in Figure B-21. If the Arrow Tool points to a corner of an object, the pointer displays an L-shaped symbol—dragging the pointer reshapes the corner of the object.

Flipping an Object

You can use an option under the Transform command to flip an object either horizontally or vertically. Select the object, click the Transform command on the Modify menu, and then choose Flip Vertical or Flip Horizontal. Other Transform options allow you to rotate and scale the selected object, and the Remove Transform command allows you to restore an object to its original state.

FIGURE B-20
Using handles to manipulate an object

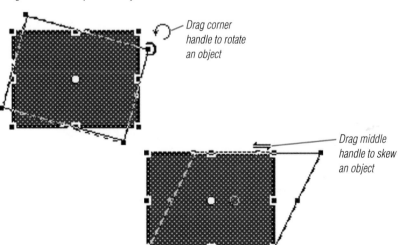

Drag corner
handle to rotate
an object

Drag middle
handle to skew
an object

FIGURE B-21
Using the Arrow Tool to distort an object

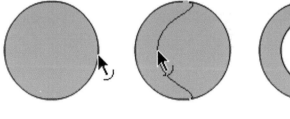

Copy and move an object

1. Click Frame 5 on the timeline.

2. Click the Arrow Tool on the toolbox, then double-click the arrow object to select it. ▶

3. Click Edit on the menu bar, click Copy, click Edit on the menu bar, click Paste, then compare your image to Figure B-22.

   Macromedia Flash pastes a copy of the arrow on the stage.

4. Drag and align the newly copied arrow under the original arrow, as shown in Figure B-23.

5. Save your work.

You used the Arrow Tool to select an object, then you copied and moved the object.

FIGURE B-22
A copy of the arrow on the stage

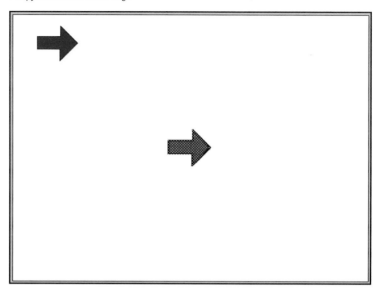

FIGURE B-23
Aligning the arrows

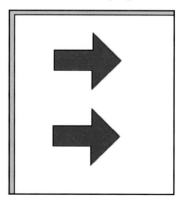

Drawing in Macromedia Flash

Resize and reshape an object

1. Verify that the arrow is selected, then click the Free Transform Tool on the toolbox.

2. Click the Scale Tool option in the Options section of the toolbox.

3. Drag each corner handle towards and then away from the center of the object, as shown in Figure B-24.

   As you drag the corner handles, the object's size is changed, but its proportions remain the same.

4. Drag each middle handle towards and then away from the center of the object.

   As you drag the middle handles, the object's size and proportions are changed.

5. Save your work.

You used the Free Transform Tool and the Scale Tool options to display an object's handles, and you used the handles to resize and reshape the object.

FIGURE B-24
Resizing an object using the corner handles

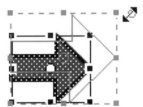

Rotate, skew, and flip an object

1. Verify that the arrow is selected, then click the Rotate and Skew Tool option in the Options section of the toolbox. ↻

2. Click the upper-right corner handle, then rotate the object clockwise as shown in Figure B-25.

3. Click the upper-middle handle, then drag it to the right.

   The arrow slants to the right.

4. Click Edit on the menu bar, click Undo, then repeat until the arrow is in its original shape.

5. Click the Arrow Tool on the toolbox, double-click the bottom arrow, click Window on the menu bar, then click Transform. ▸

6. Double-click the Rotate text box, type **45**, then press [Enter] (Win) or [return] (Mac).

7. Click Edit on the menu bar, then click Undo.

8. Close the Transform panel.

9. Verify that the arrow is selected, click Modify on the menu bar, point to Transform, then click Flip Horizontal.

10. Move the arrows to the positions shown in Figure B-26.

    > **TIP** Double-click each arrow or drag a marquee around them to select the fill and the stroke.

11. Save your work.

You used toolbox options, the Transform panel, and Modify menu commands to rotate, skew, and flip an object.

FIGURE B-25
Rotating an object clockwise

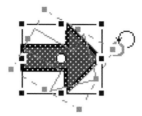

FIGURE B-26
Moving objects on the stage

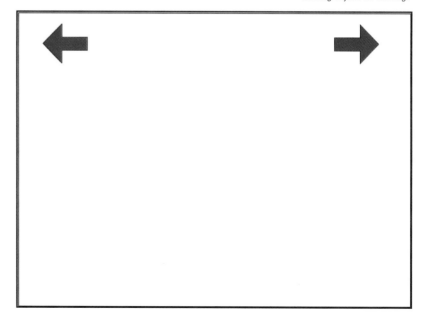

FIGURE B-27

Using the Subselection Tool to select an object

FIGURE B-28

Using the Subselection Tool to drag a handle to reshape the object

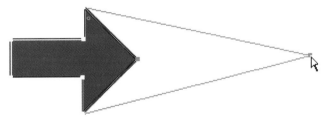

FIGURE B-29

Using the Arrow Tool to drag an edge to reshape the object

Change view and reshape an object using the Subselection Tool

1. Select the arrow in the upper-right corner of the stage, click Edit on the menu bar, click Copy, click Edit on the menu bar, then click Paste.

2. Click the Zoom Tool on the toolbox, then click the middle of the copied object to enlarge the view. Q

3. Click the Subselection Tool on the toolbox, then click the tip of the arrow to display the handles, as shown in Figure B-27.

   TIP   The handles allow you to change any segment of the object.

4. Click the handle at the tip of the arrow, then drag it as shown in Figure B-28.

5. Click the Zoom Tool on the toolbox, press and hold [Alt] (Win) or [option] (Mac), then click the middle of the arrow. Q

6. Click the Oval Tool on the toolbox, then draw a circle to the left of the middle arrow. O

7. Click the Arrow Tool on the toolbox, then point to the left edge of the circle until the Arc pointer is displayed.

8. Drag the pointer to the position shown in Figure B-29.

9. Save your work.

You used the Zoom Tool to change the view, and you used the Subselection and Arrow Tools to reshape objects.

WORK WITH TEXT

What You'll Do

Classic Car Club

You can create
and edit great
looking text
with the Text
Tool.

 In this lesson, you will enter text using text blocks. You will also resize text blocks, change text attributes, and transform text.

Learning About Text

Macromedia Flash provides a great deal of flexibility when using text. Among other settings, you can select the typeface (font), size, style (bold, italic), and color (including gradients) of text. You can transform the text by rotating, scaling, skewing, and flipping it. You can even break apart a letter and reshape its segments.

Entering Text and Changing the Text Block

It is important to understand that text is entered into a text block, as shown in Figure B-30. You use the Text Tool to place a text block on the stage and to enter and edit text. A text block expands as more text is entered and may even extend beyond the edge of the stage. You can adjust the size of the text block so that it is a fixed width by dragging the handle in the upper- right corner of the block. Figure B-31 shows the process of using the Text Tool to enter text and resize the text block. Once you select the tool, you click the pointer on the stage where you want the text to appear. An

insertion point indicates where in the text block the next character will appear when typed. You can reshape the text block by pressing [Enter] (Win) or [return] (Mac) or by dragging the circle handle. After reshaping the text block, the circle handle changes to a square, indicating that the text block now has a fixed horizontal width. Then, when you enter more text, it automatically wraps within the text block. You can resize or move the text block at any time by selecting it with the Arrow Tool and dragging the section.

Changing Text Attributes

You can use the Property inspector to change the font, size, and style of a single character or an entire text block. Figure B-32 shows the Property inspector when a text object is selected. You select text, display the Property inspector, and make the desired changes. You can use the Arrow Tool to select the entire text block by drawing a box around it. You can use the Text Tool to select a single character or string of characters by dragging the

I-beam pointer over them, as shown in Figure B-33.

Working with Paragraphs

When working on large bodies of text, such as paragraphs, Macromedia Flash provides many of the features found in a word processor. You can align paragraphs (left, right, center, justified) within a text block. You can use the Property inspector to set margins (space between the border of a text block and the paragraph text), indents for the first line of a paragraph, and line spacing (distance between paragraphs).

Transforming Text

It is important to understand that a text block is an object. Therefore, you can transform (reshape, rotate, skew, and so on) a text block as you would other objects. If you want to transform individual characters within a text block, you must first break it apart. Use the Arrow Tool to select the text block, and then click the Break Apart command on the Modify menu. Each character (or a group of characters) in the text block can now be selected and transformed.

FIGURE B-30
A text block

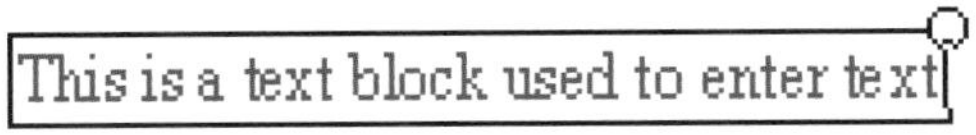

This is a text block used to enter text

FIGURE B-31
Using the Text Tool

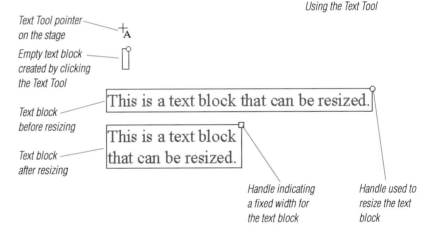

Text Tool pointer on the stage

Empty text block created by clicking the Text Tool

Text block before resizing

This is a text block that can be resized.

Text block after resizing

This is a text block that can be resized.

Handle indicating a fixed width for the text block

Handle used to resize the text block

FIGURE B-32
The Property inspector when a text object is selected

FIGURE B-33
Dragging the I-Beam pointer to select text

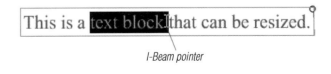

This is a text block that can be resized.

I-Beam pointer

Create text

1. Click Layer 4, click Insert on the menu bar, then click Layer to insert a new layer—Layer 5.

2. Insert a keyframe in Frame 20 on Layer 5.

3. Click the Text Tool on the toolbox, click the center of the stage, then type **You can create great looking text with the Text Tool**. A

4. Click the I-Beam pointer before the word "great," as shown in Figure B-34, then type **and edit**. I

5. Save your work.

You used the Text Tool to create text.

FIGURE B-34
Using the Text Tool to enter text

You can create great looking text with the Text Tool.

FIGURE B-35
Resizing the text block

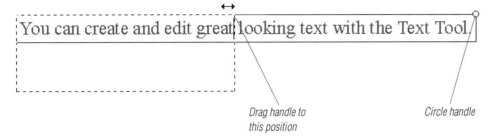

You can create and edit great looking text with the Text Tool.

Drag handle to
this position

Circle handle

FIGURE B-36
Changing text color on the Property inspector

Type Hex color
number here

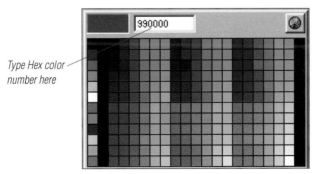

1. Position the text pointer over the circle handle until the pointer changes to a double arrow, then drag the handle to the left, as shown in Figure B-35. $\top_A$

2. Drag the I-Beam pointer across all lines of text to select all the text. $\rceil$

3. Click Window on the menu bar, then verify that Properties is checked.

4. Click the Font list arrow, click Arial Black, click the Font Size list arrow, then drag the slider to **16**.

5. Click the Text (fill) color swatch, click the Hex Edit text box, type **990000** as shown in Figure B-36, then press [Enter] (Win) or [return] (Mac). ■▾

6. Click a blank area of the stage, then save your work.

You resized the text block and changed the font and type size.

Skew text

1. Verify that the Text Tool is selected, click the pointer near the top of the stage, approximately even with Frame 20, then type **Classic Car Club**.

   The new text reflects the most recent settings changed in the Property inspector.

2. Drag the I-Beam pointer across all lines of text to select it, click the Font Size list arrow on the Property inspector, then drag the slider to **30**.

3. Click the Arrow Tool on the toolbox, click the Free Transform Tool, then click the Rotate and Skew Tool option in the Options section of the toolbox.

4. Drag the top middle handle to the right to skew the text, as shown in Figure B-37.

5. Save your work.

You skewed text using the Free Transform Tool.

FIGURE B-37
Skewing the text

FIGURE B-38
Reshaping a letter

FIGURE B-39
Applying a gradient fill to each letter

Apply a gradient to text

1. Click the Arrow Tool on the toolbox, click the text block to select it, click Modify on the menu bar, then click Break Apart.

   The words are separated into individual text blocks.

2. Click Modify on the menu bar, then click Break Apart.

   The letters are filled with a dot pattern, indicating that they can now be edited.

3. Click the Zoom Tool on the toolbox, then click the "C" in Classic.

4. Click the Subselection Tool on the toolbox, then click the edge of the letter "C" to display the object's segment handles.

5. Drag a lower handle on the "C" in Classic, as shown in Figure B-38.

   A portion of the letter extends outward.

6. Click the Arrow Tool on the toolbox, click the Fill Color Tool on the toolbox, then click the red gradient color swatch in the bottom row of the color palette.

7. Click the Paint Bucket Tool on the toolbox, then click the top of each letter to change the fill to a red gradient as shown in Figure B-39.

   | TIP   Scroll across the stage as necessary.

8. Click the Zoom Tool on the toolbox, press and hold [Alt] (Win) or [option] (Mac), then click the letter "C" in Classic to zoom out.

9. Save your work, then close the movie.

You converted and reshaped text, and added a gradient to the text.

WORK WITH LAYERS

What You'll Do

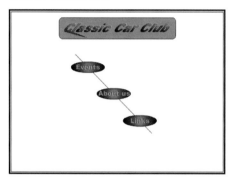

 In this lesson, you will create, rename, reorder, delete, hide, and lock layers. You will also display outline layers, use a Guide layer, distribute text to layers, and create a folder layer.

Learning About Layers

Macromedia Flash uses two types of spatial organization. First, there is the position of objects on the stage, and then there is the stacking order of objects that overlap. An example of overlapping objects is text placed on a banner. Layers are used on the timeline as a way to organize objects. Placing objects on their own layer makes them easier to work with, especially when reshaping them, repositioning them on the stage, or rearranging their order in relation to other objects. In addition, layers are useful for organizing other elements such as sounds, animations, and ActionScripts.

There are six types of layers:

Normal—The default layer type. All objects on these layers appear in the movie.

Guide (Standard and Motion)—Standard Guide layers serve as a reference point for positioning objects on the stage. Motion Guide layers are used to create a path for animated objects to follow.

Guided—A layer that contains an animated object, linked to a Motion Guide layer.

Mask—A layer that hides and reveals portions of another layer.

Masked—A layer that contains the objects that are hidden and revealed by a Mask layer.

Folder—A layer that can contain other layers.

Motion Guide and Mask layer types will be covered in a later unit.

Working with Layers

The Layer Properties dialog box allows you to specify the type of layer. It also allows you to name, show (and hide), and lock them. Naming a layer provides a clue to the objects on the layer. For example, naming a layer Logo might indicate that the object on the layer is the company's logo. Hiding a layer(s) may reduce the clutter on the stage and make it easier to work with selected objects from the layer(s) that are not hidden. Locking a layer(s) prevents the objects from being accidentally edited. Other options in the Layer Properties dialog box allow you to view layers as outlines and change the outline color. Outlines can be used to help you determine which objects are on a layer. When you turn on this feature, each layer has a colored box that corresponds with the color of the objects on its layer, as shown in Figure B-40. Icons on the Layers section of the timeline correspond to features in the Layer Properties dialog box, as shown in Figure B-41.

FIGURE B-40
Displaying outlines

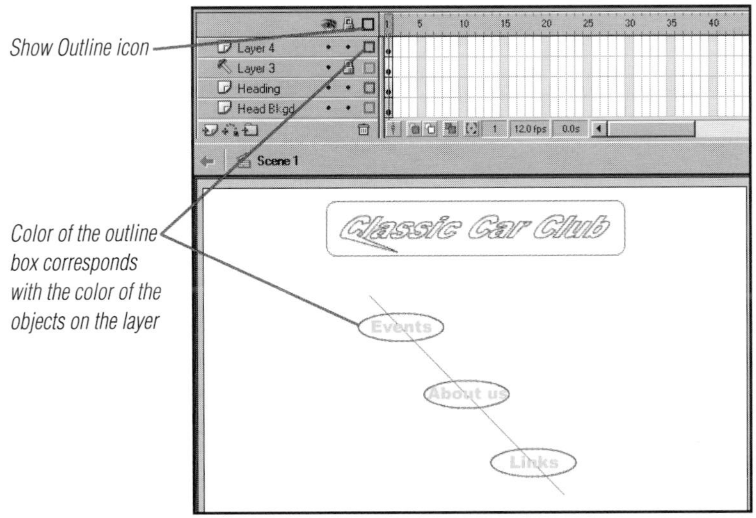

Show Outline icon

Color of the outline
box corresponds
with the color of the
objects on the layer

FIGURE B-41
The Layers section of the timeline

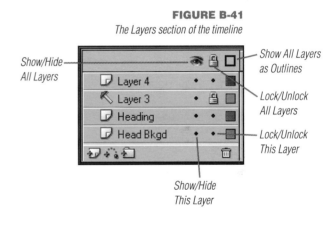

Show/Hide
All Layers

Show All Layers
as Outlines

Lock/Unlock
All Layers

Lock/Unlock
This Layer

Show/Hide
This Layer

Using a Guide Layer

Guide layers are useful in aligning objects on the stage. Figure B-42 shows a Guide layer that has been used to align three buttons along a diagonal path. The process is to insert a new layer, click the Layer command on the Modify menu to display the Layer Properties dialog box, select Guides as the layer type, and then draw a path that will be used as the guide to align objects. You then display the Guides options from the View menu, turn on Snap to Guides, and drag the desired objects to the Guide line. Objects have a registration point that is used to snap when snapping to a guide. By default, this point is at the center of the object. Figure B-43 shows the process.

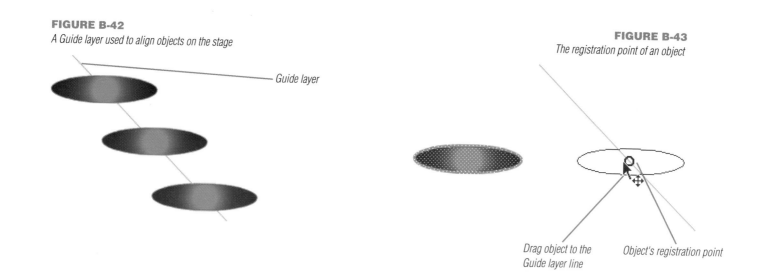

FIGURE B-42
A Guide layer used to align objects on the stage

Guide layer

FIGURE B-43
The registration point of an object

Drag object to the
Guide layer line

Object's registration point

Distributing Text to Layers

Text blocks are made up of one or more characters. When you break apart a text block, each character becomes an object that can be edited independent of the other characters. You can use the Distribute to Layers command to cause each character to automatically be placed on its own layer. Figure B-44 shows the seven layers created after the text block containing 55 Chevy has been broken apart and distributed to layers.

Using Folder Layers

As movies become larger and more complex, the number of layers increases. Macromedia Flash allows you to organize layers by creating folders and grouping other layers in them. Figure B-45 shows a layers folder—Layer 6—with seven layers in it. You can click the Folder layer triangle next to Layer 6 to open and close the folder.

FIGURE B-44

Distributing text to layers

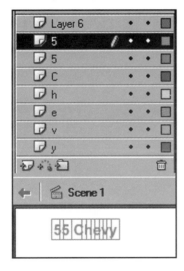

FIGURE B-45

A folder layer

Create and reorder layers

1. Open flb_1.fla, then save it as **layersB.fla**.

2. Click the Insert Layer icon on the bottom of the timeline to insert a new layer, Layer 2.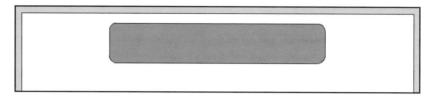

3. Click the Rectangle Tool on the toolbox, then click the Round Rectangle Radius Tool option in the Options section of the toolbox.

4. Type **10**, then click OK.

5. Click the Fill Color Tool on the toolbox, click the Hex Edit text box, type **999999**, then press [Enter] (Win) or [return] (Mac).

6. Click the Stroke Color Tool on the toolbox, click the Hex Edit text box, type **000000**, then press [Enter] (Win) or [return] (Mac).

7. Draw the rectangle shown in Figure B-46 so that it covers the text heading.

8. Drag Layer 1 above Layer 2 on the timeline, as shown in Figure B-47.

9. Save your work.

You created a layer and reordered layers.

Drawing a rectangle with a rounded corner

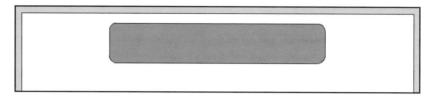

Dragging Layer 1 above Layer 2

Drag Layer 1
above Layer 2

Drawing in Macromedia Flash

FIGURE B-48
Renaming layers

1. Double-click Layer 1 on the timeline, type **Heading** in the Layer Name text box, then press [Enter] (Win) or [return] (Mac).

2. Repeat Step 1 for Layer 2, but type **Head Bkgd**, then compare your timeline to Figure B-48.

3. Click the Heading layer, then click the Delete Layer icon on the bottom of the timeline to delete the layer. 🗑

4. Click Edit on the menu bar, then click Undo.

5. Save your work.

You renamed, deleted, and restored a layer.

Hide, lock, and display layer outlines

1. Click the Show/Hide All Layers icon to hide all layers, then compare your image to Figure B-49. 👁

2. Click the Show/Hide All Layers icon to show all the layers.

3. Click the Lock/Unlock All Layers icon to lock all layers. 🔒

4. With the layers locked, try to select and edit an object.

5. Click the Lock/Unlock All Layers icon again to unlock the layers. 🔒

6. Click the Heading layer, then click the Show/Hide icon under the Show/Hide icon twice to hide and show the layer. ✚

7. Click the Show All Layers as Outlines icon twice to display and turn off the outlines of all objects. ◻

8. Save your work.

You hid and locked layers and displayed the outlines of objects in a layer.

FIGURE B-49
Hiding all the layers

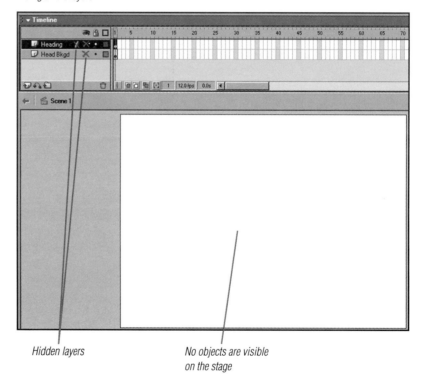

Hidden layers

No objects are visible on the stage

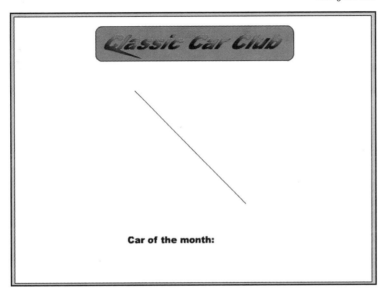

Car of the month:

1. Click the Heading layer, then click the Insert Layer icon on the timeline to add a new layer, Layer 3.

2. Click Modify on the menu bar, click Layer to display the Layer Properties dialog box, click Guide, then click OK.

3. Click the Line Tool on the toolbox, press and hold [Shift], then draw the diagonal line shown in Figure B-50.

4. Click the Lock/Unlock This Layer icon under the Lock/Unlock All Layers icon in Layer 3 to lock it, then compare your layers to Figure B-51.

5. Save your work.

You created a guide for a Guide layer.

FIGURE B-51

Layer 3 locked

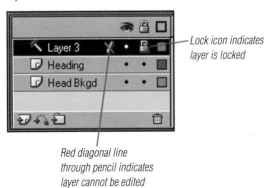

Lock icon indicates layer is locked

Red diagonal line through pencil indicates layer cannot be edited

Add objects to a Guide layer

1. Click the Insert Layer icon on the timeline to add a new layer, Layer 4.

2. Click the Fill Color Tool on the toolbox, then click the red gradient color swatch in the bottom row of the color palette, if necessary.

3. Click the Oval Tool on the toolbox, then draw the oval shown in Figure B-52. O

4. Click the Arrow Tool on the toolbox, then double-click the oval object to select it.

5. Point to the center of the oval, click, then slowly drag it to the Guide layer line, as shown in Figure B-53.

6. With the oval object selected, click Edit on the menu bar, then click Copy.

7. Click Edit on the menu bar, click Paste, then, if necessary, align the copied object to the Guide layer line beneath the first oval.

(continued)

An oval object

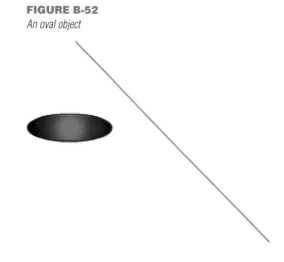

FIGURE B-53
Dragging an object to the Guide layer line

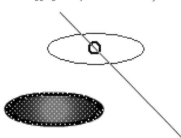

Drawing in Macromedia Flash

FIGURE B-54
Adding text to the oval objects

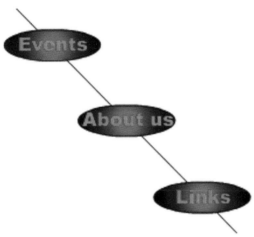

8. Click Edit on the menu bar, click Paste, then align the copied object to the bottom of the Guide layer line.

   TIP Objects are pasted in the center of the stage, and one object may cover up another object.

9. Click the Insert Layer icon on the timeline to insert a new layer, Layer 5.

10. Click the Text Tool on the toolbox, then, if necessary, click the Font list arrow on the Property inspector, click Arial Black, click the Font Size list arrow, then drag the slider to **14**. A

11. Click the Text (fill) color swatch in the Property inspector, click the Hex Edit text box, type **999999**, then press [Enter] (Win) or [return] (Mac).

12. Click on the top oval, then type **Events**.

13. Click the Arrow Tool on the toolbox, click the text box to select it, then drag the text box to center it on the oval, as shown in Figure B-54.

14. Click the text tool, click the middle oval, then type **About us**.

15. Click the text tool, click the bottom oval, then type **Links**.

16. Save your work.

You created a Guide layer and used it to align objects on the stage.

Distribute to layers and create a Folders layer

1. Insert a new layer—Layer 6—click the Text Tool on the toolbox, then type **55 Chevy** following the words "Car of the Month:".

2. Click the Arrow Tool on the toolbox, then select the 55 Chevy text block.

3. Click Modify on the menu bar, then click Break Apart.

4. Click Modify on the menu bar, then click Distribute to Layers.

   Layers are created for each letter.

5. Click Layer 6, click Modify in the menu bar, then click Layer.

   TIP You may need to use the scroll bar at the right side of the timeline to display Layer 6.

6. Click Folder in the Layer Properties dialog box, then click OK.

   Layer 6 becomes a Folder layer.

7. Click the y layer, then drag it to Layer 6, as shown in Figure B-55.

   (continued)

FIGURE B-55
Layer dragged to folder

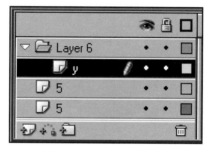

8. Repeat Step 8 for the v, e, h, C, 5, and 5 layers.

9. Click the Collapse triangle next to Layer 6 to collapse the folder, then compare your timeline to Figure B-56. ▽

10. Click the Expand triangle to expand the folder. ▷

11. Save and close the document.

You broke apart a text block and distributed the letters to a Folder layer.

FIGURE B-56
Collapsing Layer 6

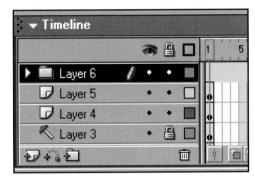

Draw objects with the drawing tools.

1. Open a new movie, then save it as **skillsdemoB.fla**.
2. Display the Grid.
3. Set the stroke color to black (hex: 000000) and the fill color to blue (hex: 0000FF).
4. Use the Oval Tool to draw an oval on the left side of the stage, then draw a circle beneath the oval.
5. Use the Rectangle Tool to draw a rectangle in the middle of the stage, then draw a square beneath the rectangle.
6. Use the Line Tool to draw a horizontal line on the right side of the stage, then draw a vertical line beneath the horizontal line and a diagonal line beneath the vertical line.
7. Use the Pen Tool to draw an arrow-shaped object above the rectangle.
8. Use the Pencil Tool to draw a freehand line above the oval, then use the Smooth Tool option to smooth out the line.
9. Save your work.

Select and edit objects.

1. Use the Arrow Tool to select the stroke of the circle, then deselect the stroke.
2. Use the Arrow Tool to select the fill of the circle, then deselect the fill.
3. Use the Lasso Tool to select several of the objects, then deselect them.
4. Use the Ink Bottle to change the stroke color of the circle to red (Hex FF0000).
5. Use the Paint Bucket to change the fill color of the square to red (Hex FF0000).
6. Change the fill color of the oval to a blue gradient.
7. Save your work.

Work with objects.

1. Copy the arrow object.
2. Move the copied arrow to another location on the stage.
3. Rescale both arrows to approximately half their original size.
4. Flip the copied arrow horizontally.
5. Rotate the rectangle to a 45° angle.
6. Skew the square to the right.
7. Copy one of the arrows and use the Subselection Tool to reshape it, then delete it.
8. Use the Arrow Tool to reshape the circle to a crescent shape.
9. Save your work.

Enter and edit text.

1. Enter the following text in a text block at the top of the stage: **Portal to the Pacific**.
2. Change the text to font: Tahoma, size: 24, color: red.
3. Use the gridlines to help align the text block to the top center of the stage.
4. Skew the text block to the right.
5. Save your work.

Work with layers.

1. Insert a layer into the movie.
2. Change the name on the new layer to **Heading Bkgnd**.
3. Draw a rounded corner rectangle that covers the words Portal to the Pacific.
4. Switch the order of the layers.
5. Lock all layers.
6. Unlock all layers.
7. Hide the Heading Bkgnd layer.
8. Show the Heading Bkgnd layer.
9. Show all layers as outlines.
10. Turn off the view of the outlines.
11. Create a Guide layer and move the arrows to it.
12. Add a layer and use the Text Tool to type **SEATTLE** below the heading.
13. Break the text block apart and distribute the text to layers.
14. Create a Folder layer and add each of the text layers to it.
15. Save your work, then compare your image to Figure B-57.

FIGURE B-57
Completed Skills Review

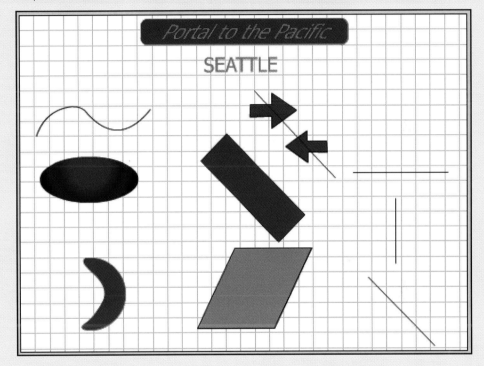

A local travel company, Ultimate Tours, has asked you to design several sample homepages for their new Web site. The goal of the Web site is to inform potential customers of their services. The company specializes in exotic treks, tours, and cruises. Thus, while their target audience spans a wide age range, they are all looking for something out of the ordinary.

1. Open a new movie and save it as **ultimatetoursB.fla**.
2. Set the movie properties, including the size and background color.
3. Create the following on separate layers and name the layers:
   - A text heading; select a font size and font color. Skew the heading, break it apart, then reshape one or more of the characters.
   - A subheading with a different font size and color.
   - A guide path.
   - At least three objects.
4. Snap the objects to the guide path.
5. On another layer, add text to the objects and place them on the guide path.
6. Compare your image to Figure B-58.
7. Save your work.

FIGURE B-58
Completed Project Builder 1

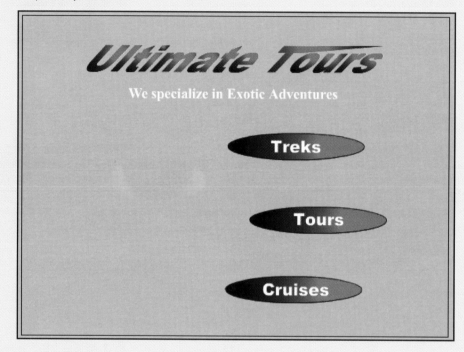

After weeks of unsuccessful job hunting, you have decided to create a personal portfolio of your work. The portfolio will be a Web site done completely in Macromedia Flash.

1. Research what should be included in a portfolio.
2. Plan the site by specifying the goal, target audience, treatment ("look and feel"), and elements you want to include (text, graphics, sound, and so on).
3. Sketch out a storyboard that shows the layout of the objects on the various screens and how they are linked together. Be creative in your design.
4. Design the homepage to include personal data, contact information, previous employment, education, and samples of your work.
5. Open a new movie and save it as **portfolioB.fla**.
6. Set the movie properties, including the size and background color, if desired.
7. Display the gridlines and rulers and use them to help align objects on the stage.
8. Create a heading with its own background, then create other text objects and drawings to be used as links to the categories of information provided on the Web site. (*Hint*: In this file, the Tahoma font is used. You can replace this font with Impact or any other appropriate font on your computer.)
9. Save your work, then compare your image to Figure B-59.

FIGURE B-59
Completed Project Builder 2

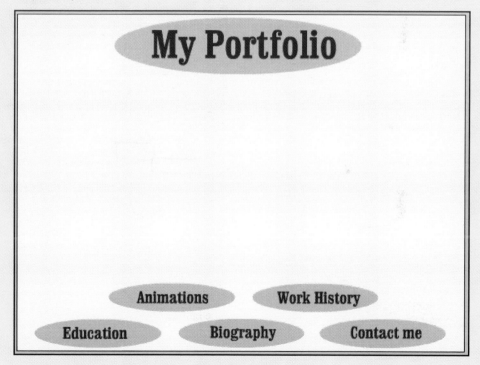

Figure B-60 shows the homepage of the Billabong Web site. Study the figure and complete the following. For each question indicate how you determined your answer.

1. Connect to the Internet, and go to *www.course.com*. Navigate to the page for this book, click the Student Online Companion, then click the link for this unit.

2. Open a document in a word processor or open a new Macromedia Flash movie, save the file as **dpuUnitB**, then answer the following questions. (*Hint*: Use the Text Tool in Macromedia Flash.)

   ■ Whose Web site is this?

   ■ What is the goal(s) of the site?

   ■ Who is the target audience?

   ■ What is the treatment ("look and feel") that is used?

   ■ What are the design layout guidelines being used (balance, movement, and so on)?

   ■ What may be animated on this homepage?

   ■ Do you think this is an effective design for the company, its products, and its target audience? Why or why not?

   ■ What suggestions would you make to improve on the design and why?

FIGURE B-60
Design Project

Your group can assign elements of the project to individual members, or work collectively to create the finished product.

Your group has been asked to create several sample designs for the homepage of a new student organization called the Jazz Club. The club is being organized to bring together music enthusiasts for social events and charitable fund-raising activities. They plan to sponsor weekly jam sessions and a show once a month. Because the club is just getting started, the organizers are looking to you for help in developing a Web site.

1. Plan the site by specifying the goal, target audience, treatment ("look and feel"), and elements you want to include (text, graphics, sound, and so on).
2. Sketch out a storyboard that shows the layout of the objects on the various screens and how they are linked together. Be creative in your design.
3. Open a new movie and save it as **jazzclub.fla**.
4. Set the movie properties, including the size and background color, if desired.
5. Display the gridlines and rulers and use them to help align objects on the stage.

6. Create a heading with a background, text objects, and drawings to be used as links to the categories of information provided on the Web site.

FIGURE B-61
Completed Group Project

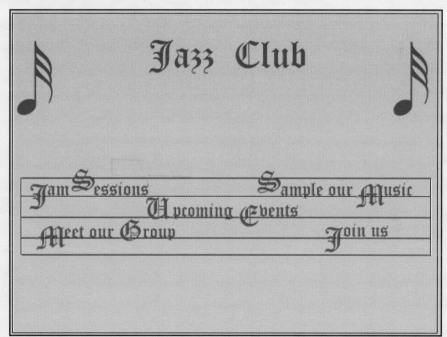

7. Save your work, then compare your image to Figure B-61.

UNIT C

WORKING WITH SYMBOLS AND INTERACTIVITY

1. Work with symbols and instances.

2. Work with Libraries.

3. Create buttons.

4. Assign actions to buttons.

UNIT C
WORKING WITH SYMBOLS
AND INTERACTIVITY

Introduction

An important feature of Macromedia Flash is its ability to create movies with small file sizes. This allows the movies to be delivered from the Web more quickly. One way to keep the file sizes small is to create reusable graphics, buttons, and movie clips. Macromedia Flash allows you to create a graphic (drawing) and then make unlimited copies, which you can use in other movies. Macromedia Flash calls the original drawing a symbol and the copied drawings instances. Using instances reduces the movie file size because Macromedia Flash needs to store only the symbol's information (size, shape, color). When you want to use a symbol in a movie, Macromedia Flash creates an instance (copy), but does not save the instance in the Macromedia Flash movie; this keeps down the movie's file size. What is especially valuable about this process is that you can change the attributes (such as color and shape) for each instance. For example, if your Web site contains drawings of cars, you have to create just one drawing, insert as many instances of the car as you like, and then change the instances accordingly. Macromedia Flash stores symbols in the Library panel—each time you need a copy of the symbol, you can open the Library panel and drag the symbol to the stage, creating an instance of the symbol.

There are three categories of symbols (called behaviors): graphic, button, and movie clip. A graphic symbol is useful because you can reuse a single image and make changes in each instance of the image. A button symbol is useful because you can create buttons for interactivity, such as starting or stopping a movie. A movie clip symbol is useful because you can create a movie within a movie. Movie clips will be covered in a later unit.

Tools You'll Use

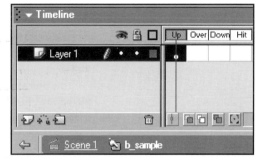

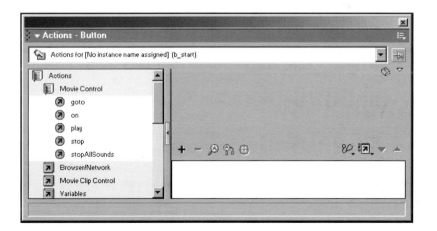

WORK WITH SYMBOLS AND INSTANCES

What You'll Do

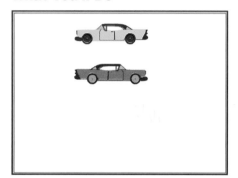

 In this lesson, you will create graphic symbols, turn them into instances, and then edit the instances.

Creating a Graphic Symbol

You can use the New Symbol command on the Insert menu to create and then draw a symbol. You can also draw an object and then use the Convert to Symbol command on the Insert menu to convert the object to a symbol. The Convert to Symbol dialog box, shown in Figure C-1, allows you to name the symbol and specify the type of symbol you want to create (Movie Clip, Button, or Graphic). When naming a symbol, it's a good idea to use a naming convention that allows you to quickly identify the type of symbol and to group like symbols together. For example, you could identify all graphic symbols by naming them g_*name*.

After you complete the Symbol Properties box, Macromedia Flash places the symbol in the Library panel, shown in Figure C-2. To create an instance of the symbol, you simply drag a symbol from the Library panel to the stage. To edit a symbol, you select it from the Library panel or use the Edit Symbol command on the Edit menu. When you edit a symbol, the changes are

reflected in all instances of that symbol in your movie. For example, you can draw a car, convert this object to a symbol, and then create several instances of the car. You can uniformly change the size of all of the cars by selecting the car symbol from the Library panel and then rescaling it to the desired size.

Working with Instances

You can have as many instances as needed in your movie, and you can edit each one to make it somewhat different than the others. You can rotate, skew (slant), and resize graphic and button instances. In addition, you can change the color, brightness, and transparency. However, there are some limitations to the editing that you can perform. An instance is a single object with no segments or parts, such as a stroke and a fill—you cannot select a part of an instance. Therefore, any changes to the color of the instance are made to the entire object. Of course, you can use layers to stack other objects on top of an instance to change its appearance. In addition, you can use the Break Apart command on the Modify menu to break the link between an instance and a symbol. Once the link is broken, you can make any changes to the object, such as changing its stroke and fill color. However, because the link is broken, the object is no longer an instance, and any changes you make to the original symbol would not affect the object.

The process for creating an instance is to open the Library panel and drag the desired symbol to the stage. You select an instance by using the Arrow Tool to draw a box around it. A blue border indicates that the object has been selected. Then, you can use the Free Transform Tool options (such as Rotate and Skew, or Scale) to modify the entire image, or you can break apart the instance and edit individual lines and fills.

QUICKTIP

You need to be careful when editing an instance. Use the Arrow Tool to draw a box around the instance, or click the object once to select it. Do not double-click the instance; otherwise, you will open an edit window that is used to edit the symbol, not the instance.

FIGURE C-1

Using the Convert to Symbol dialog box to convert a symbol

FIGURE C-2

A graphic symbol in the Library panel

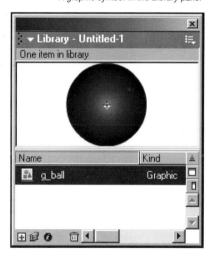

Create a symbol

1. Open flc_1, then save it as **coolcar.fla**.

2. Click the Arrow Tool on the toolbox, then drag the marquee around the car to select it.

3. Click Insert on the menu bar, then click Convert to Symbol.

4. Type **g_car** in the Name text box.

5. Click the Graphic Behavior option, as shown in Figure C-3, then click OK.

6. Click Window on the menu bar, then click Library.

7. Click the g_car symbol in the Library panel to display the car, as shown in Figure C-4.

8. Point to the Library panel title bar, then drag the panel to the right side of the screen so it does not obscure your view of the stage.

9. Save your work.

You opened a file with an object, converted the object to a symbol, and displayed the symbol in the Library panel.

FIGURE C-3
Options in the Convert to Symbol dialog box

→ Insert
→ Convert to Symbol
→ Window
→ Library

FIGURE C-4
Newly created symbol in the Library panel

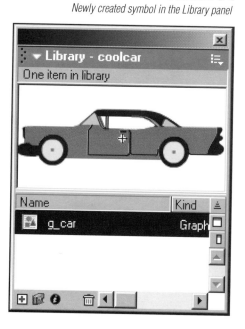

FIGURE C-5

Creating an instance

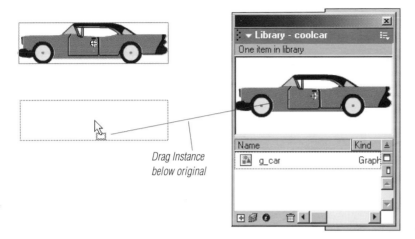

Drag Instance
below original

Create and edit an instance

1. Point to the car image in the Item Preview window, then drag the image to the stage beneath the first car, as shown in Figure C-5.

   You can also drag the name of the symbol from the Library panel to the stage.

2. Click the Arrow Tool on the toolbox, verify that the bottom car is selected, click Modify on the menu bar, point to Transform, then click Flip Horizontal. ▶

3. Click Window on the menu bar; then, if necessary, display the Property inspector.

4. Click the Color list arrow, then click Advanced.

5. Click the Settings button, double-click the Green=(text box, type **0**, then compare your dialog box to Figure C-6. Settings...

6. Click OK, then click a blank area of the stage.

   The windshield and tires become purple.

7. Save your work.

You created an instance of a symbol and edited its instance on the stage.

FIGURE C-6

The Advanced Effect dialog box

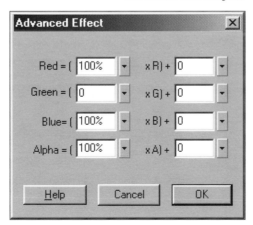

Edit a symbol in symbol-editing mode

1. Double-click the g_car symbol icon in the Library panel to enter symbol-editing mode, then compare your screen to Figure C-7.

   The g_car symbol appears on the stage below the timeline, indicating that you are editing the g_car symbol.

   TIP You can also edit a symbol by clicking Edit on the menu bar, then clicking Edit Symbols.

2. Click a blank area of the stage to deselect the car.

3. Click the Arrow Tool on the toolbox, then click the light gray hubcap inside the front wheel to select it.

4. Press and hold [Shift], then click the hubcap inside the back wheel to select the fills of both wheels.

5. Click the Fill Color Tool on the toolbox, click the blue color swatch in the left column of the color palette, then compare your image to Figure C-8.

   Changes you make to the symbol affect every instance of the symbol on the stage. The hubcap color becomes blue in the Library panel and on the stage.

6. Click Edit on the menu bar, then click Edit Document to return to movie-editing mode.

   The hubcap color of the instances on the stage reflects the color changes you made to the symbol.

7. Save your work.

You edited a symbol in symbol-editing mode.

FIGURE C-7
Symbol-editing mode

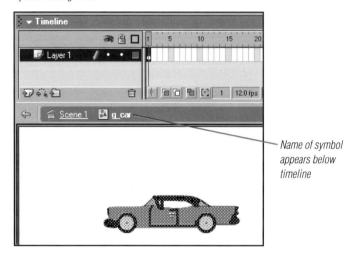

Name of symbol appears below timeline

FIGURE C-8
Edited symbol

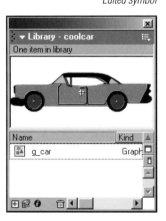

FIGURE C-9

The car with the red body selected

→ Modify
→ Break Apart
(the object is no longer linked to the symbol)

Break apart an instance

1. Click the Arrow Tool on the toolbox, then drag the marquee around the bottom car to select it. ▶

2. Click Modify on the menu bar, then click Break Apart.

   The object is no longer linked to the symbol, and its parts (strokes and fills) can now be edited.

3. Click a blank area of the stage to deselect the object.

4. Click the Arrow Tool on the toolbox, click the front hubcap, press and hold [Shift], then click the back hubcap to select both wheels. ▶

5. Click the Fill Color Tool, then click the green color swatch in the left column of the color palette. 🖲️▪️

6. Double-click the g_car symbol icon in the Library window to enter symbol-editing mode.

7. Click the red body of the car, as shown in Figure C-9.

8. Click the Fill Color Tool, then click the yellow color swatch in the left column of the color palette. 🖲️▪️

9. Click Edit on the menu bar, click Edit Document, then compare your image to Figure C-10.

   The original instance is a different color, but the one to which you applied the Break Apart command remains unchanged.

10. Save and close the movie.

You used the Break Apart command to break the link of the instance to its symbol, then you edited the object and the symbol.

FIGURE C-10

Changing the symbol affects only the one instance of the symbol

Instance of the symbol ———

Object that is no longer an ———
instance of the symbol

WORK WITH LIBRARIES

What You'll Do

In this lesson, you will use the Library panel to organize the symbols in a movie.

Understanding the Library

The Library in a Macromedia Flash movie contains the movie symbols. The Library provides a way to view and organize the symbols, and allows you to change the symbol name, display symbol properties, and add and delete symbols. Figure C-11 shows the Library panel for a movie. Refer to this figure as you read the following description of the parts of the Library.

Title bar—Names the movie with which the Library is associated. This is important because if you have multiple movies open, you could be working on one movie, but have displayed the Library panel for a different movie. In addition to the movie libraries, you can create permanent libraries that are available whenever you start Macromedia Flash. Macromedia Flash also has sample libraries that contain buttons, graphics, and movie clips. The permanent and sample libraries are accessed through the Common Libraries command in the Windows menu. All of the assets in all of the libraries are available for use in any movie.

Options menu—Shown in Figure C-12; provides access to several features used to edit symbols (such as renaming symbols) and organize symbols (such as creating a new folder).

Item preview—Displays the selected symbol. If the symbol is a movie clip, a control button appears allowing you to preview the animation.

Toggle Sorting Order icon—Allows you to reorder the list of folders and symbols within folders.

Wide Library View and Narrow Library View icons—Used to expand and collapse the Library window to display more or less of the symbol properties.

Name text box—Lists the folder and symbol names. Each symbol type has a different icon associated with it. Clicking a symbol name or icon displays the symbol in the Item Preview window.

New Symbol icon—Displays the Create New Symbol dialog box, allowing you to create a new symbol.

New Folder icon—Allows you to create a new folder.

Properties icon—Displays the Symbol Properties dialog box for the selected symbol.

Delete Item icon—Deletes the selected symbol or folder.

FIGURE C-11
The Library panel

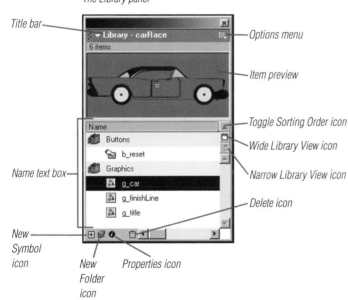

Title bar

Options menu

Item preview

Toggle Sorting Order icon

Wide Library View icon

Narrow Library View icon

Name text box

Delete icon

New Symbol icon

New Folder icon

Properties icon

FIGURE C-12
The Options menu

Create folders in the Library panel

1. Open flc_2.fla, then save it as **carRace.fla**.

2. Click Window on the menu bar, then click Library.

3. Point to the bottom of the Library panel, then when the pointer changes to a double-headed arrow (Win), drag the bottom-right corner of the window to enlarge it to the size shown in Figure C-13.

4. Click the New Folder icon.

5. Type **Graphics** in the Name text box, then press [Enter] (Win) or [return] (Mac).

6. Drag the g_finish symbol to the Graphics folder, as shown in Figure C-14.

    | TIP   You can double-click the Folder icon
    | to view the contents.

(continued)

FIGURE C-13
Enlarging the Library panel

FIGURE C-14
Moving a symbol to a folder

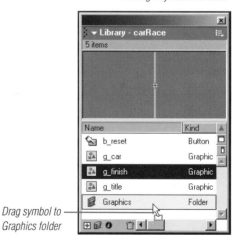

Drag symbol to ⎯
Graphics folder

Working with Symbols and Interactivity

FIGURE C-15

Folders added to the Library panel

7. Drag the g_title and g_car symbols to the Graphics folder.

8. Click the b_reset symbol, then click the New Folder icon.

9. Type **Buttons** in the Name text box, then press [Enter] (Win) or [return] (Mac).

10. Drag the b_reset symbol to the Buttons folder, then compare your panel to Figure C-15.

11. Save your work.

You opened a Macromedia Flash movie, displayed the Library panel, created folders, and organized the symbols within the folders.

Display the properties of a symbol and rename a symbol

1. Double-click the Graphics folder icon to display the symbols.

2. Click the g_finish symbol, then click the Properties icon to display the Symbol Properties dialog box. ❶

3. Type **g_finishLine** in the Name text box, as shown in Figure C-16, then click OK.

4. Save your work.

You used the Library panel to display the properties of a symbol and rename a symbol.

FIGURE C-16
Renaming a symbol

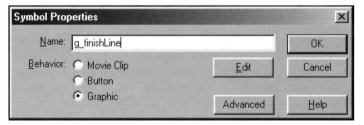

FIGURE C-17

The Library panel with the folders expanded

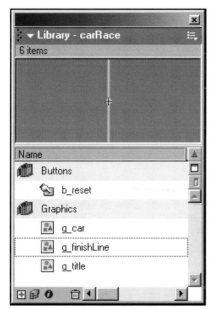

1. Click the Wide Library View icon to expand the window. ▢

2. If necessary, click the Arrow Tool on the toolbox, point to the Library panel title bar, then drag the panel to the center of the screen. ↖

3. Click the Narrow Library View icon to collapse the panel. ▯

4. Click the Graphics folder to highlight it.

5. Click the Toggle Sorting Order icon to move the Graphics folder above the Button folder. ≛

6. Click the Toggle Sorting Order icon again to move the Graphics folder below the Button folder.

7. Click the Options menu icon near the top right of the panel, then click Collapse All Folders. ▤

8. Click the Options menu icon, click Expand All Folders, then compare your Library window to Figure C-17.

9. Click the Arrow Tool on the toolbox, point to the Library panel title bar, then drag the panel to the right side of the screen. ↖

10. Save your work.

You expanded and collapsed the Library panel, and sorted folders.

CREATE BUTTONS

What You'll Do

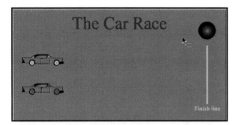

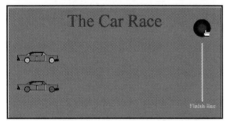

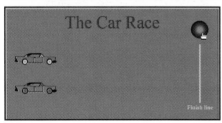

In this lesson, you will create buttons, edit the four button states, and test a button.

Understanding Buttons

Button symbols are used to provide inter-activity. When you click a button, an action occurs, such as starting an animation or jumping to another frame on the timeline. Any object, including Macromedia Flash drawings, text blocks, and imported graphic images, can be made into buttons. Unlike graphic symbols, buttons have four states: Up, Over, Down, and Hit. These states correspond to the use of the mouse and recognize that the user requires feed-back when the mouse is pointing to a but-ton and when the button has been clicked. This is often shown by a change in the but-ton (such as a different color or different shape). These four states are explained below and shown in Figure C-18.

Up—Represents how the button appears when the mouse pointer is not over it.

Over—Represents how the button appears when the mouse pointer is over it.

Down—Represents how the button appears after the user clicks the mouse.

Hit—Defines the area of the screen that will respond to the click. In most cases, you will want the Hit state to be the same or similar to the Up state in location and size.

When you create a button symbol, Macromedia Flash automatically creates a new timeline. The timeline has only four frames, one for each state. The timeline does not play; it merely reacts to the mouse pointer by displaying the appropri-ate button state and performing an action, such as jumping to a specific frame on the main timeline.

The process for creating and previewing buttons is as follows:

Create a button symbol—Draw an object or select an object that has already been created and placed on the stage. Use the Convert to Symbol command on the Insert menu to convert the object to a button symbol and to enter a name for the button.

Edit the button symbol—Select the button and choose the Edit Symbols command on the Edit menu. This displays the button timeline, shown in Figure C-19, which allows you to work with the four button states. The Up state is the original button symbol that Macromedia Flash automatically places in Frame 1. You need to determine how the original object will change for the other states. To change the button for the Over state, click Frame 2 and insert a keyframe. This automatically places a copy of the button in Frame 1 into Frame 2. Then, alter the button's appearance for the Over state. Use the same process for the Down state. For the Hit state, you insert a keyframe on Frame 4 and then specify the area on the screen that responds to the pointer.

Return to the main timeline—Once you've finished editing a button, choose the Edit Document command on the Edit menu to return to the main timeline.

Preview the button—By default, Macromedia Flash disables buttons so that you can manipulate them on the stage. You can preview a button by choosing the Enable Simple Buttons command on the Control menu. You can also click the Test Movie command on the Control menu to play the movie and test the buttons.

FIGURE C-18
The four button states

FIGURE C-19
The button timeline

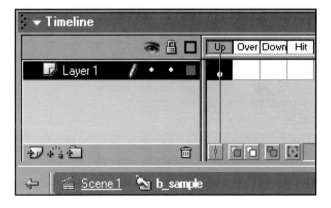

Lesson 3   Create Buttons

Create a button

1. Click the title layer on the timeline.

2. Click the Insert Layer icon on the timeline.

   | TIP   The number of your newly created layer will vary.

3. Double-click the new layer number, type **signal**, then press [Enter] (Win) or [return] (Mac).

4. Click the Oval Tool on the toolbox, click the Stroke Color Tool on the toolbox, then click the black color swatch in the left column of the color palette.

5. Click the Fill Color Tool on the toolbox, then click the red gradient color swatch in the bottom row of the color palette.

6. Draw the circle shown in Figure C-20.

7. Click the Arrow Tool on the toolbox, then drag the marquee around the circle to select it.

8. Click Insert on the menu bar, then click Convert to Symbol.

9. Type **b_signal** in the Name text box, click the Button option, then click OK.

10. Drag the b_signal symbol to the Buttons folder in the Library panel.

11. Save your work.

You created a button symbol on the stage and dragged it to the Buttons folder in the Library panel.

FIGURE C-20
The circle object

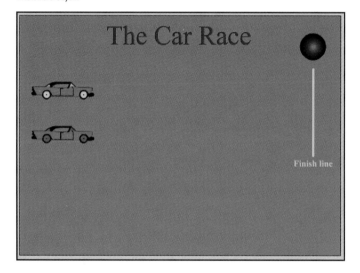

Working with Symbols and Interactivity

FIGURE C-21
The button states on the timeline

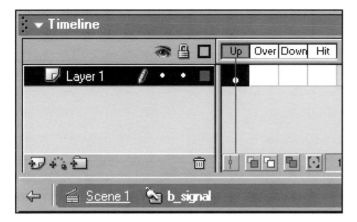

Edit a button and specify a Hit area

1. Click Edit on the menu bar, click Edit Symbols, then compare your timeline to Figure C-21.

   Macromedia Flash switches to symbol-editing mode, and the timeline contains four button states.

2. Insert a keyframe in the Over frame on Layer 1.

3. Click the Fill Color Tool on the toolbox, then click the blue gradient color swatch on the bottom of the color palette.

4. Insert a keyframe in the Down frame on Layer 1.

5. Click the Fill Color Tool on the toolbox, then click the green gradient color swatch on the bottom of the color palette.

6. Insert a keyframe in the Hit frame on Layer 1.

7. Click the Oval Tool on the toolbox, then draw a circle that covers the button, as shown in Figure C-22.

   TIP   The Hit area is not visible on the stage.

8. Click Edit on the menu bar, then click Edit Document.

9. Save your work.

You edited a button by changing the color of its Over and Down states, and you specified the Hit area.

FIGURE C-22
Designating the Hit state for the button

Start dragging here

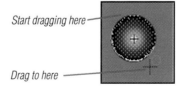

Drag to here

Test a button

1. Click the Arrow Tool on the toolbox, then click a blank area of the stage.

2. Click Control on the menu bar, then click Enable Simple Buttons.

3. Point to the signal button on the stage; notice that the button changes to a blue gradient, the color you selected for the Over state, then compare your image to Figure C-23.

4. Press and hold the mouse, then notice that the button changes to a green gradient, the color you selected for the Down state, as shown in Figure C-24.

(continued)

FIGURE C-23
The button's Over state

FIGURE C-24
The button's Down state

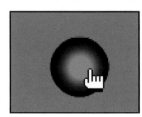

FIGURE C-25

The button's Up state

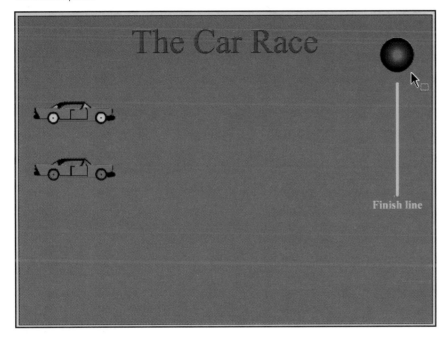

5. Release the mouse and notice that the button changes to the Over state color.

6. Move the mouse away from the signal button, and notice that the button returns to a red gradient, the Up state color, as shown in Figure C-25.

7. Click Window on the menu bar, then click Library to close the Library panel.

You used the mouse to test a button and view the button states.

ASSIGN ACTIONS TO BUTTONS

What You'll Do

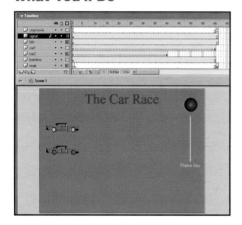

 In this lesson, you will use ActionScripts to assign actions to frames and buttons.

Understanding Actions

In a basic movie, Macromedia Flash plays the frames sequentially, repeating the movie without stopping for user input. However, you may often want to provide users with the ability to interact with the movie by allowing them to perform actions such as starting and stopping the movie or jumping to a specific frame. One way to provide user interaction is to assign an action to the Down state of a button or preferably to the instance of a button. Then, whenever the user clicks on the button, the action occurs. Macromedia Flash provides a scripting language, called ActionScript, that allows you to add actions to buttons and frames within a movie. For example, you can place a stop action in a frame that pauses the movie and then assign a play action to a button that starts the movie when the user clicks the button.

Analyzing ActionScript

ActionScript is a powerful scripting language that allows those with programming expertise to create very sophisticated actions. For example, you can create order forms that capture user input, or volume controls that display when sounds are played. A basic ActionScript involves an event (such as a mouse click) that causes some action to occur by triggering the script. Following is an example of a basic ActionScript:

```
on (release) {gotoAndPlay
(10);}
```

In this example, the event is a mouse click (indicated by the word `release`) that causes the movie's playback head to go to Frame 10 and play the frame. This is a simple ActionScript and is easy to follow. Other ActionScripts can be quite complex and may require programming expertise to understand. Fortunately, Macromedia Flash provides an easy way to use ActionScripts without having to learn the scripting language. The Actions panel allows you to assign basic actions to frames and objects, such as buttons. Figure C-26 shows the Actions panel displaying an ActionScript indicating that when the user clicks on the selected object (a button), the movie plays.

The process for assigning actions to buttons, shown in Figure C-27, is as follows.

- Select the desired button on the stage.
- Display the Actions panel.
- Select the appropriate category. Macromedia Flash provides several Action categories. The Movie Control category allows you to create scripts for controlling movies and navigating within movies. You can use these actions to start and stop movies, jump to specific frames, and respond to user mouse movements and keystrokes.
- Select the desired action.

Button actions respond to one or more of the following mouse events:

Press—With the pointer inside the button Hit area, the user presses the mouse button.

Release—With the pointer inside the button Hit area, the user presses and releases (clicks) the mouse button.

Release Outside—With the pointer inside the button Hit area, the user presses and holds down the mouse button, moves the pointer outside the Hit area, and releases the mouse button.

Key Press—With the Macromedia Flash button displayed, the user presses a predetermined key on the keyboard.

Roll Over—The user moves the pointer into the button Hit area.

Roll Out—The user moves the pointer out of the button Hit area.

Drag Over—The user holds down the mouse button, moves the pointer out of the button Hit area and then back into the Hit area.

Drag Out—With the pointer inside the button Hit area, the user holds down the mouse button and moves the pointer outside the Hit area.

FIGURE C-26

The Actions panel displaying an ActionScript

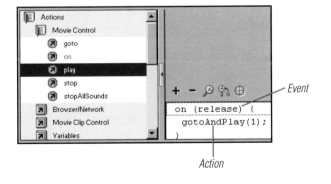

Event

Action

FIGURE C-27

The process for assigning actions to buttons

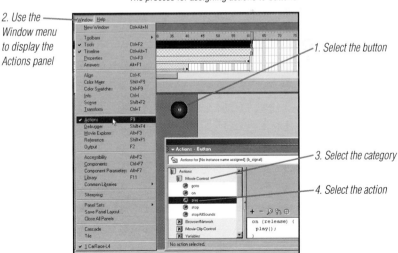

2. Use the Window menu to display the Actions panel

1. Select the button

3. Select the category

4. Select the action

Assign a stop action to frames

1. Click Control on the menu bar, then click Test Movie.

   The movie plays and continues to loop.

2. Click File on the menu bar, then click Close.

   TIP You can also click the Close button on the Test Movie window to close the window, but be careful not to click the Close button for the Macromedia Flash window.

3. Click the Insert Layer icon on the timeline to insert a new layer.

4. Double-click the new layer's name, type **stopmovie**, then press [Enter] (Win) or [return] (Mac).

5. Click Frame 1 on the stopmovie layer.

6. Click Window on the menu bar, then click Actions to display the Actions panel, as shown in Figure C-28.

   TIP Close or minimize the Property inspector if it is open and obscures your view of the stage.

   (continued)

FIGURE C-28

The Actions panel

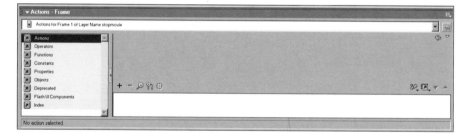

FIGURE C-29

Assigning an action to Frame 1 on the stopmovie layer

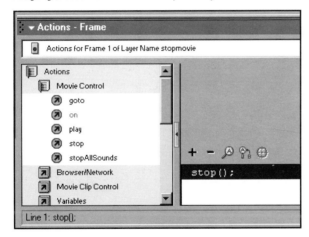

7. Click Actions (if necessary), click Movie Control, double-click stop, then compare your Actions panel to Figure C-29.

8. Insert a keyframe in Frame 61 on the stopmovie layer.

9. Double-click stop in the Actions panel.

10. Click Frame 1 on the timeline, click Control on the menu bar, then click Test Movie.

   The movie does not play because there is a stop action assigned to Frame 1.

11. Click File on the menu bar, then click Close to close the test movie window.

12. Save your work.

You inserted a layer and assigned a stop action to the first and last frames on the layer.

Assign a start action to a button

1. Click the Arrow Tool on the toolbox, then drag the pointer around the signal button on the stage to select it.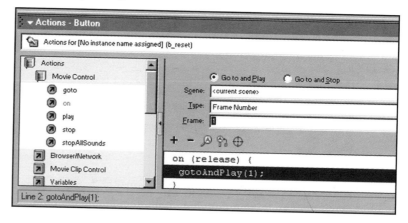

2. Double-click play in the Actions panel.

3. Click Control on the menu bar, then click Test Movie.

4. Click Control on the menu bar, then click Loop to turn it off.

5. Click the signal button.

   The movie plays and stops. The reset button appears but it does not have an action assigned to it.

6. Close the test movie window and save your work.

You assigned a start action to a button.

Assign a goto frame action to a button

1. Click Frame 61 on the timeline to display the Reset button.

2. Click the Arrow Tool on the toolbox, then drag the marquee around Reset to select it.

3. Double-click goto in the Actions panel to display the goto settings shown in Figure C-30.

   TIP The default settings for the goto action are release (click the mouse button and release it) for the event, and Frame 1 for the frame to which the movie jumps. You can specify another frame, change the event, or add multiple events.

   (continued)

FIGURE C-30

The default settings for the goto *action*

FIGURE C-31

Displaying the list of events

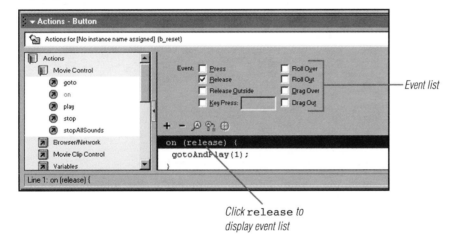

Click release *to display event list*

4. Click release in the ActionScript to display the list of events, as shown in Figure C-31.

   TIP   Expand the Actions panel, if necessary and use the scroll bar at the lower right of the Actions panel to display the release line.

5. Click the Key Press check box, then type **r** in the text box.

   TIP   The letter you specify for the key press is case-sensitive.

6. Click Control on the menu bar, then click Test Movie.

7. Click Control on the menu bar, then click Loop to turn it off.

8. Click the signal button to start the movie, then when the movie stops, click Reset or press **r**.

9. Close the test window, then save and close the movie.

You assigned a start action to a button and a goto *frame action to another button. You also added an event that triggers the action.*

Create a symbol.

1. Open flc_3.fla and save it as **skillsdemoC.fla**.
2. Add a new layer above the ballspin layer and name it **title-bkgnd**.
3. Draw a black rectangle behind the title text Color Spin, using the Rounded Rectangle Radius Tool option, and set the corner radius points to 10.
4. Select the rectangle, convert it to a graphic symbol, then name it **g_bkgnd**.
5. Save your work.

Create and edit an instance.

1. Add a new layer above the titlebkgnd layer and name it **vballs-sm.**
2. Display the Library panel.
3. Drag the g_vball-sm symbol to the upper-left corner of the stage.
4. Drag the g_vball-sm symbol three more times to each of the other corners.
5. Double-click the g_vball-sm symbol icon in the Library panel to switch to symbol-editing mode.
6. Change the color of the ball to red.
7. Return to the document and notice how all instances have been changed to red.
8. Select the ball in the upper-right corner of the stage and break apart the object.

9. Change the color to blue.
10. Select, break apart, and change the bottom-left ball to green and the bottom-right ball to yellow.
11. Save your work.

Create a folder in the Library panel.

1. Use the Options menu in the Library panel to create a new folder.
2. Name the folder **Graphics**.
3. Move the three graphic symbols to the Graphics folder.
4. Expand the Graphic folder.
5. Save your work.

Work with the Library window.

1. Rename the g_bkgnd symbol to g_title-bkgnd in the Library panel.
2. Expand and narrow your view of the Library panel.
3. Collapse and expand the folder.
4. Save your work.

Create a button.

1. Add a new layer above the vballs-sm layer and name it **start**.
2. Drag the g_title-bkgnd symbol from the Library panel to the bottom center of the stage.

3. Create a white 30-pt Arial text block on top of the title-bkgnd object, then type **Start**. (*Hint*: Center the text block in the background object.)
4. Select the rectangle and the text. (*Hint*: Select the Arrow Tool, then press and hold [Shift].)
5. Convert the selected objects to a button symbol and name it **b_start**.
6. Create a new folder named **Buttons** in the Library panel and move the button symbol to the folder.
7. Display the button timeline.
8. Insert a keyframe in the Over frame.
9. Select the text and change the color to gray.
10. Insert a keyframe in the Down frame.
11. Select the text and change the color to blue.
12. Insert a keyframe in the Hit frame.
13. Draw a rectangular object that covers the area for the Hit state.
14. Return to movie-editing mode.
15. Save your work.

Test a button.

1. Turn on Enable Simple Buttons.
2. Point to the button and notice the color change.
3. Click the button and notice the other color change.

Stop a movie.

1. Insert a new layer and name it **stopmovie**.
2. Insert a keyframe in Frame 40 on the new layer.
3. With Frame 40 selected, display the Actions panel.
4. Assign a stop action to the frame.
5. Click Frame 1 on the new layer.
6. Assign a stop action to Frame 1.
7. Save your work.

Assign an action to a button.

1. Click Control on the menu bar, then click Enable Simple buttons to turn off this feature.
2. Use the Arrow Tool to select the button on the stage.
3. Use the Actions panel to assign a play action to the button.
4. Test the movie.
5. Save your work, then compare your image to Figure C-32.

FIGURE C-32
Completed Skills Review

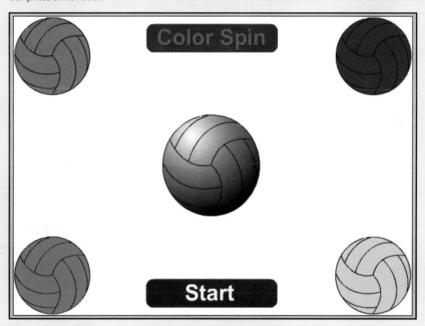

The Ultimate Tours travel company has asked you to design a sample navigation scheme for its Web site. The company wants to see how its homepage will link with one of its main categories (Treks). Figure C-33 shows a sample homepage and Treks screen. Using these or the homepage you created in Unit B as a guide, you will add a Treks screen and link it to the homepage. (*Hint*: Assume that all of the drawings on the homepage are on Frame 1, unless noted.)

1. Open ultimatetoursB.fla (the file you created in Unit B Project Builder 1) and save it as **utlimatetoursC.fla**. (*Hint*: If you did not create ultimatetoursB.fla in Unit B, see your instructor.)
2. Select the layer that the Ultimate Tours is on, and insert a keyframe on a frame at least five frames further along the timeline.
3. Add a new layer, add a keyframe on the last frame of the movie, then create the Treks screen, except for the home graphic, using layers for each of the elements on the screen.
4. Convert the Treks graphic on the homepage to a button symbol, and edit the symbol so that different colors appear for the different states.
5. Assign a goto action that jumps the playhead to the Treks screen when the button is clicked.

6. Add a new layer and name it **stopmovie**. Add stop actions that cause the movie to stop after displaying the homepage and after displaying the Treks page.
7. Insert a new layer and name it **homeButton**, insert a keyframe on the appropriate frame, and draw the home button image with the Home text.

FIGURE C-33
Completed Project Builder 1

8. Convert the image to a button symbol, and edit the symbol so that different colors appear for the different states. Assign a goto action for the button that jumps the movie to Frame 1.
9. Test the movie.
10. Save your work, then compare your Web page to Figure C-33.

This is a continuation of Project Builder 2 in Unit B, which is the development of a personal portfolio. If you did not create portfolioB.fla in Unit B, see your instructor. The homepage has several categories, including the following:

- Personal data
- Contact information
- Previous employment
- Education
- Samples of your work

In this project, you will create a button that will be used to link the homepage of your portfolio to the animations page. Next, you will create another button to start the animation.

1. Open portfolioB.fla (the file you created in Project Builder 2, Unit B) and save it as **portfolioC.fla**. (*Hint*: In this file, the Tahoma font is used. You can replace this font with Impact or any other appropriate font on your computer.)
2. Add a new layer, insert a keyframe on Frame 3 (or one frame past the last frame of the movie), and create an animation using objects that you create.
3. Add a new layer, insert a keyframe on Frame 2 (or one frame before the animation frame), and create a Sample Animation screen.

4. Convert the title into a button symbol and edit the symbol so that different colors appear for the different states. Assign an action that jumps to the frame that plays an animation.
5. Change the Animations graphic on the homepage to a button, and edit the symbol so that different colors appear for the different states. Assign an action that jumps to the Sample Animation screen.

FIGURE C-34
Completed Project Builder 2

6. Add a new layer and name it **stopmovie**. Insert keyframes and assign stop actions to the appropriate frames.
7. Test the movie.
8. Save your work, then compare your movie to Figure C-34.

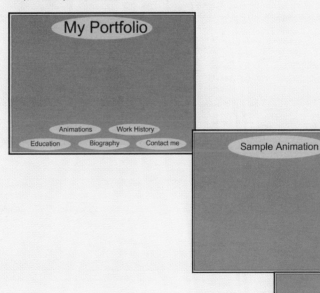

Figure C-35 shows the homepage of a Web site. Study the figure and complete the following questions. For each question, indicate how you determined your answer.

1. Connect to the Internet, and go to *www.course.com*. Navigate to the page for this book, click the Student Online Companion, then click the link for this unit.

2. Open a document in a word processor or open a new Macromedia Flash movie, save the file as **dpuUnitC**, then answer the following questions. (*Hint*: Use the Text Tool in Macromedia Flash.)

   ▪ Whose Web site is this?
   ▪ What is the goal(s) of the site?
   ▪ Who is the target audience?
   ▪ What is the treatment ("look and feel") that is used?
   ▪ What are the design layout guidelines being used (balance, movement, and so on)?
   ▪ What animations would you suggest to enhance this site?
   ▪ Do you think this is an effective design for the company, its products, and its target audience? Why or why not?
   ▪ What suggestions would you make to improve on the design, and why?

FIGURE C-35
Design Project

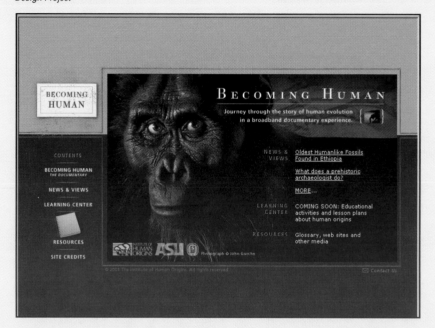

Your group can assign elements of the project to individual members, or you can work collectively to create the finished product.

Your group has been asked to assist your school's International Student Association (ISA). The association sponsors a series of monthly events, each focusing on a different culture from around the world. The events are led by a guest speaker who makes a presentation, followed by a discussion. The events are free and they are open to everyone. ISA would like you to design a Macromedia Flash movie that will be used with its Web site. The movie starts by providing information about the series, and then provides a link to the upcoming event.

1. Open a new movie and save it as **isa.fla**. (*Hint*: In this file, the CloisterBack BT font is used. You can replace this font with Georgia or any other appropriate font on your computer.)
2. Create an initial screen with Information about the association's series.
3. Assign an action that stops the movie.
4. Add a button on the Information screen that jumps the movie to a screen that presents information about the next event.
5. Add a button on the Information screen that jumps the movie to a screen that lists the series (all nine events for the school year-September through May).
6. On the next Event and Series screens, add a Return button that jumps the movie back to the Information screen.

7. Specify different colors for each state of each button.
8. Test the movie.
9. Save your work, then compare your movie to Figure C-36.

FIGURE C-36
Completed Group Project

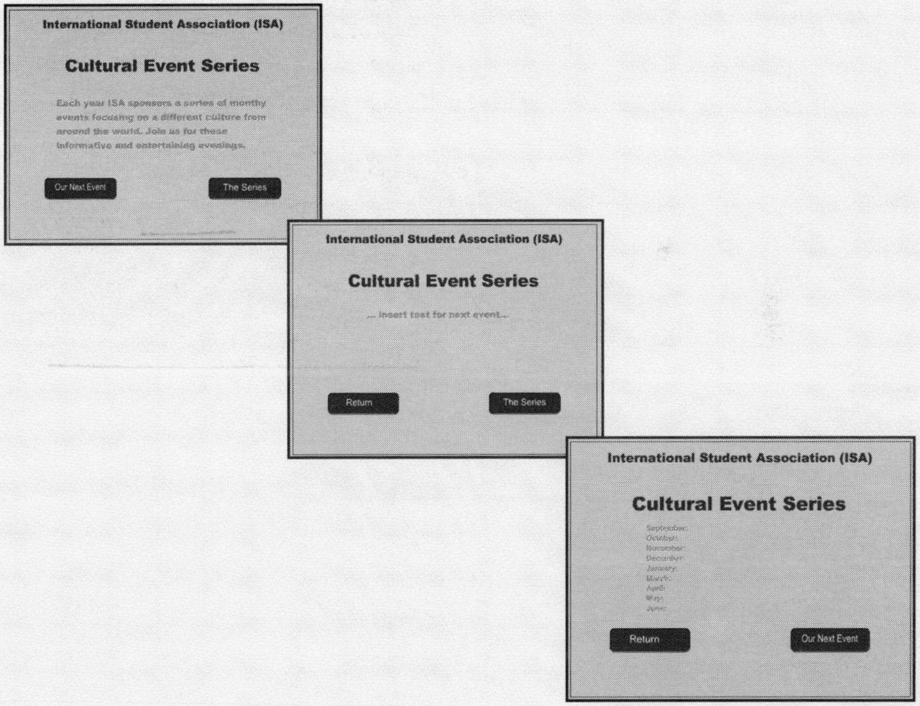

UNIT D

CREATING ANIMATIONS

1. Create frame animations.

2. Create motion-tweened animation.

3. Work with motion guides.

4. Create motion animation effects.

5. Animate text.

UNIT D
CREATING ANIMATIONS

Introduction

Animation can be an important part of your Web site, whether the site focuses on e-commerce (attracts attention and provides product demonstrations), education (simulates complex processes such as DNA replication), or entertainment (provides interactive games).

How Does Animation Work?

The perception of motion in an animation is actually an illusion. Animation is like a motion picture in that it is made up of a series of still images. Research has found that our eye captures and holds an image for one-tenth of a second before processing another image. By retaining each impression for one-tenth of a second, we perceive a series of rapidly displayed still images as a single, moving image. This phenomenon is known as persistence of vision and provides the basis for the frame rate in animations. Frame rates of 10–12 frames-per-second (fps) generally provide an acceptably smooth computer-based animation. Lower frame rates result in a jerky image, while higher frame rates may result in a blurred image. Macromedia Flash uses a default frame rate of 12 fps.

Macromedia Flash Animation

Creating animation is one of the most powerful features of Macromedia Flash, yet developing basic animations is a simple process. Macromedia Flash allows you to create animations that can move and rotate an object around the stage, and change its size, shape, or color. You can also use the animation features in Macromedia Flash to create special effects, such as an object zooming or fading in and out. You can combine animation effects so that an object changes shape and color as it moves across the stage. Animations are created by changing the content of successive frames. Macromedia Flash provides two animation methods: frame-by-frame animation and tweened animation.

Tools You'll Use

Transform options

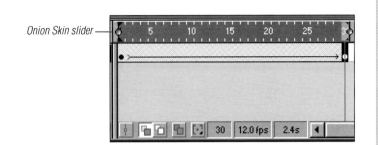

Onion Skin slider

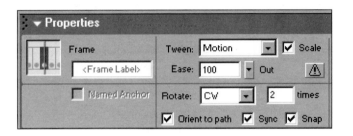

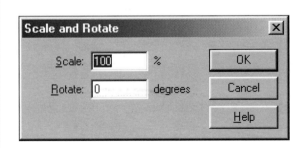

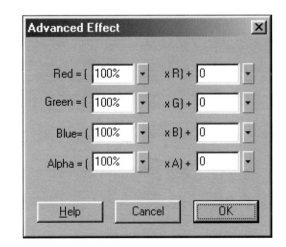

CREATE FRAME ANIMATIONS

What You'll Do

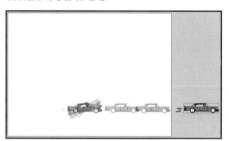

▶ In this lesson you will create frame animations.

Understanding Frame Animations

A frame animation (also called a frame-by-frame animation) is created by specifying the object that is to appear in each frame of a sequence of frames. Figure D-1 shows three images that are variations of a cartoon character. In this instance, the head and body remain the same, but the arms and legs change to represent a walking motion. If these individual images are placed into succeeding frames (with keyframes), an animation is created.

Frame-by-frame animations are useful when you want to change individual parts of an image. The images in Figure D-1 are simple—only three images are needed for the animation. However, depending on the complexity of the image and the desired movements, the time needed to display each change can be large. When creating a frame-by-frame animation, you need to consider the following points:

- The number of different images. The more images there are, the more time is needed to create them. However, the greater the number of images, the less change you need to make in each image. Therefore, the movement in the animation may seem more realistic.
- The number of frames in which each image will appear. If each image appears in only one frame, the animation may appear rather jerky, since the changes are made very rapidly. In some instances, you may want to give the impression of a rapid change in an object, such as rapidly blinking colors. The number of frames creates varied results.
- The movie frame rate. Frame rates below 10 may appear jerky, while those above 30 may appear blurred.

Keyframes are critical to the development of frame animations because they signify a change in the object. Because frame animations are created by changing the object, all frames in a frame animation may need to be keyframes. The exception is when you want an object displayed in several frames before it changes.

Creating a Frame Animation

To create a frame animation, select the frame on the layer where you want the animation to begin, insert a keyframe, and then place the object on the stage. Next, select the frame where you want the change to occur, insert a keyframe, and then change the object. You can also add a new object in place of the original one. Figure D-2 shows

the first six frames of an animation in which the front end of a car raises up and down in place. The movement of the animation is visible because the Onion Skin feature is turned on; this feature will be discussed later in this unit. In this case, the car stays in place during the animation. A frame animation can also involve movement of the object around the stage.

FIGURE D-1
Three images used in an animation

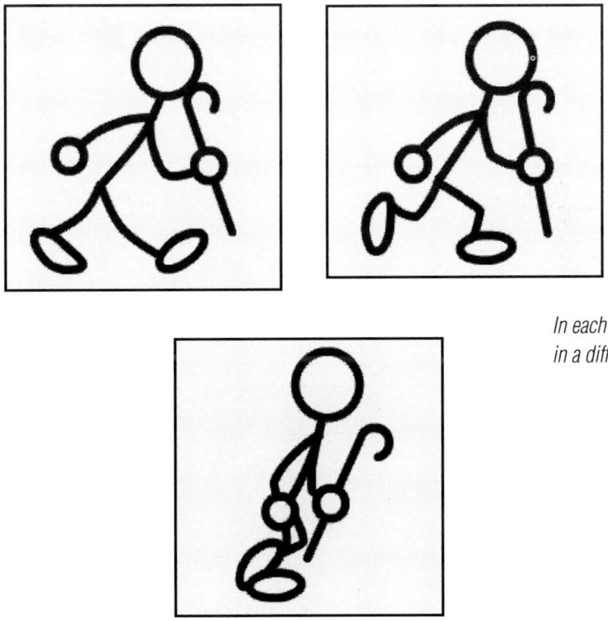

FIGURE D-2
The first six frames of an animation

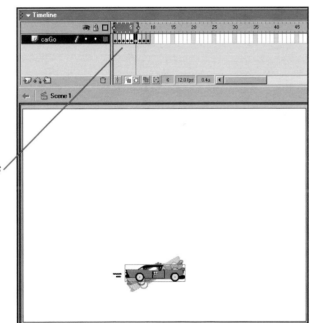

In each frame, the car is in a different position

Create an in-place frame animation

1. Open fld_1.fla, then save it as **frameAn.fla**.

2. Insert a keyframe in Frame 2 on the carGo layer.

3. Verify that the car is selected, click the Free Transform Tool on the toolbox, then click the Rotate and Skew Tool option in the Options section of the toolbox.

4. Drag the top-right handle up one position, as shown in Figure D-3.

5. Insert a keyframe in Frame 3 on the carGo layer.

6. Drag the top-right handle up one more position.

7. Insert a keyframe in Frame 4 on the carGo layer, then drag the top-right handle down one position.

8. Insert a keyframe in Frame 5 on the carGo layer, then drag the top-right handle down to position the car to its original horizontal position.

9. Insert a keyframe in Frame 6 on the carGo layer, then compare your timeline to Figure D-4.

10. Save your work.

You created an in-place frame animation.

FIGURE D-3
Rotating the car

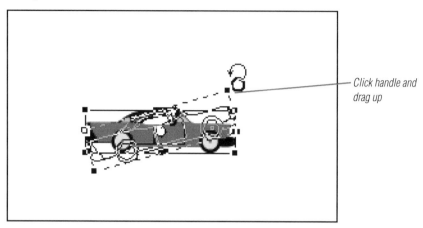

Click handle and drag up

FIGURE D-4
The timeline with keyframes

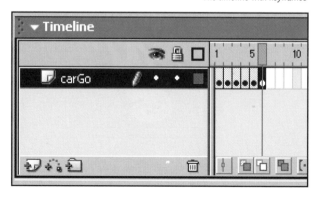

Creating Animations

Add detail to the animation

1. Click the Pencil Tool on the toolbox, click the Stroke Color Tool on the toolbox, then select the black color swatch in the left column of the color palette. ✏

   | TIP Adjust the Zoom percentage as needed.

2. Draw the two lines shown in Figure D-5.

3. Click Control on the menu bar, then click Play.

4. Save your work.

You added lines to the animation that indicate motion.

FIGURE D-5

Adding lines to the object

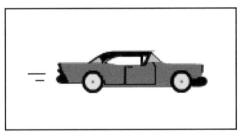

Create a moving frame animation

1. Insert a keyframe in Frame 7 on the carGo layer.

2. Click the Arrow Tool on the toolbox, drag a marquee around the car and the lines, then drag the car and the two lines to the right approximately half the distance to the right edge of the stage.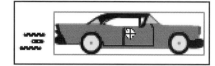

3. Insert a keyframe in Frame 8 on the carGo layer.

4. Click the Pencil Tool on the toolbox, then draw a third line as shown in Figure D-6.

5. Click the Arrow Tool on the toolbox, drag a marquee around the car and lines, then drag the car and the three lines to the right, as shown in Figure D-7.

(continued)

MACROMEDIA FLASH D-8

FIGURE D-6
The car with a third line

FIGURE D-7
The car and three lines after dragging them to the right

Creating Animations

6. Insert a keyframe in Frame 9 on the carGo layer, then drag the car and the three lines completely off the right side of the stage, as shown in Figure D-8.

7. Play the movie, then save your work.

You created a moving frame animation.

Change the frame rate

1. Double-click the Frame Rate icon on the timeline, type **6** in the Frame Rate text box, click OK, then play the movie. 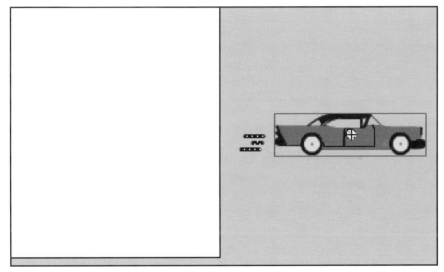 12.0 fps

2. Repeat Step 1, typing **18** and **12** in the Frame Rate text box, respectively.

3. Save your work, then close the movie.

You changed the frame rate for the movie.

FIGURE D-8

Positioning the car off the stage

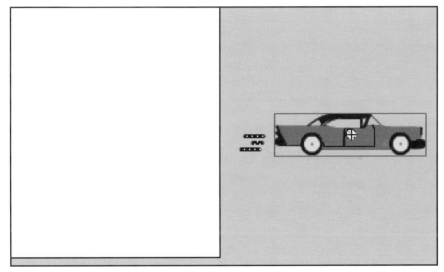

CREATE MOTION-TWEENED ANIMATION

What You'll Do

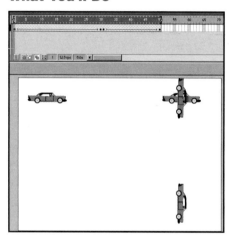

 In this lesson, you will create motion-tweened animations.

Understanding Motion Tweening

Frame-by-frame animation can be a tedious process, especially if you have to alter an object's position an infinitesimal amount in every frame. Fortunately, once you create start and end frames, Macromedia Flash can fill in the in-between frames, a process called tweening. In tweened animation, Macromedia Flash stores only the attributes that change from frame to frame. For example, if you have an object that moves across the stage, Macromedia Flash stores the location of the object in each frame, but not the other attributes of the object, such as its dimensions and color. In contrast, for frame animation, all of the attributes for the object need to be stored in each frame. Frame animations have larger file sizes than tweened animations.

There are two types of tweened animation: shape and motion. Shape animations are similar to the process of image morphing in which one object slowly turns into another—often unrelated—object, such as a robot that turns into a man. Shape-tweened animations will be covered in the next unit. You can use motion tweening to create animations in which objects move and in which they are resized, rotated, and recolored. Figure D-9 shows a motion-tweened animation of a car moving diagonally across the screen. There are only two keyframes needed for this animation: a keyframe in Frame 1 where the car starts, and a keyframe in Frame 30 where the car ends. Macromedia Flash automatically fills in the other frames.

To create a motion-tweened animation, select the starting frame and, if necessary, insert a keyframe. Position the object on the stage and verify that it is selected. Next, choose the Create Motion Tween command from the Insert menu, then insert a keyframe in the ending frame of the animation. Figure D-10 shows the timeline after creating a Motion Tween and specifying an ending keyframe. Motion tweening is represented by black dots displayed in the keyframes and a black arrow linking the keyframes against a light blue background. The final step is to move the object and/or make changes to the object, such as changing its size or rotating it. Keep in mind the following points as you create motion-tweened animations.

- If you change the position of the object, it will move in a direct line from the starting position to the ending position. To move the object on a predetermined path, you can create several motion-tweened animations in succeeding frames, or you can use a motion guide as explained in the next lesson.
- If you reshape an object in the ending keyframe, the object will slowly change from the starting to the ending keyframes. If this is not the effect you want, you can add a keyframe immediately after the tweened animation and reshape the object at that point.
- When you select an object and create a motion tween, Macromedia Flash automatically creates a symbol and names it Tween 1.

QUICKTIP

Make sure that you add a keyframe at the beginning and at the end of each animation. By default, the first frame in a layer is a keyframe.

FIGURE D-9
Sample motion-tweened animation

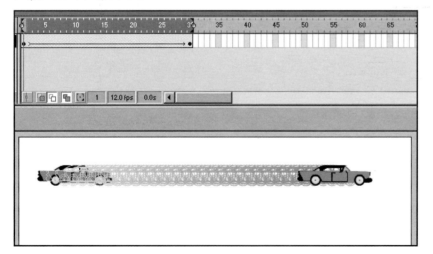

FIGURE D-10
Motion tweening as it appears on the timeline

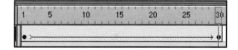

Create a motion-tweened animation

1. Open fld_2.fla, then save it as **carAn**.

2. Click Frame 1 on the carTurn layer, click Insert on the menu bar, then click Create Motion Tween.

3. Insert a keyframe in Frame 30 on the carTurn layer.

4. Click the Arrow Tool on the toolbox (if necessary), then drag the car to the position on the stage shown in Figure D-11. ▶

5. Play the movie, then save your work.

You created a motion-tweened animation.

FIGURE D-11
Final position of the first motion tween

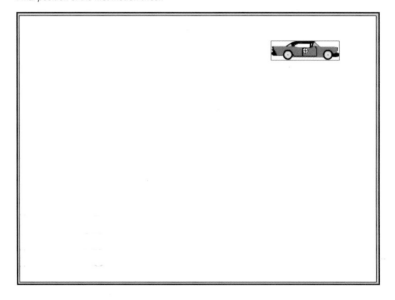

FIGURE D-12

Final position of the combined motion tween

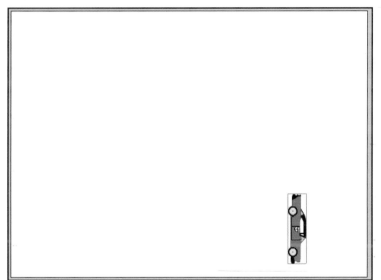

Combine motion-tweened animations

1. Insert a keyframe in Frame 31 on the carTurn layer.

2. Verify that the car is selected, click Modify on the menu bar, point to Transform, then click Rotate 90° CW.

3. Insert a keyframe in Frame 50 on the carTurn layer.

4. Click the Arrow Tool on the toolbox (if necessary), then drag the car to the location shown in Figure D-12.

5. Play the movie.

6. Save your work, then close the movie.

You combined two motion-tweened animations with a rotation between the animations.

WORK WITH MOTION GUIDES

What You'll Do

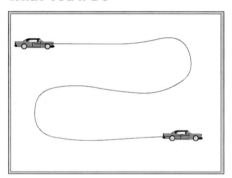

In this lesson, you will create a motion guide and attach an animation to it.

Understanding Motion Guides

In the previous lesson, you combined two animations to cause an object to change directions. Macromedia Flash provides a way for you to create a path that will guide moving objects around the stage in any direction, as shown in Figure D-13. Motion guide layers allow you to draw a path and attach motion-tweened animations to the path. The animations are placed on their own layer beneath the motion guide layer. There are two ways to work with motion guides. First, you can create the guide layer and draw a path, then create an animation and attach the animated object to the path. Second, you can create an animation, create a motion guide layer and draw a path, then attach the animated object to the path. The process for using the second method is as follows:

- Create a motion-tweened animation.
- Select a layer and insert a motion guide layer. The selected layer is indented below the motion guide layer, as shown in Figure D-14. This indicates that the selected layer is associated with the motion guide layer.

- Draw a path using the Pen, Pencil, Line, Circle, Rectangle, or Brush Tools.
- Attach the object to the path by dragging the object by its registration point to the beginning of the path in the first frame, and to the end of the path in the last frame.

Depending on the type of object you are animating and the path, you may need to orient the object to the path. This means that the object will rotate in response to the direction of the path. The Property inspector is used to specify that the object will be oriented to the path. The advantages of using a motion guide are that you can have an object move along any path, including a path that intersects itself, and you can easily change the shape of the path, allowing you to experiment with different motions. A disadvantage of using a motion guide is that, in some instances, orienting the object along the path may result in an unnatural-looking animation. You can fix this by stepping through the animation one frame at a time until you reach the frame where the object is positioned poorly. You

can then insert a keyframe and adjust the
object as desired.

Working with the Property Inspector When Creating Motion-Tweened Animations

You can adjust the following motion-
tweened options on the Property inspector:

- Tween—specifies Motion, Shape,
  or None.
- Scale—tweens the size of an object.

Select this option when you want an
object to grow smaller or larger.

- Ease—specifies the rate of change
  between tweened frames. For
  example, you may want to have an
  object—such as a car—start out slowly
  and accelerate gradually. Ease values
  are between –100 (slow) to 100 (fast).
- Rotate—specifies the number of times
  an object rotates clockwise (CW) or
  counterclockwise (CCW).

- Orient to path—orients the baseline of
  the object to the path.
- Sync—ensures that the object loops
  properly.
- Snap—attaches the object to the path
  by its registration point, the point
  around which the object rotates and
  the point that snaps to a motion guide.

FIGURE D-13
Comparing orientations

FIGURE D-14
A motion guide layer

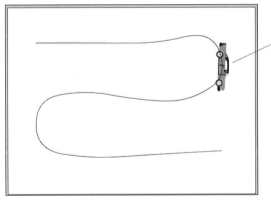

Object oriented to path

Object not oriented to path

Create an animation without a motion guide

1. Open fld_3.fla, then save it as **carPath.fla**.

2. Make sure that the car is selected, click Insert on the menu bar, then click Create Motion Tween.

3. Insert a keyframe in Frame 40 on the carRoute layer.

4. Drag the car to the lower-right corner of the stage, as shown in Figure D-15.

5. Play the movie.

6. Click Frame 1 on the timeline, then save your work.

   The car moves diagonally down to the corner of the stage.

You created a motion animation without a motion guide.

FIGURE D-15
Positioning the car

FIGURE D-16

Motion path

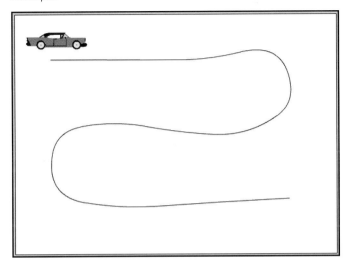

FIGURE D-17

Snapping an object to the path

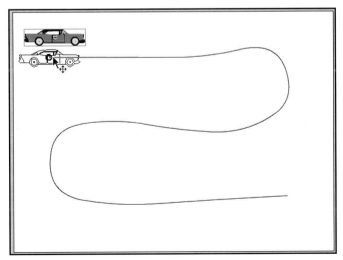

Add a motion guide to an animation

1. Click Frame 1 on the carRoute layer.

2. Click Insert on the menu bar, then click Motion Guide.

   The carRoute layer is indented beneath the guide layer on the timeline.

3. Click the Pencil Tool on the toolbox, click the Smooth Tool option in the Options section of the toolbox, then draw a path similar to the one shown in Figure D-16. ⟋S

   > **TIP**   You can smooth out a path by selecting it with the Arrow Tool, then clicking the Smooth Tool option several times.

4. Click the Arrow Tool on the toolbox. ↖

5. If the car does not snap to the beginning of the path, click the car to select it, click the registration point of the car, then drag it to the beginning of the path, as shown in Figure D-17.

   > **TIP**   An object is snapped to the beginning or end of a motion path when the start or end point of the motion path intersects the car's registration point.

6. Click Frame 40 on the carRoute layer.

7. If the car does not snap to the end of the path, click the Arrow Tool on the Tools panel, click the registration point of the car, then drag it to the end of the path.

8. Play the movie, then save your work.

You created a motion guide on a path and attached an animation to it.

Orient an object to the path

1. Play the movie again and notice how the car does not turn front-first in response to the turns in the path.

2. Make sure the Property inspector is displayed, then click Frame 1 on the carRoute layer.

3. Make sure the car is selected, click the Orient to path check box, then compare your Property inspector to Figure D-18 (Win).

4. Play the movie, then save your work.

   Notice the car is oriented front-first to the turns in the path and that CarRoute appears on the timeline to identify the animation.

You used the Property inspector to specify that the object is oriented to the path.

FIGURE D-18

Orient to path option

FIGURE D-19

Setting the Ease value

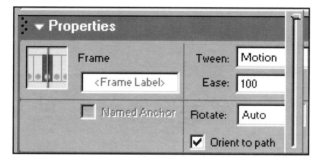

1. Play the movie and notice the speed of the car is constant.

2. Click Frame 1 on the carRoute layer.

3. Click the Ease list arrow in the Property inspector, then drag the slider up to 100, as shown in Figure D-19.

4. Click a blank area outside the stage.

5. Play the movie and notice how the car starts out fast and decelerates as it moves toward the end of the path.

6. Click Frame 1 on the carRoute layer.

7. Click the Ease list arrow in the Property inspector, drag the slider down to −100, then click a blank area outside the stage.

8. Play the movie and notice how the car starts out slow and accelerates as it moves toward the end of the path.

9. Save your work.

You set Ease values to alter the starting and ending speed of the car.

CREATE MOTION ANIMATION EFFECTS

What You'll Do

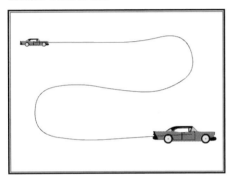

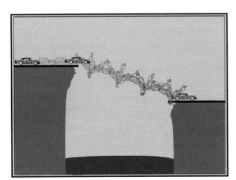

 In this lesson, you will use motion tween-ing to resize, rotate, and change the color of animated objects.

Creating Motion Animation Effects

Up to this point, you have created motion-tweened animations that cause an object to move around the stage. There are several other effects that you can create using motion tweening, including resizing, rotating, and changing the color of an object as it is in motion.

Resizing an Object Using a Motion Tween

The simplest process for resizing an object during a motion tween is to select a frame as the starting frame, draw or place an object on the stage, and then create a motion tween. You can select an ending frame and resize the object using the resize handles that are displayed when you select the Free Transform Tool and the Scale Tool options on the toolbox. The results of this process are shown in Figure D-20. By moving and resizing an object, you can create the effect that it is moving away from you or towards you. If you have the object remain stationary while it is being resized, the effect is similar to zooming in or out.

Rotating an Object Using a Motion Tween

You have several options when rotating an object using a motion tween. You can cause the object to rotate clockwise or counterclockwise any number of degrees and any number of times. You can also stipulate an Ease value to cause the rotation to accelerate or decelerate. These effects can be specified using the Rotate Tool option of the Free Transform Tool on the toolbox, adjusting settings in the Property inspector, or clicking a Transform option on the Modify menu. Notice that these options include Flip Vertical and Flip Horizontal. Choosing these options causes the object to slowly flip throughout the length of the animation. You can combine effects so that they occur simultaneously during the animation. For example, you can have a car rotate and get smaller as it moves across the stage. The Scale and Rotate dialog box allows you to specify a percentage for scaling and a number of degrees for rotating.

Changing an Object's Color Using a Motion Tween

Macromedia Flash provides several ways in which you can alter the color of objects using a motion tween. The most basic change involves starting with one color for the object and ending with another color. The tweening process slowly changes the color across the specified frames. When the movie is played, the colors are blended as the object moves across the stage. If you start with a red color and end with a blue color, at the middle of the animation, the object's color is purple with equal portions of the blue and red colors mixed together. Figure D-21 displays the animation using the Onion Skin feature. Normally, Macromedia Flash displays one frame of an animation sequence at a time on the stage. Turning on the Onion Skin feature allows you to view an outline of the object(s) in any number of frames. This can help in positioning animated objects on the stage.

More sophisticated color changes can be made using the Property inspector. You can adjust the brightness; tint the colors; adjust the transparency (Alpha option); and change the red, green, and blue values of an object. One of the most popular animation effects is to cause an object to slowly fade in. You can accomplish this by motion tweening the object, setting the Alpha value to 0 (transparent) in the starting frame, and then setting it to 100 in the ending frame. To make the object fade out, just reverse the values.

Combining Various Animation Effects

Macromedia Flash allows you to combine the various motion-tween effects so that you can rotate an object as it moves across the stage, changes color, and changes size. Macromedia Flash allows you to combine motion-tweened animations to create various effects. For example, if you create an airplane object, you can apply the following aerial effects:

- enter from off stage and perform a loop;
- rotate the plane horizontally to create a barrel roll effect;
- grow smaller as it moves across the screen to simulate the effect of the plane speeding away;
- change colors on the fuselage to simulate the reflection of the sun.

FIGURE D-20
Resizing an object using a motion tween

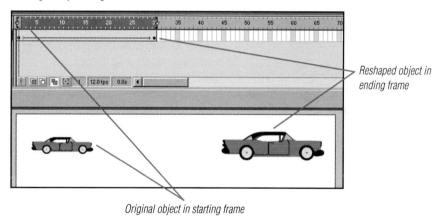

Reshaped object in ending frame

Original object in starting frame

FIGURE D-21
Onion Skin feature

Use motion tweening to resize an object

1. Make sure that the carPath.fla movie is open.

2. Click Frame 1 on the carRoute layer.

3. Make sure the car is selected, click the Free Transform Tool on the toolbox, then click the Scale Tool option in the Options section of the toolbox.

4. Drag the upper-left corner handle inward until the car is approximately half the original size, as shown in Figure D-22.

5. Click Frame 40 on the carRoute layer.

6. Make sure the car is selected, then click the Scale Tool option in the Options section of the toolbox.

7. Drag the upper-right corner handle outward until the car is approximately twice the original size, as shown in Figure D-23.

8. Play the movie and notice how the car is resized.

9. Save your work, then close the movie.

You used the Scale Tool option to resize an object in a motion animation.

Using the handles to reduce the size of the car

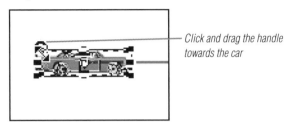

Click and drag the handle towards the car

Using the handles to increase the size of the car

Click and drag the handle away from the car

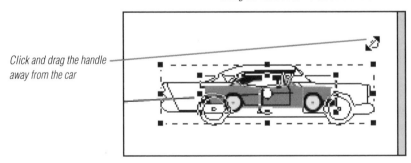

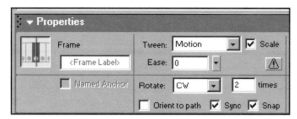

Use motion tweening to rotate an object

1. Open fld_4.fla, then save it as **carRotate**.

2. Click Frame 5 on the carJump layer.

3. Make sure the car is selected, click Insert on the menu bar, then click Create Motion Tween.

4. Click the Rotate list arrow in the Property inspector, click CW, double-click the times text box, then type **2**, as shown in Figure D-24.

5. Insert a keyframe in Frame 20 on the carJump layer.

6. Play the movie; notice the car moves forward, then rotates in place at the edge of the cliff.

7. Click Frame 20 on the carJump layer, then drag the car across the stage to the edge of the right cliff, as shown in Figure D-25.

8. Play the movie; notice that the car rotates as it moves to the new location, then save your work.

You created a motion animation and rotated the object.

FIGURE D-25

Repositioning the car

Use motion tweening to change the color of an object

1. Click Frame 20 on the carJump layer.

2. Click the Arrow Tool on the toolbox (if necessary), then single-click the car to select it. ▸

3. Click the Color list arrow in the Property inspector, click Advanced, then click the Settings button. `Settings...`

4. Click the xB)+ list arrow, then drag the slider to **255**, as shown in Figure D-26.

5. Click OK.

6. Play the movie and notice how the color slowly changes from red to fuchsia.

    TIP   Because motion tweening is performed on instances of symbols and text blocks, changing the color of a motion-tweened object affects the entire object. To make changes in individual areas of an object, you must first select the object and choose the Break Apart command from the Modify menu.

7. Save your work.

You used the Property inspector to change the color of an object as it was being animated.

FIGURE D-26
Changing the color settings

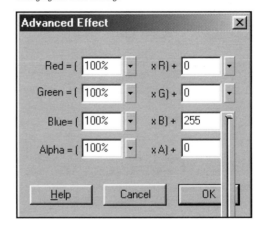

Use the Onion Skin feature

1. Click Frame 1 on the carJump layer, then click the Onion Skin icon on the timeline.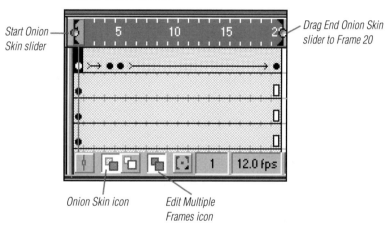

2. Click the Edit Multiple Frames icon on the timeline.

3. Drag the End Onion Skin slider to Frame 20, then compare your image to Figure D-27.

   Each frame of the animation is visible on the stage.

4. Click the Onion Skin icon and the Edit Multiple Frames icon on the timeline to turn off these features.

5. Save and close the movie.

You displayed the animation using the Onion Skin feature.

FIGURE D-27
Using the Onion Skin feature

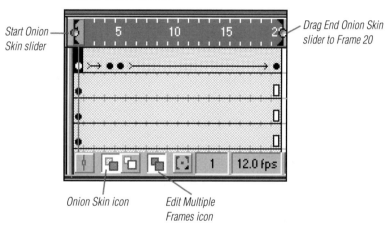

Start Onion Skin slider

Drag End Onion Skin slider to Frame 20

Onion Skin icon

Edit Multiple Frames icon

ANIMATE TEXT

What You'll Do

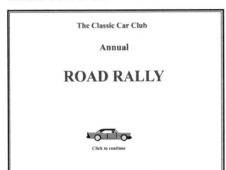

The Classic Car Club

Annual

ROAD RALLY

Click to continue

 In this lesson, you will animate text by scrolling, rotating, zooming, and resizing it.

Animating Text

You can motion tween text block objects just as you do graphic objects. You can resize, rotate, reposition, and change their colors. Figure D-28 shows three examples of animated text. When the movie starts, each of the following can occur one after the other:

■ The Classic Car Club text block scrolls in from the left side to the top center of the stage. This is done by positioning the text block off the stage and creating a motion-tweened animation that moves it to the stage.

■ The Annual text block appears and rotates five times. This occurs after you create the Annual text block, position it in the middle of the stage under the heading, and use the Property inspector to specify a clockwise rotation that repeats five times.

- The ROAD RALLY text block slowly zooms out and appears in the middle of the stage. This occurs after you create the text block and use the Free Transform Tool handles to resize it to a small block. You use the Property inspector to specify a transparent value. Finally, the text block is resized to a larger size at the end of the animation.

Once you create a motion animation using a text block, the text block becomes a symbol and you are unable to edit individual characters within the text block. You can, however, edit the symbol as a whole.

FIGURE D-28
Three examples of animated text

Text scrolls from off the stage to the stage

Text rotates

Text zooms

Select, copy, and paste frames

1. Open frameAn.fla.

2. Click Frame 10 on the carGo layer, then drag left to Frame 1 until you select all the frames, as shown in Figure D-29.

3. Click Edit on the menu bar, then click Cut Frames.

4. Click Frame 71 on the carGo layer.

5. Click Edit on the menu bar, then click Paste Frames.

6. Play the movie, then save your work.

You selected, copied, and pasted frames on the timeline.

FIGURE D-29
Selecting frames

Drag to here — 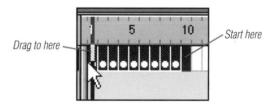 Start here

Positioning the Text Tool pointer outside the stage

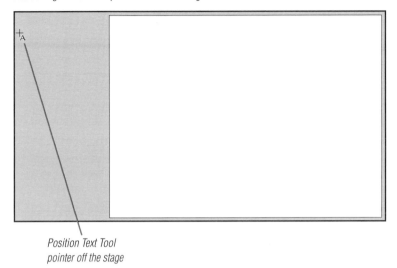

Position Text Tool
pointer off the stage

Positioning the text block

Create animated text

1. Insert a new layer, rename it **scrollText**, then press [Enter] (Win) or [return] (Mac).

2. Click Frame 1 on the scrollText layer, then verify that the Property inspector is displayed.

3. Click the Text Tool on the toolbox, click the Font list arrow in the Property inspector, then click Times New Roman. $\boxed{A}$

4. Click the Font Size list arrow in the Property inspector, then drag the slider to **20**.

5. Click the Text (fill) color swatch in the Property inspector, then click the blue color swatch on the left column of the color palette. ■

6. Click the Text Tool pointer outside the stage in the upper-left corner of the workspace, as shown in Figure D-30. $\top_A$

7. Type **The Classic Car Club**.

8. Click the Arrow Tool on the toolbox, click the text box, click Insert on the menu bar, then click Create Motion Tween. ▶

9. Insert a keyframe in Frame 20 on the scrollText layer.

10. Drag the text block horizontally to the center of the stage, as shown in Figure D-31.

11. Insert a keyframe in Frame 80 on the scrollText layer.

12. Play the movie, then save your work.

    The text moves to center stage from offstage left.

You created a text block object and applied a motion tween animation to it.

Create rotating text

1. Insert a new layer, rename it **rotateText**, then press [Enter] (Win) or [return] (Mac).

2. Insert a keyframe in Frame 21 on the rotateText layer.

3. Click the Text Tool on the toolbox, click the font size list arrow in the Property inspector, drag the slider to **24**, position the pointer beneath the "a" in "Classic", type **Annual**, then compare your image to Figure D-32. A

4. Click the Arrow Tool on the toolbox, click Insert on the menu bar, then click Create Motion Tween. ▶

5. Click Frame 21 on the rotateText layer, click the Rotate list arrow in the Property inspector, click CW, drag the pointer to select 1 in the times text box, then type **2**.

6. Insert keyframes in Frames 40 and 80 on the rotateText layer.

7. Play the movie, then save your work.

   The text rotates clockwise two times.

You created a rotating text block.

FIGURE D-32
Positioning the text for rotation

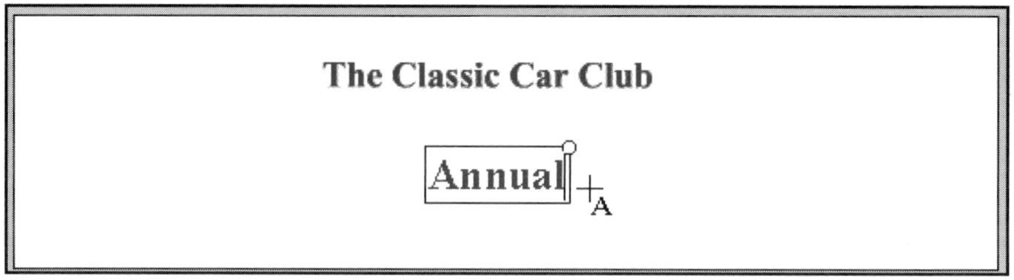

FIGURE D-33

Using the Text Tool to type ROAD RALLY

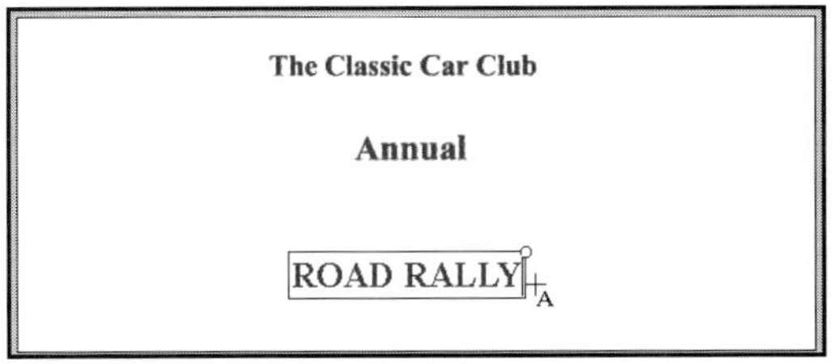

The Classic Car Club

Annual

ROAD RALLY

FIGURE D-34

Resizing and repositioning the text block

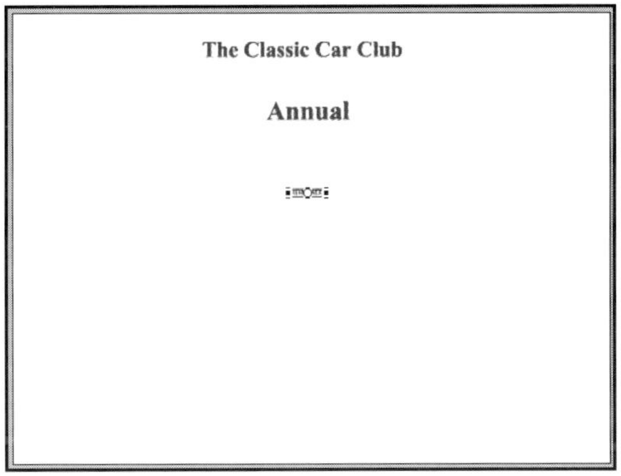

The Classic Car Club

Annual

FIGURE D-35

Resizing the text block

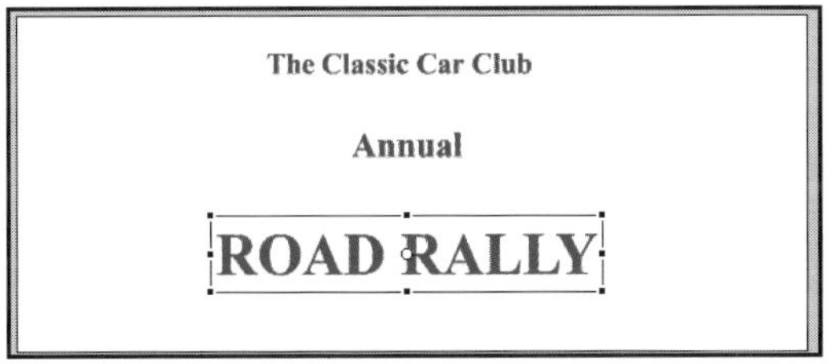

The Classic Car Club

Annual

ROAD RALLY

1. Insert a new layer, rename it **fadeinText**, then press [Enter] (Win) or [return] (Mac).

2. Insert a keyframe in Frame 40 on the fadeinText layer.

3. Click the Text Tool on the toolbox, position the pointer beneath the Annual text block and even with the "T" in "The", type **ROAD RALLY**, then compare your image to Figure D-33. **A**

4. Click the Free Transform Tool on the toolbox, then click the Scale Tool option in the Options section of the toolbox. ▦

5. Drag the upper-left corner handle inward to resize the text block, then position the text block as shown in Figure D-34. ▦

6. Click Insert on the menu bar, then click Create Motion Tween.

7. Click the Color list arrow in the Property inspector, click Alpha, click the Alpha Amount list arrow, drag the slider to **0**, then click a blank area outside the stage.

8. Insert a keyframe in Frame 60 on the fadeinText layer, then click the Arrow Tool on the toolbox (if necessary). ▸

9. Click the Alpha Amount list arrow in the Property inspector, then drag the slider to **100**.

10. Click the Free Transform Tool on the toolbox, click the Scale Tool option in the Options section of the toolbox, drag the upper-left corner handle outward to resize the text block, then position it as shown in Figure D-35. ▣

(continued)

MACROMEDIA FLASH D-31

11. Insert a keyframe in Frame 80 on the fadeinText layer.

12. Play the movie, then save your work.

You created a motion animation that caused a text block to fade in and zoom out.

Add a play button

1. Insert a new layer, rename it **continue**, then press [Enter] (Win) or [return] (Mac).

> TIP Scroll up the timeline to view the new layer.

2. Insert a keyframe in Frame 71 on the continue layer.

3. Click the Text Tool on the toolbox, click the Font Size list arrow in the Property inspector, drag the slider to **12**. A

4. Make sure the bottom of the stage is visible, position the Text Tool pointer beneath the back wheel of the car, click the text tool, type **Click to continue**, then compare your image to Figure D-36. +A

5. Click the Arrow Tool on the toolbox to select the text block, click Insert on the menu bar, click Convert to Symbol, type **b_continue** in the Name text box, make sure the Button option is selected, then click OK.

6. Click the Arrow Tool on the toolbox (if necessary), then double-click the text block to edit the button.

(continued)

FIGURE D-36
Adding a button

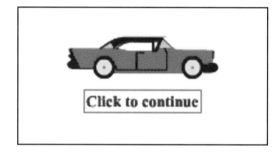

FIGURE D-37

The rectangle that defines the hit area

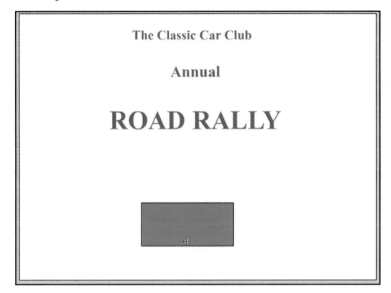

The Classic Car Club

Annual

ROAD RALLY

FIGURE D-38

Adding a stop action

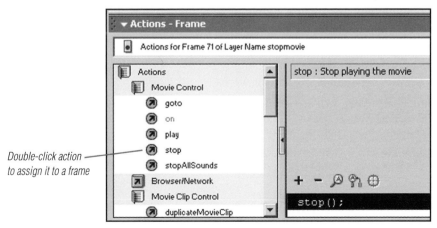

Double-click action to assign it to a frame

7. Insert a keyframe in the Over frame, click the Fill Color Tool on the toolbox, then click the black color swatch in the left column of the color palette.

8. Insert a keyframe in the Down frame, click the Fill Color Tool on the toolbox, then click the bright green color swatch in the left column of the color palette.

9. Insert a keyframe in the Hit frame, click the Rectangle Tool on the toolbox, then draw a rectangle that covers the text block and the car, as shown in Figure D-37.

10. Click Edit on the menu bar, click Edit Document, then save your work.

You inserted a play button.

Add an action to the button

1. Click the Arrow Tool on the toolbox, click Window on the menu bar, then click Actions.

2. Double-click `play` in the Actions panel to assign a `play` action to the button.

3. Insert a new layer, rename the layer **stopmovie**, then insert a keyframe in Frame 71.

4. Double-click `stop` in the Actions panel to assign a `stop` action to Frame 71 on the stopmovie layer, as shown in Figure D-38.

5. Close the Actions panel.

6. Test the movie, then save and close the movie.

   The movie plays the animated text blocks, then plays the animated car when you click the ActionScript text.

You inserted a play button and added a `stop` *action to it.*

Create a frame animation.

1. Open fld_5.fla and save it as **skillsdemoD.fla**.
2. Insert a keyframe in Frame 22 on the v-ball layer.
3. Resize the object to approximately one-fourth its original size.
4. Insert a keyframe in Frame 23 on the v-ball layer.
5. Resize the object back to approximately its original size.
6. Insert a keyframe in Frame 24 on the v-ball layer, then drag the object to the upper-left corner of the stage.
7. Insert a keyframe in Frame 25 on the v-ball layer, then drag the object to the lower-left corner of the stage.
8. Insert a keyframe in Frame 26 on the v-ball layer, then drag the object to the upper-right corner of the stage.
9. Insert a keyframe in Frame 27 on the v-ball layer, then drag the object to the lower-right corner of the stage.
10. Change the movie frame rate to 3 frames per second, then play the movie.
11. Change the movie frame rate to 12 frames per second, play the movie, then save your work.

Create a motion-tweened animation.

1. Insert a new layer and name it **ballAn**.
2. Insert a keyframe in Frame 28 on the ballAn layer.
3. Display the Library panel, then drag the g_vball graphic symbol to the lower-left corner of the stage.
4. Make sure the object is selected, then create a Motion Tween.
5. Insert a keyframe in Frame 60 on the ballAn layer.
6. Drag the object to the lower-right corner of the stage.
7. Play the movie, then save your work.

Create a motion guide.

1. Click Frame 28 on the ballAn layer.
2. Insert a Motion Guide layer.
3. Use the Pencil Tool to draw a motion path in the shape of an arc, as shown in Figure D-39.
4. Attach the object to the left side of the path in Frame 28 on the ballAn layer.
5. Attach the object to the right side path in Frame 60 on the ballAn layer.
6. Use the Property inspector to orient the object to the path.
7. Play the movie, then save your work.

Accelerate the animated object.

1. Click Frame 28 on the ballAn layer.
2. Use the Property inspector to change the Ease value to –100.
3. Play the movie, then save your work.

Create motion animation effects.

1. Click Frame 60 on the ballAn layer, and use the Free Transform Tool and the Scale Tool option handles to resize the object to approximately one-fourth its original size.
2. Click Frame 28 on the ballAn layer, and use the Property inspector to specify a clockwise rotation that plays five times.
3. Play the movie.
4. Select Frame 60 on the ballAn layer, then select the ball.
5. Use the Advanced Color option in the Property inspector to change the color of the object to green.
6. Play the movie, then save your work.

Animate text.

1. Click the guide layer, then insert a new layer and name it **heading**.
2. Click Frame 1 on the heading layer.
3. Use the Text Tool to type **Having fun with a** in a location off the top-left of the stage.
4. Change the text to Arial, 20 point, red, and boldface.
5. Insert a motion tween.
6. Insert a keyframe in Frame 10 on the heading layer.
7. Drag the text to the top center of the stage.
8. Insert a keyframe in Frame 60 on the heading layer.
9. Play the movie and save your work.
10. Add a layer and name it **zoom**.
11. Insert a keyframe in Frame 11 on the zoom layer.
12. Use the Text Tool to type **Volleyball** below the heading, then center it as needed.

13. Create a motion tween.
14. Insert a keyframe in Frame 20 on the zoom layer.
15. Click Frame 11 on the zoom layer and select the text block.
16. Use the Property inspector to set the Alpha color option to 0.

17. Resize the text block to approximately one-half inch in Frame 11 on the zoom layer.
18. Select Frame 20 on the zoom layer, and resize the text block to approximate the size shown in Figure D-39.

19. Insert a keyframe in Frame 60 of the zoom layer.
20. Test the movie, then save your work.

FIGURE D-39
Completed Skills Review

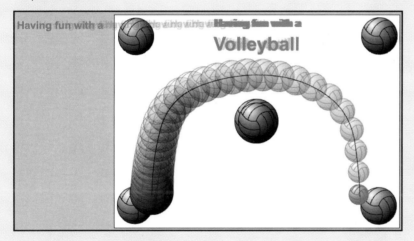

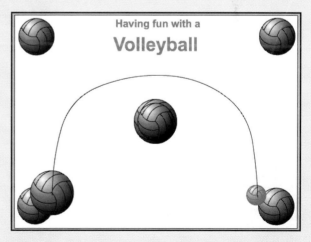

The Ultimate Tours travel company has asked you to design several sample animations for their Web site. Figure D-44 shows a sample homepage and the Cruises screen. Using these (or one of the homepages you created in Unit C) as a guide, complete the following:

For the Ultimate Tours homepage:

1. Open ultimatetoursC.fla (the file you created in Unit C Project Builder 1) and save it as ultimatetoursD.fla. (*Hint*: If you did not create ultimatetoursC.fla in Unit C, see your instructor.)

2. Have the heading **Ultimate Tours** zoom out from a transparent text block.

3. After the heading appears, make the subheading **We Specialize in Exotic Adventures** appear.

4. Make each of the buttons (Treks, Tours, Cruises) scroll from off the bottom of the stage to their positions on the stage. Stagger the buttons so that each one scrolls after the other.

5. Make the logo text appear.

6. Assign a stop action after the homepage appears.

7. Assign a go-to action to the Cruises button to jump to the frame that has the Cruises screen.

8. Add a Cruises screen, then display the heading, subheading, and logo.

9. Create a motion-tweened animation that moves a boat across the screen.

10. Add a motion path that has a dip in it.

11. Attach the boat to the motion path, and orient it to the path.

FIGURE D-40
Completed Project Builder 1

12. Add the three placeholders (Cruise 1, Cruise 2, Cruise 3).

13. Add the Home button.

14. Test the movie, then compare your movie to Figure D-40.

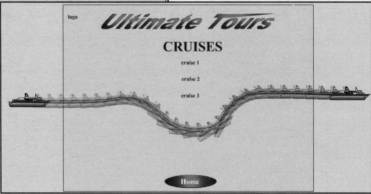

This is a continuation of Project Builder 2 in Unit C, which is the development of a personal portfolio. If you have not completed the previous project, see your instructor. The homepage has several categories, including the following:

- Personal data
- Contact information
- Previous employment
- Education
- Samples of your work

In this project, you will create several buttons for the sample animations screen and link them to the animations.

1. Open portfolioC.fla (the file you created in Project Builder 2, Unit C) and save it as **portfolioD.fla**. (*Hint*: In this file, the Tahoma font is used. You can replace this font with Impact or any other appropriate font on your computer.)

2. Display the Sample Animation screen and change the heading to Sample Animations.

3. Add layers and create buttons for the tweened animation, frame-by-frame animation, motion path animation, and animated text.

4. Create a tweened animation or use the passing cars animation from Unit C, and link it to the appropriate button on the Sample Animations screen.

5. Create a frame-by-frame animation, and link it to the appropriate button on the Sample Animations screen.

6. Create a motion path animation, and link it to the appropriate button on the Sample Animations screen.

7. Create several text animations, using scrolling, rotating, and zooming; link them to the appropriate button on the Sample Animations screen.

8. Add a layer and create a Home button that links the Sample Animation screen to the Home screen.

9. Create frame actions that cause the movie to return to the Sample Animations screen after each animation has been played.

10. Test the movie.

11. Save your work, then compare sample pages from your movie to Figure D-41.

FIGURE D-41
Completed Project Builder 2

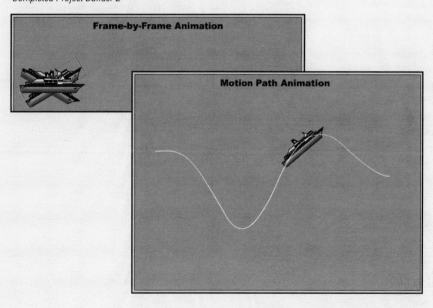

Figure D-42 shows the homepage of a Web site. Study the figure and complete the following. For each question, indicate how you determined your answer.

1. Connect to the Internet and go to *www.course.com*. Navigate to the page for this book, click the Student Online Companion, then click the link for this unit.

2. Open a document in a word processor or open a new Macromedia Flash movie, save the file as **dpuUnitD**, then answer the following questions. (*Hint*: Use the Text Tool in Macromedia Flash.)

   - What seems to be the purpose of this site?
   - Who would be the target audience?
   - How might a frame animation be used in this site?
   - How might a motion-tweened animation be used?
   - How might a motion guide be used?
   - How might motion animation effects be used?
   - How might text be animated?

FIGURE D-42
Design Project

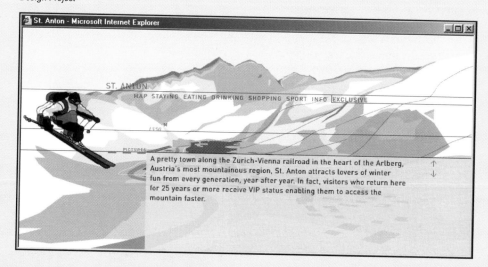

Your group can assign elements of the project to individual members, or work collectively to create the finished product.

Your group has been asked to develop a Web site for the school's summer basketball camp. The camp caters to kids from 6 to 12 years old. Participants are grouped by ability and given instruction on the fundamentals of basketball such as dribbling, passing, and shooting; the rules of the game; teamwork; and sportsmanship. A tournament is played at the end of the two-week camp.

Include the following in the Web site:

1. An initial screen with information about the camp (you provide the camp name, dates, and so on).
2. A black border around the stage.
3. A frame-by-frame animation.
4. A motion-tweened animation.
5. One or more animations that has an object(s) change location on the stage, rotate, change size, and change color.
6. One or more animations that has a text block(s) change location on the stage, rotate, change size, change color, zoom in or out, and fade in or out.
7. An animation that uses a motion guide.
8. An animation that changes the Ease setting.
9. Save the movie as **summerBB**, then compare your image to Figure D-43.

FIGURE D-43
Completed Group Project

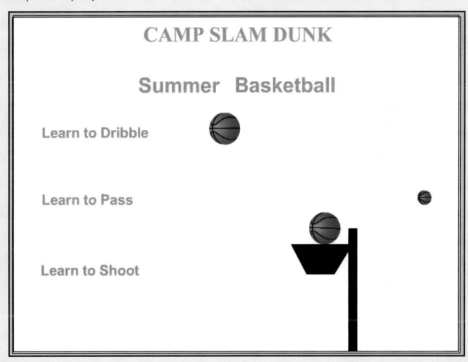

Creating Animations

UNIT E

CREATING SPECIAL EFFECTS

1. Create shape-tweened animations.

2. Create a mask effect.

3. Add sound.

4. Add scenes.

5. Create a slide show presentation.

UNIT E
CREATING SPECIAL EFFECTS

Introduction

Now that you are familiar with the basics of Macromedia Flash, you can begin to apply some of the special features that can enhance a movie. Special effects can provide variety and add interest to a movie, as well as draw the viewer's attention to a location or event in the movie. One type of special effect is a <u>morph</u>. That is, making one shape appear to change into another shape over time, such as an airplane changing into a hot air balloon as it flies across the sky. Another special effect is a spotlight that highlights an area(s) of the movie or reveals selected contents on the stage. You can use sound effects to enhance a movie by creating moods and dramatizing events.

In addition to working with special effects, you now also have experience in developing several movies around one theme, Classic Car Club, and are ready to incorporate these individual movies into a single movie with several scenes. Scenes provide a way to organize a large movie that has several parts, such as a Web site.

Tools You'll Use

Sound settings

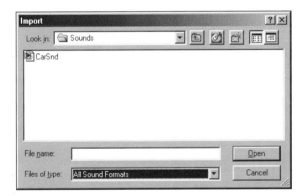

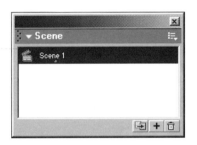

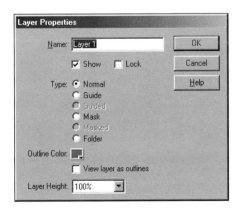

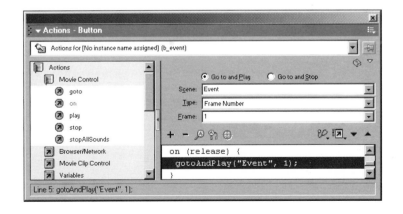

CREATE SHAPE TWEEN ANIMATIONS

What You'll Do

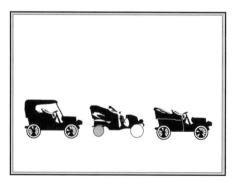

In this lesson, you will create a shape-tweened animation and specify shape hints.

Shape Tweening

In Unit D, you learned that you can use motion tweening to change the shape of an object. You accomplish this by selecting the Free Transform Tool and then dragging the handles. This process allows you to resize and skew the object. While this is easy and allows you to include motion along with the change in shape, there are two drawbacks. First, you are limited in the type of changes (resizing and skewing) that can be made to the shape of an object. Second, you must work with the same object throughout the animation. When you use shape tweening, however, you can have an animation change the shape of an object to any form you desire, and you can include two objects in the animation with two different shapes. As with motion tweening, you can use shape tweening to change other properties of an object, such as the color, location, and size.

Using Shape Tweening to Create a Morphing Effect

Morphing involves changing one object into another, sometimes unrelated, object. For example, you could turn a robot into a man, or turn a football into a basketball. The viewer sees the transformation as a series of incremental changes. In Macromedia Flash, the first object appears on the stage and changes into the second object as the movie plays. The number of frames included from the beginning to the end of this shape-tweened animation determines how quickly the morphing effect takes place. The first frame in the animation displays the first object and the last frame displays the second object. The in-between frames display the different shapes that are created as the first object changes into the second object.

When working with shape tweening you need to keep the following points in mind:

- Shape tweening can be applied only to editable graphics. To apply shape tweening to instances, groups, symbols, text blocks, or bitmaps, you can use the Break Apart command on the Modify menu to break apart an object and make it editable. When you break apart an instance of a symbol, it is no longer linked to the original symbol.

- You can shape tween more than one object at a time as long as all the objects are on the same layer. However, if the shapes are complex and/or if they involve movement in which the objects cross paths, the results may be unpredictable.
- You can use shape tweening to move an object in a straight line, but other options, such as rotating an object, are not available.
- You can use the settings in the Property inspector to set options (such as acceleration or deceleration) for a shape tween.
- Shape hints can be used to control more complex shape changes.

Properties Panel Options

Figure E-1 shows the Property inspector options for a shape tween. The options allow you to adjust several aspects of the animation, as described below.

- Adjust the rate of change between frames to create a more natural appearance during the transition by setting an ease value. Setting the value between -1 and -100 will begin the shape tween gradually and accelerate it toward the end of the animation. Setting the value between 1 and 100 will begin the shape tween rapidly and decelerate it toward the end of the animation. By default, the rate of change is set to 0, which causes a constant rate of change between frames.
- Choose a blend option. The Distributive option creates an animation in which the in-between shapes are smoother and more irregular. The Angular option preserves the corners and straight lines and works only with objects that have these features. If the objects do not have corners, Macromedia Flash will default to the Distributive option.

Shape Hints

You can use shape hints to control the shape's transition appearance during animation. Shape hints allow you to specify a location on the beginning object that corresponds to a location on the ending object. Figure E-2 shows two shape animations of the same objects, one using shape hints and the other not using shape hints. The figure also shows how the object being reshaped appears in one of the in-between frames. Notice that with the shape hints the object in the in-between frame is more recognizable.

FIGURE E-1

The Property inspector options for a shape tween

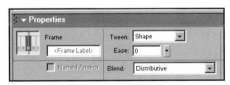

FIGURE E-2

Two shape animations: with and without shape hints

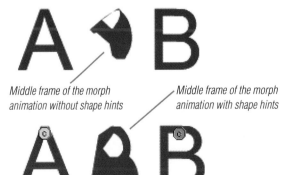

Middle frame of the morph animation without shape hints

Middle frame of the morph animation with shape hints

Create a shape tween animation

1. Open fle_1.fla, then save it as **antiqueCar.fla**.

2. Insert a keyframe in Frame 30 on the shape layer.

3. Click a blank area outside the stage, point to the left side of the top of the car, then drag the car top to the shape shown in Figure E-3.

4. Click anywhere on the shape layer between Frames 1 and 30.

5. Make sure the Property inspector is displayed, click the Tween list arrow, then click Shape.

6. Click Frame 1 on the shape layer, then play the movie.

7. Click Frame 30 on the shape layer.

8. If necessary, click the Arrow Tool on the toolbox, then drag a marquee around the car to select it.

9. Drag the car to the right side of the stage.

10. Play the movie, then save and close it.

You created a shape-tweened animation.

FIGURE E-3
The reshaped object

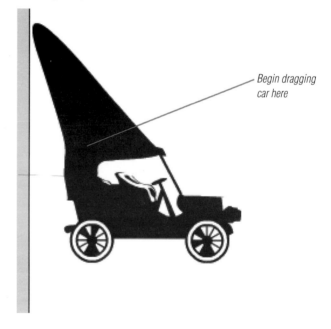

Begin dragging car here

FIGURE E-4

Positioning the car instance on the stage

1. Open fle_2.fla, then save it as **morphCar.fla**.

2. Insert a blank keyframe in Frame 40 on the morph layer.

   > TIP   Inserting a blank keyframe prevents the object in the preceding keyframe from automatically being inserted into the blank frame.

3. Click the Edit Multiple Frames icon on the timeline.

   Turning on the Edit Multiple Frames will allow you to align the two objects to be morphed.

4. Make sure the Library panel is open.

5. Drag the g_antiqueCarTopDown graphic symbol from the Library panel directly on top of the car on the stage, as shown in Figure E-4.

   > TIP   Use the arrow keys to move the object in small increments.

6. Make sure that the antiqueCarTopDown object is selected, click Modify on the menu bar, then click Break Apart.

7. Click the Edit Multiple Frames icon on the timeline to turn off the feature.

8. Click anywhere between Frames 1 and 40 on the morph layer, click the Tween list arrow on the Property inspector, then click Shape.

9. Play the movie, then save your work.

   The first car morphs into the second car.

You created a morphing effect.

Adjust the rate of change in a shape-tweened animation

1. Click Frame 40 on the morph layer.

2. If necessary, click the Arrow Tool on the toolbox, then drag a marquee around the car to select it. ▸

3. Drag the car to the right side of the stage.

4. Click Frame 1 on the morph layer.

5. Click the Ease list arrow in the Property inspector, then drag the slider down to **–100**, as shown in Figure E-5.

6. Click Frame 1 on the timeline, then play the movie.

7. Repeat Steps 4 and 5, but change the value to 100.

8. Click Frame 1 on the timeline, then play the movie.

   The car starts out fast and slows down as the morph process is completed.

9. Save your work, then close the movie.

You added motion to a shape-tweened animation and changed the Ease values.

FIGURE E-5
Changing the Ease value for the morph

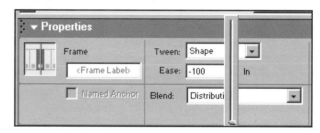

FIGURE E-6

Positioning a shape hint

FIGURE E-7

Adding shape hints

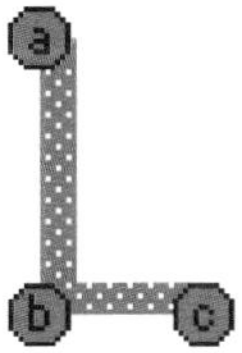

FIGURE E-8

Matching shape hints

1. Open fle_3.fla, then save it as **shapeHints.fla**.

2. Play the movie and notice how the L morphs into a Z.

3. Click Frame 15 on the timeline, the midpoint of the animation, then notice the shape.

4. Click Frame 1 on the hints layer to display the first object.

5. Make sure the object is selected, click Modify in the menu bar, point to Shape, then click Add Shape Hint.

6. Drag the Shape Hint icon to the location shown in Figure E-6. (a)

7. Repeat Steps 5 and 6 to set a second and third Shape Hint icon, as shown in Figure E-7.

8. Click Frame 30 on the hints layer, then drag the Shape Hint icons to match Figure E-8.

   TIP   The shape hints are stacked on top of each other.

9. Click Frame 15 on the hints layer, then notice how the object is more recognizable now that the shape hints have been added.

10. Play the movie.

11. Save your work, then close the movie.

You added shape hints to a morph animation.

CREATE A MASK EFFECT

What You'll Do

Cla

'ar

'lul

 In this lesson, you will apply a mask effect.

Understanding Mask Layers

A mask layer allows you to cover up the objects on another layer(s) and, at the same time, create a window through which you can view various objects on the other layer. You can determine the size and shape of the window and specify whether it moves around the stage. Moving the window around the stage can create effects such as a spotlight that highlights certain contents on the stage, drawing the viewer's attention to a specific location. Because the window can move around the stage, you can use a mask layer to reveal only the area of the stage and the objects you want the viewer to see.

You need at least two layers on the timeline when you are working with a mask layer. One layer, called the mask layer, contains the window object through which you view the objects on the second layer below. The second layer, called the masked layer, contains the object(s) that are viewed through the window. Figure E-9 shows how a mask layer works: The top part of the figure shows the mask

layer with the window in the shape of a circle. The next part of the figure shows the layer to be masked. The last part of the figure shows the results of applying the mask. Figure E-9 illustrates the simplest use of a mask layer. In most cases, you want to have other objects appear on the stage and have the mask layer affect only a certain portion of the stage.

Following is the process for using a mask layer:

- Select an original layer that will become the masked layer—it contains the objects that you want to display through the mask layer window.
- Insert a new layer above the masked layer that will become the mask layer. A mask layer always masks the layer(s) immediately below it.
- Draw a filled shape, such as a circle, or create an instance of a symbol that will become the window on the mask layer. Macromedia Flash will ignore bitmaps, gradients, transparency colors, and line styles on a mask layer. On a mask layer, filled areas become

Creating Special Effects

transparent and non-filled areas become opaque.

- Select the new layer and open the Layer Properties dialog box after selecting the Layer command on the Modify menu, then choose Mask. Macromedia Flash converts the layer to become the mask layer.

- Select the original layer and open the Layer Properties dialog box after selecting the Layer command on the Modify menu, then choose Masked. Macromedia Flash converts the layer to become the masked layer.
- Lock both the mask and masked layers.
- To mask additional layers: Drag an existing layer to beneath the mask

layer, or create a new layer beneath the mask layer and use the Layer Properties dialog box to convert it to a masked layer.

- To unlink a masked layer: Drag it above the mask layer, or select it and select Normal from the Layer Properties dialog box.

FIGURE E-9

A mask layer with a window

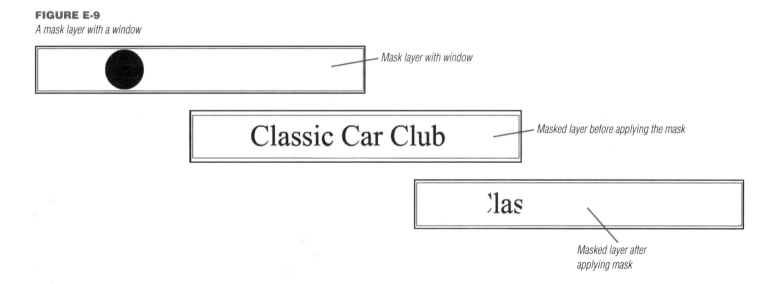

Mask layer with window

Masked layer before applying the mask

Masked layer after applying mask

Create a mask layer

1. Open fle_4.fla, then save it as **classicCC.fla**.

2. Create a new layer on top of the heading layer, then rename it **mask**.

3. Click the Oval Tool on the toolbox, click the Stroke Color Tool, then click the No Stroke icon on the top row of the color palette.

4. Click the Fill Color Tool on the toolbox, then click the black color swatch in the left column of the color palette.

5. Draw the circle shown in Figure E-10, click the Arrow Tool on the toolbox, draw a marquee around the circle to select it, click Insert on the menu bar, then click Create Motion Tween.

6. Insert a keyframe in Frame 40 on the mask layer, then drag the circle to the position shown in Figure E-11.

7. Click the mask layer on the timeline to select it, click Modify on the menu bar, then click Layer to open the Layer Properties dialog box.

8. Verify that the Show option is selected in the Name section, click the Lock option, click the Mask option in the Type section, then click OK.

   The mask layer has a shaded mask icon next to it on the timeline.

9. Play the movie and notice how the circle object covers the text in the heading layer as it moves across the stage.

10. Save your work.

You created a mask layer.

Classic Car Club

Classic Car Club

FIGURE E-12

The completed Layer Properties dialog box

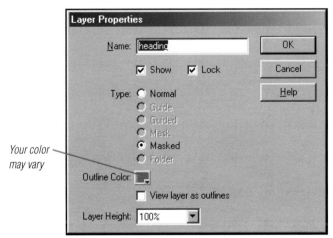

Your color may vary

Create a masked layer

1. Click the heading layer to select it, click Modify on the menu bar, then click Layer to open the Layer Properties dialog box.

2. Verify that the Show option is selected in the Name section, click the Lock option, click the Masked option in the Type section, compare your dialog box to Figure E-12, then click OK.

   The heading layer appears indented and has a shaded masked icon next to it on the timeline.

3. Play the movie and notice how the circle object acts as a window to display the text on the heading layer.

4. Save your work, then close the movie.

You created a masked layer.

ADD SOUND

What You'll Do

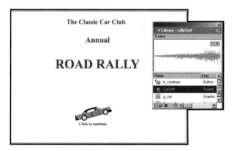

In this lesson, you will add sound to an animation.

Incorporating Animation and Sound

Sound can be extremely useful in a Macromedia Flash movie. Sounds are often the only effective way to convey an idea, elicit an emotion, dramatize a point, and provide feedback to a user's action, such as clicking a button. How would you describe in words or show in an animation the sound a whale makes? Think about how chilling it is to hear the footsteps on the stairway of the haunted house. Consider how useful it is to hear the pronunciation of "Buenos Dias" as you are studying Spanish. All types of sounds can be incorporated into a Macromedia Flash movie: for example, CD-quality music that might be used as background for a movie; narrations that help explain what the user is seeing; various sound effects, such as a car horn beeping; and recordings of special events such as a presidential speech or a rock concert.

Following is the process for adding a sound to a movie:

- Import a sound file into the movie; Macromedia Flash places the sound into the movie's Library.
- Create a new layer.
- Select the desired frame in the new layer and drag the sound symbol to the stage.

You can place more than one sound file on a layer, and you can place sounds on layers with other objects. However, it is recommended that you place each sound on a separate layer as though it were a sound channel, as shown in Figure E-13. In Figure E-13, the sound layer shows a wave pattern that extends from Frame 1 to Frame 40. The wave pattern gives some indication of the volume of the sound at any particular frame. The higher spikes in the pattern indicate a louder sound. The wave pattern also gives some indication of the pitch. The denser the wave pattern, the lower the pitch. You can alter the sound by adding or removing frames. However, removing frames may create undesired effects. It is best to make changes to a sound file using a sound-editing program.

You can use options in the Property inspector (shown in Figure E-14) to synchronize a sound to an event—such as clicking a button—and to specify special effects—such as fade in and fade out. You can import the following sound file formats into Macromedia Flash:
- WAV (Windows only)
- AIFF (Macintosh only)
- MP3 (Windows or Macintosh)

If you have QuickTime 4 or later installed on your computer, you can import these additional sound file formats:
- AIFF (Windows or Macintosh)
- Sound Designer II (Macintosh only)
- Sound Only QuickTime Movies (Windows or Macintosh)
- Sun AU (Windows or Macintosh)
- System 7 Sounds (Macintosh only)
- WAV (Windows or Macintosh)

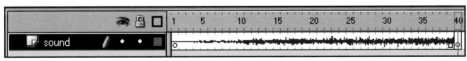

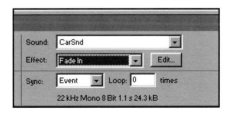

Add sound to a movie

1. Open fle_5.fla, then save it as **rallySnd.fla**.

2. Click the stopmovie layer, insert a new layer, then rename it **carSnd**.

3. Insert a keyframe in Frame 72 on the carSnd layer.

4. Click File on the menu bar, then click Import.

5. Use the Import dialog box to locate the CarSnd.wav file, then click Open.

6. Click Window on the menu bar, then click Library.

7. Drag the CarSnd sound symbol to the stage, as shown in Figure E-15.

8. Test the movie, then close the test movie window.

9. Save your work.

You imported a sound and added it to a movie.

FIGURE E-15
Dragging the CarSnd symbol to the stage

Drag the CarSnd symbol to the stage

Creating Special Effects

FIGURE E-16
The button timeline with the sound layer

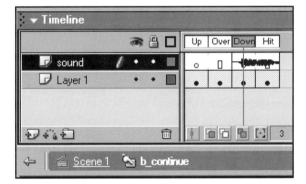

1. Click Frame 71 on the carSnd layer.

2. Click the Arrow Tool on the toolbox, drag a marquee around "Click to continue" to select this button, then double-click the selection to display the button's timeline.

3. Create a new layer above Layer 1, then rename it **sound**.

4. Click the Down frame on the sound layer, click Insert on the menu bar, then click Blank Keyframe.

5. Click File on the menu bar, then click Import.

6. Use the Import dialog box to locate the beep.wav file, then click Open.

7. Drag the beep.wav sound symbol to the stage, then compare your timeline to Figure E-16.

8. Click Edit on the menu bar, then click Edit Document.

9. Test the movie, then close the test movie window.

10. Save your work, then close the movie.

You added sound to a button.

ADD SCENES

What You'll Do

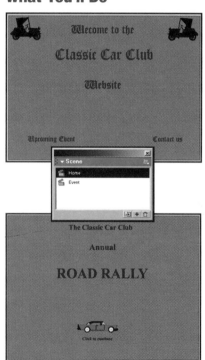

 In this lesson, you will add scenes to a movie and combine scenes from multiple movies into one movie.

Understanding Scenes

Until now you have been working with relatively short movies that have only a few layers and less than 100 frames. However, movies can be quite complex and extremely large. One way to help organize large movies is to use scenes. Just as with their celluloid equivalent, Macromedia Flash scenes are discrete parts of a movie. They have their own timeline and they can be played in any order you specify, or they can be linked through an interactive process that lets the user navigate to a desired scene.

QUICKTIP

There are no guidelines for the length or number of scenes appropriate for any size movie. The key is to determine how best to break down a large movie so that the individual parts are easier to develop, edit, and combine.

Working with Scenes

To add a scene to a movie, you choose Scene from the Insert menu or use the Scene command from the Modify menu. This displays the Scene panel and allows you to add a new scene. The Scene panel can be used to accomplish the following:

- Rename a scene by double-clicking the scene name, then typing in the new name.
- Duplicate a scene by selecting it, then clicking the Duplicate Scene icon.
- Add a scene by clicking the Add Scene icon.
- Delete a scene by selecting it, then clicking the Delete scene icon.
- Reorder the scenes by dragging them up or down the list of scenes.

When a movie is played, the scenes are played in the order they are listed in the Scene panel. You can use the interactive features of Flash, such as a stop action and buttons with `goto` actions to allow the user to jump to various scenes.

Following is the process for combining scenes from several movies into one movie:
- Open the movie that will be used as Scene 1.
- Insert a new scene into the movie.
- Open the movie that will be used as Scene 2.
- Copy the frames from the second movie into Scene 2 of the first movie.
- Continue the process until the scenes for all the movies have been copied into one movie.

The home page for the Classic Car Club Web site, shown in Figure E-17, will become the first scene of a multi-scene movie.

FIGURE E-17
The Classic Car Club home page

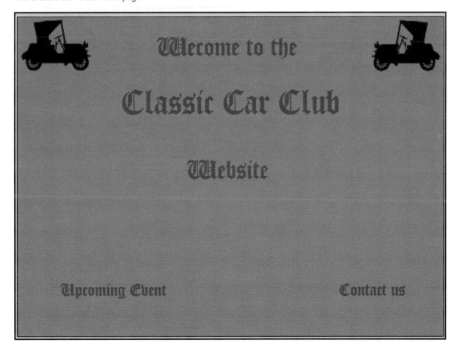

Add and name a scene

1. Open fle_6 movie, then save it as **cccHome.fla**.

2. Click Modify on the menu bar, then click Scene to open the Scene panel.

3. Double-click Scene 1 in the Scene panel, type **Home**, then press [Enter] (Win) or [return] (Mac).

4. Click the Add scene icon, double-click Scene 2, type **Event**, compare your Scene panel with Figure E-18, then press [Enter] (Win) or [return] (Mac). ➕

   The stage is blank when the new scene, Event, is created.

5. Click Home in the Scene panel and notice that the timeline changes to the Home scene.

6. Click Event in the Scene panel and notice that the timeline changes to the Event scene, which is blank.

7. Test the movie and notice how the movie moves from Scene 1 to the blank Scene 2.

8. Close the test movie window, then save your work.

You added a scene and used the Scene panel to rename the scenes.

FIGURE E-18
Changes to the Scene panel

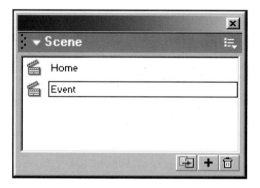

1. Open rallySnd.fla.
2. Click Edit on the menu bar, then click Select All Frames to select all the frames in all the layers, as shown in Figure E-19.
3. Click Edit on the menu bar, then click Copy Frames.
4. Close rallySnd.fla without saving the changes.
5. Click Window on the menu bar, then click cccHome.fla.
6. Make sure that the Event scene is selected.
7. Click Frame 1 on Layer 1 of the Event scene.
8. Click Edit on the menu bar, then click Paste Frames.

   The layers and frames from rallySnd.fla appear in the timeline.
9. Click Home in the Scene panel.
10. Test the movie and notice how the Home scene is played, followed by the Event scene.
11. Close the test movie window, then save your work.

You copied frames from one movie into a scene of another movie.

FIGURE E-19

Selecting all the frames

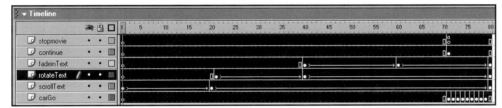

Add interactivity to scenes

1. Make sure that the Home scene is displayed.

2. If necessary, click the Arrow Tool on the toolbox, then click the Upcoming Event text button on the stage. ▶

3. Click Window on the menu bar, then click Actions.

4. If necessary, click Actions, click Movie Control, then double-click `goto` in the Actions panel.

5. Click the Scene list arrow in the Actions panel, click Event, then compare your Actions panel to Figure E-20.

(continued)

FIGURE E-20

The completed Actions panel

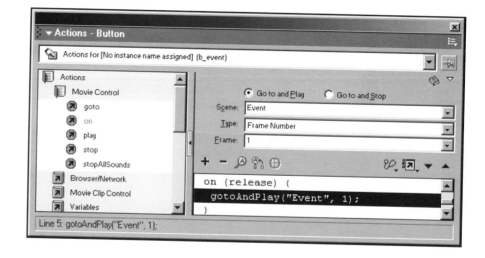

6. Click Frame 1 on the stopmovie layer, double-click **stop** in the Actions panel, then compare your Actions panel to Figure E-21.

7. Test the movie, click the Upcoming Event button, then notice how the Event scene plays.

8. Close the test movie window.

9. Save your work, then close the movie.

You added a scene, used the Scene panel to rename the scenes, and added interactivity to jump from one scene to another.

FIGURE E-21

Adding a stop *action*

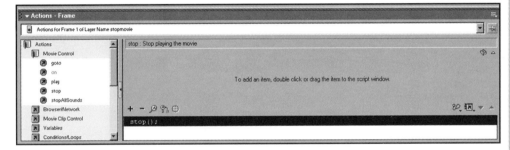

CREATE A SLIDE SHOW PRESENTATION

What You'll Do

 In this lesson, you will make changes to a slide show presentation by adding interactivity and transition effects.

Electronic Slide Shows

Electronic slide shows are useful when making presentations, such as a salesperson to potential buyers, a businessperson to interested investors, an executive to the Board of Directors, keynote speaker to an audience, or a professor to a group of students. The slide show can be stored on the hard drive or CD-ROM/DVD of a computer and projected on a large screen or simply delivered through the Internet to individual viewers. Slide shows—especially those that incorporate multimedia, including animation—can greatly enhance a presentation. The slides can include graphics that help illustrate specific content, bullets that summarize the main points, and sounds that add variety. Slide shows help in keeping the viewer interested in the content and in keeping them on track throughout the presentation.

There are various programs, such as Microsoft PowerPoint, that are specifically designed to create electronic slide shows. These programs have several advantages. They are relatively inexpensive, easy to

learn, and easy to use. They come with templates for the layout of the slides, color scheme, and overall design, as shown in Figure E-22. In addition, they can include sound, video, and animation developed with other programs. Despite this, there are some disadvantages to using these programs. The programs create presentations that are primarily linear, with limited ability to jump easily from one slide to any other except the previous or next slide. The slide shows are designed to be controlled by a presenter or to self-run, with no interaction by the viewer. If you use a design template, the slide show may resemble others in its look and feel. Finally, these programs allow you to assemble various elements, but are limited in their capabilities to create or edit these elements, especially animations.

You can use Macromedia Flash to create an electronic slide show that provides the viewer more flexibility. Each scene in a movie could be a slide. The show could be designed to be controlled by either a presenter or a viewer by providing navigation buttons that allow them to jump to any scene. Alternately, the show could be self-running and include only start and stop buttons. In addition, you can use special effects, such as dissolves or wipes, to transition from one scene to another. A dissolve transition effect could be created with a motion tween that includes a zoom out and an alpha setting that goes from 0 to 100. A wipe transition effect could be created by using a mask that reveals each scene by moving from off the stage to covering the stage from various angles.

Macromedia Flash provides a great deal of flexibility and sophistication when designing and developing electronic slide shows and can be used to create compelling and unique presentations.

FIGURE E-22

Templates provided by a slide show program

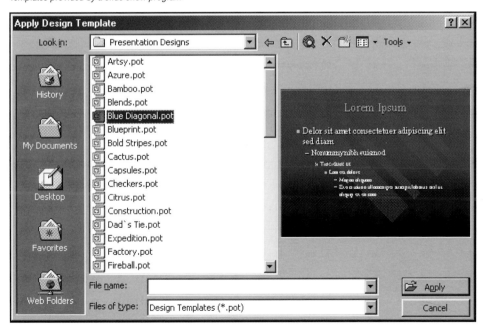

Test a slide show presentation

1. Open fle_7.fla, then save it as **coolCars.fla**.

2. Verify that the Scene panel is open, then click Car1 to display the Car1 scene.

3. Repeat Step 2 for the other scenes, then click Start to display the Start scene.

4. Click Control on the menu bar, then click Test Movie.

5. Click the go button on the road sign to display the next scene.

6. Click the navigation buttons to display each scene, as shown in Figure E-23.

7. Close the test movie window.

8. Click View on the menu bar, point to Magnification, then click 50%.

9. Save your work.

You tested a slide show presentation.

FIGURE E-23
The navigation buttons

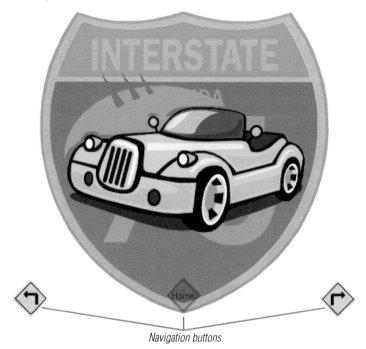

Navigation buttons

FIGURE E-24

Positioning the rectangle

1. Click Car1 in the Scene panel, then add a new layer named **mask** above the image layer.

2. Click the Fill Color Tool on the toolbox, then click the black color swatch in the top left column of the color palette.

3. Click the Rectangle Tool on the toolbox, draw a black rectangle over the stage, then drag it to the left of the stage, as shown in Figure E-24.

4. Create a motion tween using Frames 1 through 20 that scrolls the rectangle to the right until it covers the entire stage.

5. Click the mask layer on the timeline, click Modify on the menu bar, click Layer, click the Lock check box, click the Mask option, then click OK.

6. Click the image layer on the timeline, click Modify on the menu bar, click Layer, click Lock, click Masked, then click OK.

7. Repeat Step 5 for the backgrnd layer.

8. Test the movie and notice the transition effect (wipe from left to right) when the Car1 scene is displayed.

9. Close the test movie window.

10. Repeat Steps 1 through 6 for the Car2 and Car3 scenes, but have the mask (rectangle) scroll in from top to bottom for Car2, and diagonally from left to right for Scene 3.

11. Test the movie, close the test movie window, then save your work.

You created transition effects.

Create a shape-tweened animation.

1. Open fle_8.fla, then save it as **skillsdemoE.fla**.
2. Insert a keyframe in Frames 45 and 65 on the face2 layer.
3. Use the Arrow Tool to drag and reshape the mouth of face2 into a smile.
4. Display the Properties panel.
5. Click anywhere between Frames 45 and 65.
6. Use the Properties panel to specify a Shape Tween.
7. Play the movie.
8. Save your work.

Create a morphing effect.

1. Insert a keyframe in Frame 65 on the number1 layer.
2. Use the Arrow Tool to select 1, then break it apart.
3. Insert a blank keyframe in Frame 85 on the number1 layer.
4. Display the Library panel.
5. Click Edit Multiple Frames on the timeline to turn on this feature.
6. Drag the g_number2 symbol and place it directly over the 1.
7. Break apart the 2 symbol.
8. Turn off the Edit Multiple Frames feature.
9. Click anywhere between Frames 65 and 85 on the number1 layer.

10. Use the Properties panel to specify a Shape tween.
11. Play the movie, then save your work.

Use shape hints.

1. Click Frame 65 of the number1 layer.
2. With the 1 selected, add two shape hints, one at the top and one at the bottom of the 1.
3. Click Frame 85 of the number1 layer, then position the shape hints accordingly.
4. Play the movie, then save your work.

Create and apply a mask layer.

1. Insert a layer above the heading layer, then name it **mask**.
2. Click Frame 1 on the mask layer.
3. Drag the g_face graphic from the Library panel to the left side of the word "How".
4. Insert a Motion tween.
5. Insert a keyframe in Frame 45 on the mask layer.
6. Drag the face to the right side of the word "faces?".
7. Click the mask layer on the timeline, click Modify on the menu bar, then click Layer.
8. Use the Layer Properties dialog box to specify a Mask layer that is locked.
9. Click heading in the timeline, then use the Layer Properties dialog box to specify a Masked layer that is locked.
10. Play the movie, then save your work.

Add and name a scene.

1. Display the Scene panel.
2. Rename Scene 1 **faces**.
3. Add a new scene, then rename it **correct**.
4. Type a heading, **That's correct**, with red, Arial, 72 pt, and center it near the top of the stage.
5. Change the name of Layer1 to **heading**.
6. Insert a keyframe in Frame 30 on the heading layer.
7. Test the movie.
8. Save your work.

Add interactivity to a scene.

1. Display the faces scene, add a new layer above the face2 layer, and rename it **stopmovie**.
2. Insert a keyframe in Frame 85 on the stopmovie layer and add a `stop` action to it.
3. Use the Arrow Tool to select the Continue button on the stage.
4. Use the Actions panel to assign a `goto` action to the Continue button that jumps the movie to the message scene.
5. Test the movie.
6. Save your work.

Add sound to a movie.

1. Use the Scene panel to display the correct scene.
2. Add a layer and name it **applause**.
3. Click Frame 1 on the applause layer.
4. Display the Library panel and drag the applause sound symbol to the stage.
5. Test the movie.
6. Save your work.

Add a transition effect.

1. Display the correct scene.
2. Add a layer, name it mask, then specify it as a mask layer.
3. Draw a rectangle, then create a motion tween that causes the rectangle to move from above the stage to covering the stage.
4. Specify the heading as a masked layer.
5. Test the movie.
6. Save your work, then compare your images to Figure E-25.

FIGURE E-25
Completed Skills Review

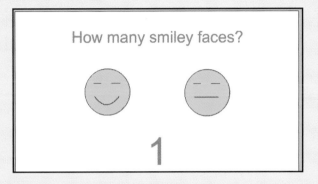

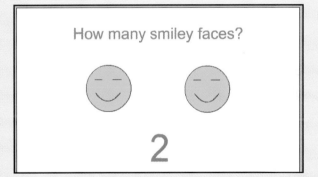

Creating Special Effects

The Ultimate Tours travel company has asked you to design several sample animations for their Web site. Figure E-26 shows a sample Cruises screen with morphed and shape-tweened animations, as well as a mask effect. Using these or one of the sites you created in Unit D as a guide, complete the following for the Cruises screen of the Ultimate Tours Web site:

1. Open ultimatetoursD.fla (the file you created in Unit D Project Builder 1) and save it as **utlimatetoursE.fla**. (*Hint*: If you did not create ultimatetoursD.fla in Unit D, see your instructor.)
2. Create a morph animation.
3. Create a shape-tweened animation.
4. Create a button that goes to another scene.

For the new scene:

5. Create a scene and give it an appropriate name.
6. Rename Scene 1.
7. Create an animation using a mask effect in the new scene.
8. Add a sound to the scene.
9. Add an action to go to the Cruises screen when the animation is done.
10. Test the movie, then compare your image to Figure E-26.

FIGURE E-26
Completed Project Builder 1

Creating Special Effects

This is a continuation of Project Builder 2 in Unit D, which is the development of a personal portfolio. If you have not completed the previous project, see your instructor. The homepage has several categories, including the following:

- Personal data
- Contact information
- Previous employment
- Education
- Samples of your work

In this project, you will create several buttons for the Sample Animations screen and link them to the animations.

1. Open portfolioD.fla (the file you created in Project Builder 2, Unit D) and save it as **portfolioE.fla**. (*Hint*: In this file, the Tahoma font is used. You can replace this font with Impact or any other appropriate font on your computer.)
2. Display the Sample Animations screen.
3. Add layers and create buttons for a shape-tweened animation, morph animation, and an animation using shape hints.
4. Add a new scene and create the morph animation in this scene.
5. Rename the new scene and Scene 1 using appropriate names.
6. Add a sound to the scene.

7. Create frame actions that cause the movie to return to the Sample Animations screen after each animation has been played.
8. Test the movie.

FIGURE E-27
Completed Project Builder 2

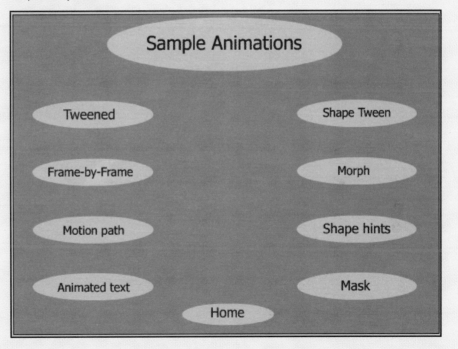

9. Save your work, then compare your image to Figure E-27.

Figure E-28 shows the homepage of a Web site. Study the figure and complete the following questions. For each question, indicate how you determined your answer.

1. Connect to the Internet and go to *www.course.com*. Navigate to the page for this book, click the Student Online Companion, then click the link for this unit.

2. Open a document in a word processor or open a new Macromedia Flash movie, save the file as **dpuUnitE**, then answer the following questions. (*Hint*: Use the Text Tool in Macromedia Flash.)

   - What seems to be the purpose of this site?
   - Who would be the target audience?
   - How might a shape-tweened animation be used in this site?
   - How might a morph animation be used?
   - How might a mask effect be used?
   - How might sound be used?
   - What suggestions would you make to improve the design and why?

FIGURE E-28
Design Project

Your group can assign elements of the project to individual members, or work collectively to create the finished product.

Your group has been asked to develop a Web site illustrating the signs of the zodiac. The introductory screen will have a heading with a mask effect and links to the 12 zodiac signs. Selecting a sign will display another screen with a different graphic to represent the sign and information about the sign, as well as special effects such as sound, shape animation, and morphing. Each information screen will be linked to the introductory screen.

1. Open a new movie, then save it as **zodiac.fla**. (*Hint*: In this file, the Stonehenge font is used. You can replace this font with any appropriate font on your computer.)
2. Create an introductory screen for the Web site with the following:
   - A heading
   - A mask layer that creates a spotlight effect
   - Several graphics
   - Two graphics that are buttons that jump to another scene when clicked
3. Create a second scene that has
   - A morph animation using two graphics
   - A sound
   - A Home button with a sound when clicked

4. Create a third scene that has
   - A shape animation using shape hints
   - A Home button with a sound when clicked

FIGURE E-29
Completed Group Project

5. Rename all of the scenes.
6. Test the movie.
7. Save the movie, then compare your image to Figure E-29.

UNIT F
PREPARING AND PUBLISHING MOVIES

1. Publish movies.

2. Reduce file size to optimize a movie.

3. Use HTML Publish Settings.

4. Create a remote Web site.

UNIT F
PREPARING AND PUBLISHING MOVIES

Introduction

During the planning process for a Macromedia Flash movie, you are concerned with, among other things, how the target audience will view the movie. The most common use of Macromedia Flash is to develop movies that provide Web content and applications. Macromedia Flash provides several features that help you generate the files that are necessary for delivering movies over the Internet. When you deliver content over the Internet, you want to provide compelling movies but you need to keep the file size down so that the movies play smoothly given the user's connection speed. Macromedia Flash allows you to test movies to determine where problems might arise during download and to make changes to optimize the movies.

Tools You'll Use

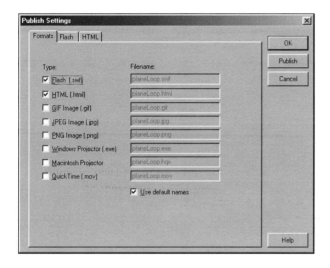

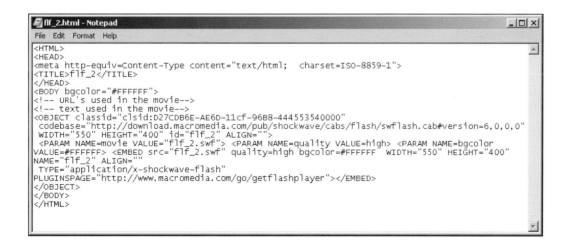

PUBLISH MOVIES

What You'll Do

 In this lesson, you will use the Publish Settings feature of Macromedia Flash to publish a movie, create a GIF animation, and create a JPEG image from a movie.

Using Publish Settings

The Publish feature in Macromedia Flash generates the files necessary to deliver the movies on the Web. When you publish a movie using the default settings, a Macromedia Shockwave (.swf) file is created that can be viewed using the Macromedia Flash Player. In addition, an HTML file is created with the necessary code to instruct the browser to play the Macromedia Shockwave file using the Macromedia Flash Player. If you are not distributing the movie over the Internet, or if a Macromedia Flash Player is not available, you can use the Publish feature to create alternate images and stand-alone projector files.

Figure F-1 shows the Publish Settings dialog box with a list of the available formats for publishing a Macromedia Flash movie. You can choose a combination of formats, and you can specify a different name (but not file extension) for each format. The GIF, JPEG, and PNG formats create still images that can be delivered on the Web. The projector formats are executable files and the QuickTime format requires a QuickTime player. After selecting a format(s), a tab appears allowing you to display a dialog box with settings specifically for the format. Figure F-2 shows the Flash tab of the Publish Settings dialog box. You can choose settings for the following options:

- The version of the Macromedia Flash Player
- The Load Order (for example, Bottom up starts loading from Frame 1 of the bottom layer)
- Other options, such as compressing the movie
- The quality for JPEG images and audio

FIGURE F-1
The Publish Settings dialog box

FIGURE F-2
The Flash tab

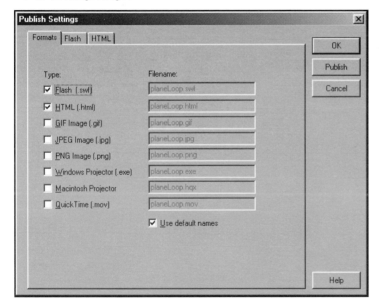

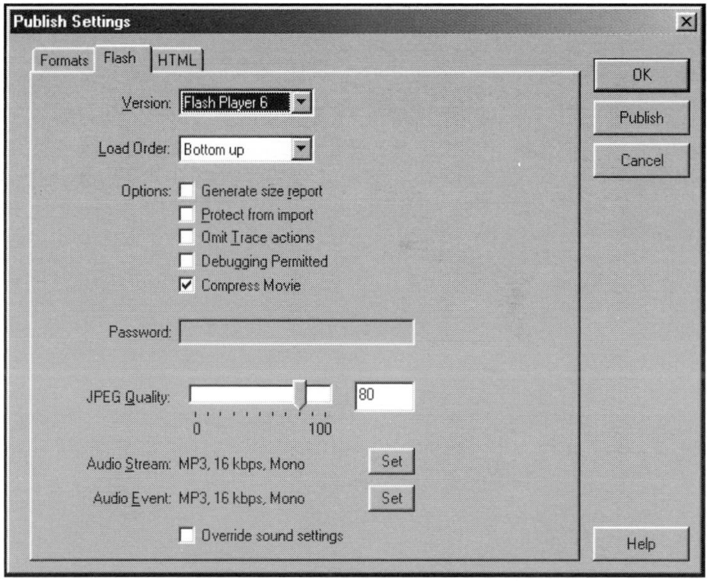

Figure F-3 shows the Publish Settings dialog box for the GIF format. GIF files, which are compressed bitmaps, provide an easy way to create images and simple animations for delivery on the Web. GIF animations are frame-by-frame animations created from Flash movie frames. Using this dialog box, you can change several settings, including these:

- The dimensions in pixels (or you can match the movie dimensions)
- Specifying a static image or animated GIF
- Selecting from a range of appearance settings, such as optimizing colors and removing gradients

Using Publish Preview

You can use the Publish Preview command on the File menu to publish a movie and display the movie in either your default browser or the Macromedia Flash Player. In addition, you can use this command to view HTML, GIF, JPEG, PNG, Projector, and QuickTime files.

FIGURE F-3
The GIF tab

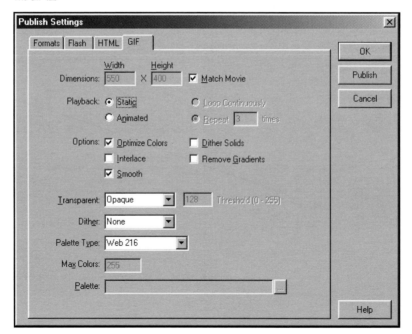

FIGURE F-4

The three planeLoop files

planeLoop.fla	68KB	Flash Document
planeLoop.html	1KB	Microsoft HTML Document 5.0
planeLoop.swf	6KB	Flash Movie

Your browser icon may vary

Publish using the default settings

1. Open flf_1.fla, then save it as **planeLoop.fla**.
2. Click File on the menu bar, then click Publish Settings, then click the Formats tab (if necessary).
3. Verify that the Flash and HTML check boxes are the only ones selected, then click the Flash tab.
4. Verify that the version is Flash Player 6, that the Load Order is Bottom up, and that the Compress Movie check box is selected.
5. Accept the remaining default settings, click Publish, then click OK.
6. Open the file management tool that is on your operating system, navigate to the folder where you save your Macromedia Flash movies, then notice the three files whose file names start with "planeLoop", as shown in Figure F-4.

   The three files are planeLoop.fla, the Macromedia Flash document; planeLoop.html, the HTML document; and planeLoop.swf, the Macromedia Shockwave file.
7. Display the Macromedia Flash program, click File on the menu bar, point to Publish Preview, click Default - (HTML), then notice how the movie plays in a browser or in an HTML editor.

   TIP Netscape users may have difficulty viewing the files, depending on the version of Netscape that is loaded on your computer.
8. Close the browser or the HTML editor.

You published a movie using the default publish settings.

Create a GIF animation from a movie

1. Click File on the menu bar, click Publish Settings, then click the Formats tab.

2. Click the GIF Image (.gif) check box, then click the GIF tab.

3. Click the Match Movie check box to turn off this setting, double-click the Width text box, type **275,** double-click the Height text box, then type **200**.

4. Click the Animated option, click the Repeat option, click the text box, type **3,** accept the remaining default settings, then compare your dialog box with Figure F-5.

5. Click Publish, then click OK.

6. Navigate to the folder where you save your Macromedia Flash movies, then notice the planeLoop.gif file.

7. Open your browser, open planeLoop.gif, then notice the GIF animation plays in the browser with the modified settings.

   Because the GIF file is not a Macromedia SWF (or Flash) file, it does not require Macromedia Flash Player in order to play—it can be displayed directly in a Web browser.

8. Close the browser.

9. Save your work.

You created a GIF animation and viewed it in your Web browser.

FIGURE F-5

The completed GIF format dialog box

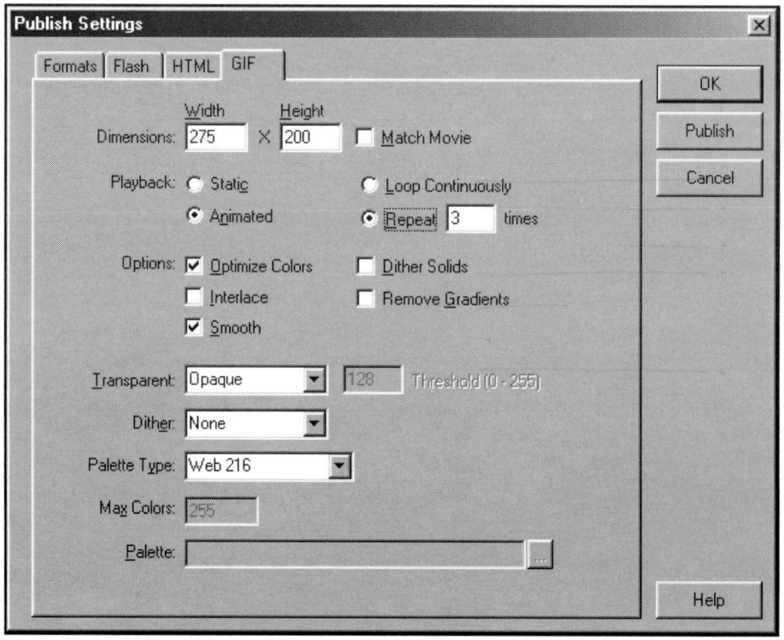

FIGURE F-6

The JPEG image displayed in the browser

Your browser may vary

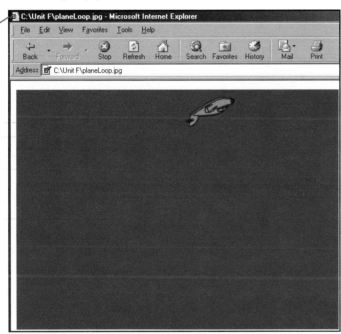

1. Click Frame 10 on the plane layer.

2. Click File on the menu bar, then click Publish Settings.

3. Click the Formats tab, click the GIF check box to deselect it, then click the JPEG check box.

4. Click the JPEG tab, accept the default settings, click Publish, then click OK.

5. Navigate to the folder where you save your Macromedia Flash movies, then notice the planeLoop.jpg file.

6. Open your browser, open planeLoop.jpg, then notice that the static JPEG image appears in the browser, as shown in Figure F-6.

7. Close your browser.

8. Save your work, then close the movie.

You created a JPEG image and viewed it in your Web browser.

REDUCE FILE SIZE TO OPTIMIZE A MOVIE

What You'll Do

In this lesson, you will test a movie and reduce its file size.

Testing a Movie

The goal in publishing a movie is to provide the most effective playback for the intended audience. This requires that you pay special attention to the download time and playback speed. Users are turned off by long waits to view content, jerky animations, and audio that skips. These events can occur as the file size increases in relation to the user's diminished Internet connection speed.

Macromedia Flash provides various ways to test a movie to determine where changes can improve its delivery. Following are guidelines for optimizing movies:

- Use symbols for every element that appears in a movie more than once.
- When possible, use tweened animations rather than frame-by-frame animations.
- For animation sequences, use movie clips rather than graphic symbols.

- Confine the area of change to a keyframe so that the action takes place in as small an area as possible.
- Use bitmap graphics as static elements rather than in animations.
- Group elements, such as related images.
- Limit the number of fonts and font styles.
- Use gradients and alpha transparencies sparingly.

When you publish a movie, Macromedia Flash optimizes it using default features, including compressing the entire movie, which is later decompressed by the Macromedia Flash Player.

Using the Bandwidth Profiler

When a movie is delivered over the Internet, the contents of each frame are sent to the user's computer. The Macromedia Flash Player tries to match the movie's frame rate. However, depending on the amount of data in the frame and the user's connection speed, the movie may pause while the frame's contents download. The first step in optimizing a movie is to test the movie and determine which frames may create a pause during playback. The test should be done using a simulated Internet connection speed that is representative of the speed of your target audience. You can set a simulated speed using the Bandwidth Profiler, shown in

Preloading a movie
One way to improve playback performance of large or complex movies is to preload frames. Preloading frames prevents Macromedia Flash from playing a specified frame or series of frames until all of the frames have been downloaded. One process for creating a preload sequence is to insert two blank frames at the beginning of the movie. Frame 1 contains an ActionScript that checks whether or not the last frame of the movie has been loaded. If not, the playhead moves to Frame 2, which contains a goto action that jumps the playhead back to Frame 1. This looping continues until the last frame of the movie has been loaded. While a movie is preloading you can display a short animation (using a movie clip) or a static graphic so that the viewer knows what is happening.

Figure F-7. The Bandwidth Profiler allows you to view a graphical representation of the size of each frame. Each bar represents a frame of the movie, and the height of the bar corresponds to the frame's size. If a bar extends above the red baseline, the movie may need to pause to allow the frame's contents to be downloaded. Figure F-7 shows the following:

- Movie information: dimensions, frame rate, file size, duration, and preload

- Settings: simulated bandwidth (specified in the Debug menu option)
- State: selected frame number and size of contents in the frame

The Bandwidth Profiler indicates that downloading the contents of Frames 1 and 20 will result in a pause because of the large size of the contents in these frames in relationship to the connection speed and the frame rate. Frame 1 is not as crucial as other frames, because the movie will not

start until its contents are downloaded. If the specified connection speed is correct for your target audience and the frame rate is needed to ensure acceptable animation quality, then the only change that can be made is in the contents of the frame.

FIGURE F-7
The Bandwidth Profiler

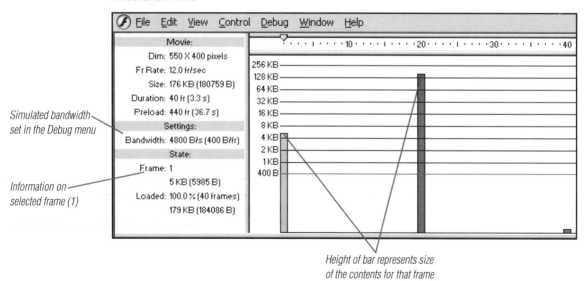

Simulated bandwidth set in the Debug menu

Information on selected frame (1)

Height of bar represents size of the contents for that frame

FIGURE F-8

A pause in the movie

Display a movie in a browser

1. Open flf_2.fla, then save it as **planeFun.fla**.

2. Click File on the menu bar, then click Publish Settings.

3. Make sure the Flash and HTML check boxes are selected, click Publish, then click OK.

4. Open your browser.

5. Navigate to the folder where you save your Macromedia Flash movies, then open planeFun.html.

6. Click the Start button and notice how the animation runs smoothly until the middle of the morph animation, where there is a noticeable pause, as shown in Figure F-8.

   The pause in the animation is caused by the time it takes your browser to download the remaining contents of the movie.

7. Close your browser.

You displayed a movie in a browser.

Test a movie

1. Display, then test the movie to view the movie in the Macromedia Flash Player window.

2. Click Control on the menu bar of the test movie window, then click Loop to turn off this feature.

3. Click Debug on the menu bar, then verify that 56K (4.7KB/s) is selected, if necessary, to simulate the Internet connection speed.

   The actual simulation speed is set to 4.7KB per second, which is more realistic than the 56K per second that is used as the optimal speed.

4. Click View on the menu bar, then click Bandwidth Profiler.

5. Click View on the menu bar, then click Frame By Frame Graph.

6. Click Control on the menu bar, then click Rewind.

7. Click the Start button in the movie, then notice that the morph animation pauses in Frame 38.

   > TIP The movie may not pause the second time it plays, because the contents have already been downloaded. You can close the Macromedia Flash Player window and then test the movie again to view the pause.

8. Click Frame 37 on the timeline, notice there is no JPEG image (balloons image), click Frame 38, then notice the large color image that is over 512KB, as shown in Figure F-9.

9. Close the test window, then save your work.

You tested a movie and used the Bandwidth Profiler to analyze the movie.

FIGURE F-9

A large image shown in the Bandwidth Profiler

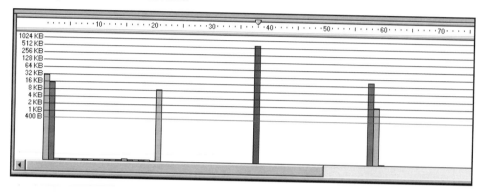

FIGURE F-10

Positioning the cloud image

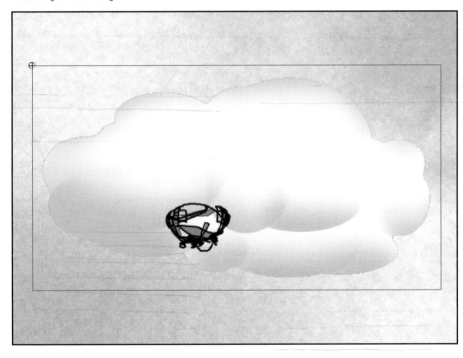

1. Click Frame 38 on the balloons-image layer.

   TIP If the layer name appears cut off, position the mouse over the right border of the layer section until the pointer changes to a double-arrow pointer, then drag the border to the right until the name is fully visible. ⟶⟵

2. Click the balloon photographic image on the stage, click Edit on the menu bar, then click Cut.

   TIP The balloon image is no longer visible on the stage.

3. Click Window on the menu bar, then click Library.

4. Drag the cloud graphic symbol from the Library panel to the center of the stage, as shown in Figure F-10.

5. Test the movie, click the Start button, then notice that the morph animation does not pause at Frame 38.

6. Click Frame 38 on the timeline and notice that the contents are now just above the 8KB line.

7. Close the test window.

8. Save your work.

You replaced a large image to help optimize a movie.

USE HTML PUBLISH SETTINGS

What You'll Do

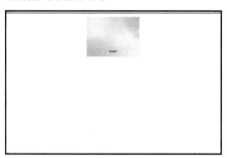

 In this lesson, you will use the HTML Publish Settings to align the movie window in a browser window and change the code of an HTML document.

Understanding HTML Publishing Options

During the publishing process, Macromedia Flash automatically creates an HTML document that allows a Macromedia Flash movie to be displayed on the Web. The HTML document specifies, among other things, the movie's background color, its size, and its placement in the browser. In addition, the attributes for the OBJECT (Internet Explorer for WIN) and EMBED (all other browsers for WIN and MAC) tags are specified in the HTML document. These tags are used to direct the browser to load the Macromedia Flash Player. The HTML options from the Publish Settings dialog box can be used to change these settings.

Following is a description of the HTML options:

Template—Macromedia Flash provides several templates that create different HTML coding. For example, you could choose the Detect for Macromedia Flash 6 option, which uses browser scripting to detect the presence of the Macromedia Flash Player. If Macromedia Flash Player 6 or above is not installed on the user's computer, a static image is displayed in lieu of the movie.

Dimensions—This option sets the values for the WIDTH and HEIGHT attributes in the OBJECT and EMBED tags and is used to set the size of the movie display window in the browser. You can choose to match the size of the movie, enter the size in pixels, or set the movie dimensions as a percentage of the browser window.

Playback—These options control the movie's playback and features, including:

- Paused at Start—pauses the movie until the user takes some action.
- Loop—repeats the movie.
- Display Menu—displays a shortcut menu (with options such as zoom in and out, step forward and back, rewind, and play) when the user right-clicks (Win) or [control] clicks (Mac) the movie in the browser.
- Device Font (Win)—allows you to substitute system fonts for fonts not installed on the user's computer.

Quality—This option allows you to specify the quality of the appearance of objects within the frames. Selecting low quality increases playback speed, but reduces image quality, while selecting high quality results in the opposite effect.

Window Mode—This option allows you to specify settings for transparency, positioning, and layering.

HTML Alignment—This option allows you to position the movie in the browser.

Scale—If you have changed the movie's original width and height, you can use this option to place the movie within specified boundaries.

Flash Alignment—This option allows you to align the movie within the movie window.

Determining Movie Placement in a Browser

When you publish a movie for delivery on the Internet, you need to be concerned with where in a browser window the movie will appear. The placement is controlled by settings in the HTML document. You can specify the settings when you publish the movie. A Macromedia Flash movie is displayed within a movie window. You can have the movie window match the size of the movie or use the HTML panel in the Publish Settings dialog box to specify a different size. Figure F-11 shows the relationships among the movie dimensions, the movie display window, the browser window, and the HTML settings. In this example, the user's screen resolution is set to Width: 800 pixels, Height: 600 pixels.

The movie dimensions are Width: 400 pixels, and Height: 400 pixels. You can adjust the following settings in the HTML Publish Settings dialog box:

- Movie window width: 400 pixels, Height: 100 pixels
- HTML alignment: right
- Flash alignment: right

When you reduce the size of one movie window dimension below the size of the corresponding movie dimension, the other movie dimension is reduced in order to keep the same aspect ratio. In this example, the movie window height of 100 causes the movie height to be resized to 100. Then, the movie width is resized to 100 to maintain the same 1:1 aspect ratio.

FIGURE F-11

Relationships among the movie dimensions, movie and browser windows, and the HTML settings

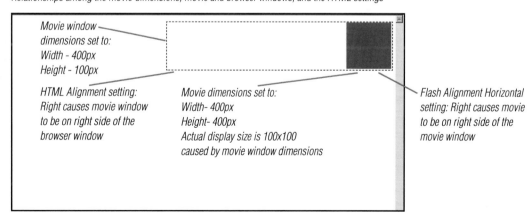

Movie window dimensions set to:
Width - 400px
Height - 100px

HTML Alignment setting: Right causes movie window to be on right side of the browser window

Movie dimensions set to:
Width- 400px
Height- 400px
Actual display size is 100x100 caused by movie window dimensions

Flash Alignment Horizontal setting: Right causes movie to be on right side of the movie window

Change HTML publish settings

1. Click File on the menu bar, then click Publish Settings.

2. Click the HTML tab.

3. Click the Dimensions list arrow, then click Percent.

4. Double-click the Height box, type **30**, then compare your dialog box to Figure F-12.

   Specifying 100 percent for the width and 30 percent for the height causes the Macromedia Flash Player window to be as wide as the browser window and approximately one-third the height.

5. Click OK.

6. Click File on the menu bar, point to Publish Preview, then click Default-(HTML).

7. Click the Start button, then view the movie.

   TIP The movie is centered within the Macromedia Flash Player window because both the horizontal and vertical alignments were specified as centered in the HTML settings.

8. Close the browser, then save your work.

You changed the HTML publish settings.

FIGURE F-12
Changing the HTML publish settings

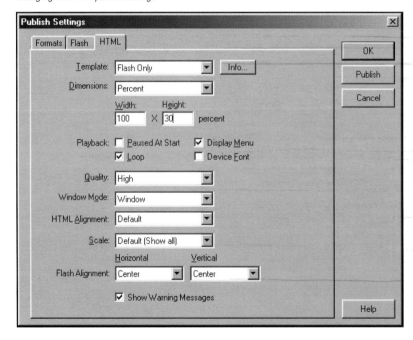

Edit an HTML document

1. Open a text editor such as Notepad (Win) or SimpleText or TextEdit (Mac).

2. Open planeFun.html.

3. Insert a blank line above the second tag from the bottom, </BODY>.

4. Type **
**, then press [Enter] (Win) or [return] (Mac).

5. Type ** <font color="red"> Having PlaneFun!!!</font> **, then compare your screen with Figure F-13.

6. Save the file, then close the text editor.

7. Open your browser, then open planeFun.html.

   The text you added appears in red.

8. Close your browser.

9. Save your work, then close the movie.

You edited an HTML document.

FIGURE F-13

Changing the HTML code

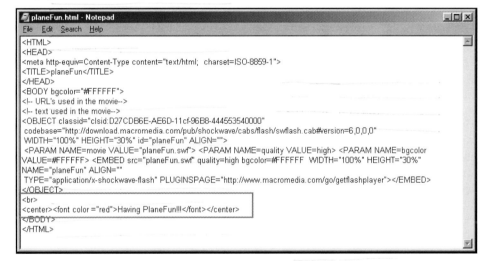

Lesson 3 *Use HTML Publish Settings*

MACROMEDIA FLASH F-19

CREATE A REMOTE WEB SITE

What You'll Do

▶ In this lesson, you will set up access to a Web server and upload files to the server.

Uploading Files to a Web Server

In order to make a Web site available to anyone browsing the Web, the site and all of its referenced files must reside on a Web server. The Web server, a computer dedicated to hosting Web sites, is connected to the Internet and configured with software to handle requests from browsers. Maintaining a Web server and its connections can be a complex and expensive endeavor. A large business or university may maintain its own server for hosting its Web sites. For the rest of us, businesses that offer Web hosting provide these services. Hosting services vary by the businesses that offer them. Your Internet Service Provider (ISP) may offer Web hosting as part of your Internet access package, giving you an account that allows you to upload files to the Web server it manages. An organization with a complex Web site or intranet might put its own server at a hosting company that would provide maintenance and network connections. In all cases, some method must be used to transfer, or upload, files from the development site to the Web server.

A standard method for transferring files from a development site to a Web server is through the File Transfer Protocol (FTP). FTP is a language that enables you to access a remote server and send and receive files efficiently. The company hosting your Web site (or your instructor) will provide you with an FTP server address and a username and password to gain access to the server. The hosting company (or your instructor) may provide you with the path to the folder where your Web files should reside, or you may be automatically directed to the appropriate folder after submitting the username you are assigned. With this information, you can use FTP to upload Web files to the Web server, where the files can be viewed by anyone browsing the Web.

Using the FTP feature Macromedia Dreamweaver MX

Several FTP programs, such as WS-FTP or CuteFTP, allow you to upload your files to a server. In addition, Web development programs such as Macromedia Dreamweaver provide an FTP feature. To create a remote Web site using Dreamweaver, you establish the site on a local disk and then upload the files to a server. Organization of the site structure is critical. Figure F-14 shows a basic structure that includes folders containing categories of files. For example, the Assets folder contains all the graphics, audio, Macromedia Shockwave, and other files. The entire file structure uploads at one time. You can add or modify individual files at a later time.

FIGURE F-14
A basic structure for a Web site

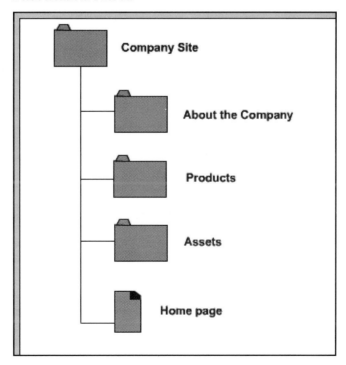

In Macromedia Dreamweaver, the Site menu option is used to create the local site, define the remote site, and transfer files between the sites. Figure F-15 shows the Site window with the folders and files for the local site and the remote site. The index.htm file is not in a folder because it is the default name for the file that the host server displays when anyone accesses the Web site. Figure F-16 shows the Site menu options that allow you to, among other things, create a new site, define (edit) a site, and transfer files (Put and Get) between the local and remote sites.

FIGURE F-15
The Site window

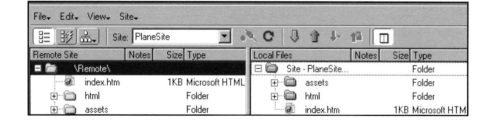

FIGURE F-16
The Site menu options

FIGURE F-17

The local site

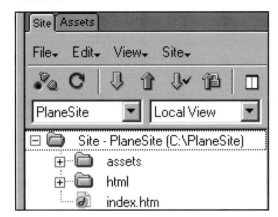

This lesson requires that you have Macromedia Dreamweaver MX installed on your computer.

1. Create a folder on your hard drive and name it **PlaneSite**.

2. Create two folders within the PlaneSite folder and name them **assets** and **html**.

3. Navigate to the drive and folder where you save your Macromedia Flash movies, then copy the following files into the PlaneSite folder: index.htm (root folder), planeGo.swf (assets folder), and planeGo.html (html folder).

4. Start Macromedia Dreamweaver MX.

5. Click Site in the menu bar, click New Site, then click the Advanced tab.

6. Make sure that the Site Name box is high-lighted, then type **PlaneSite**.

   | TIP Check with your instructor if you need to use a different site name.

7. Click the Local Root Folder icon and navigate to the folder you created in Step 1.

8. Click Select (Win) or Choose (Mac) to close the Choose Local Folder for PlaneSite dialog box, then click OK to close the Site Definition for PlaneSite dialog box.

   You created a local site using files already created.

9. If necessary, click Window on the menu bar, then click Site to display the Site panel, as shown in Figure F-17.

(continued)

10. Verify that the Local View in the Site panel is displayed.

> TIP If the Site panel is not set to Local View, click the View list arrow, then click Local View (Win).

You created a local site in Macromedia Dreamweaver MX.

Create a remote site and use FTP to transfer the files

1. Obtain the following from your instructor: the server address, the path to the folder where your Web site files should reside, and a username and password to gain access to the server.

2. Click Site on the Dreamweaver menu bar, then click Edit Sites.

3. Make sure that PlaneSite is highlighted, then click Edit.

4. Click Remote Info in the Category list, click the Access list arrow, then click FTP.

5. Complete the Remote Info section of the dialog box, click OK, then click Done.

6. Click Site on the Site panel menu bar, then click Connect (Win), or click the Connects to remote host button on the Site window (Mac).

   The files are uploaded from the local site to the remote site.

7. Click the View list arrow in the Site panel, then click Remote View, as shown in Figure F-18, or click the Site Files button on the Site window (Mac).

8. Open your browser, then open the index.htm file on the remote site.

9. Close your browser.

You created a remote site and transferred files.

FIGURE F-18

Displaying the remote site

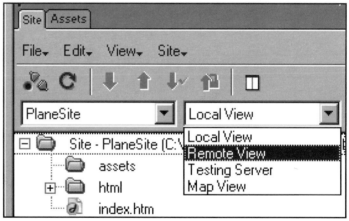

FIGURE F-19

Uploading the edited file

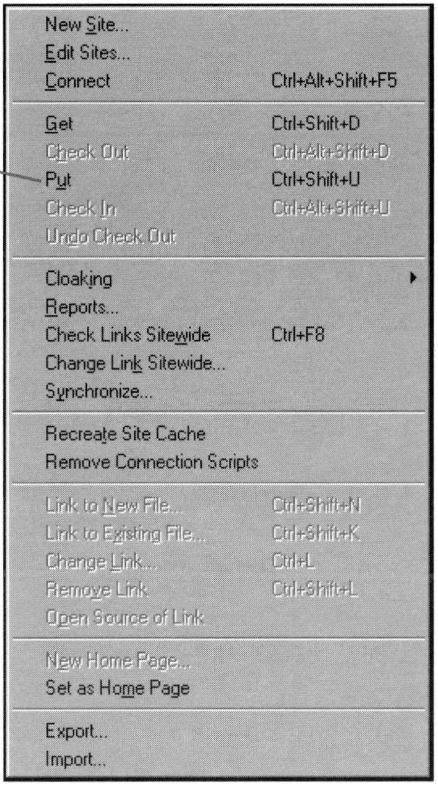

Click Put to transfer files to server

New Site...	
Edit Sites...	
Connect	Ctrl+Alt+Shift+F5
Get	Ctrl+Shift+D
Check Out	Ctrl+Alt+Shift+D
Put	Ctrl+Shift+U
Check In	Ctrl+Alt+Shift+U
Undo Check Out	
Cloaking	▶
Reports...	
Check Links Sitewide	Ctrl+F8
Change Link Sitewide...	
Synchronize...	
Recreate Site Cache	
Remove Connection Scripts	
Link to New File...	Ctrl+Shift+N
Link to Existing File...	Ctrl+Shift+K
Change Link...	Ctrl+L
Remove Link	Ctrl+Shift+L
Open Source of Link	
New Home Page...	
Set as Home Page	
Export...	
Import...	

Change a Macromedia Flash animation and upload it to the server

1. If necessary, start Macromedia Flash, then open planeGo.fla.

2. Click the background layer, then click the Insert Layer icon.

3. Rename the new layer **cloud**.

4. Click Window on the menu bar, then click Library.

5. Drag the cloud graphic symbol to the center of the stage.

6. Save your work, then publish the movie.

7. Copy the newly published Macromedia FlashSWF file (planeGo.swf) to the folder (assets) containing your local Web site files.

8. Display the Dreamweaver Site window.

9. Make sure that the Local View is displayed in the Site panel.

10. Click + next to the Assets folder, then click planeGo.swf to select it (Win), or click the right arrow to expand the Assets folder, then click planeGo.swf (Mac).

11. Click Site in the menu bar, then click Put, as shown in Figure F-19.

12. Click Yes for the overwrite message.

13. Open your browser, then open the index.htm file on the remote site.

14. Close the browser.

You changed a file and uploaded it to the server.

Publish using default settings.

1. Open flf_3.fla, then save it as **skillsdemoF.fla**.
2. Display the Publish Settings dialog box.
3. Verify that the Flash and HTML options are the only ones checked.
4. Click Publish and close the dialog box.
5. Navigate to the folder where you save your work, and display the folder with the skillsdemoF.swf and skillsdemoF.html files.
6. Return to the Macromedia Flash program.
7. Use the Publish Preview feature to display the movie in a browser or HTML editor.
8. Close your browser or HTML editor.
9. Save your work.

Create a GIF animation.

1. Display the Publish Settings dialog box.
2. Display the formats.
3. Select the GIF Image (.gif) format and display the GIF format dialog box.
4. Change the width to **275** and the height to **200**.
5. Select the Animated option and have the animation repeat three times.
6. Publish the movie and click OK to close the dialog box.
7. Display the folder with the GIF animation.
8. Open your browser and play the GIF animation.

9. Close the browser.
10. Save your work.

Create a JPEG image.

1. Select the last frame in the timeline.
2. Display the Publish Settings dialog box.
3. Display the formats and choose the JPEG tab.
4. Select Publish and click OK to close the dialog box.
5. Display the folder with the JPEG image.
6. Open your browser and open the JPEG file.
7. Close the browser.
8. Save your work.

Test a movie.

1. Use the Publish Preview feature to view the movie in your browser and note the pause.
2. Close the browser.
3. Use the Test Movie option from the Control menu to view the movie in the Macromedia Flash Player window.
4. Turn off the loop feature.
5. Set the simulated connection speed to 28.8K.
6. Display the Bandwidth Profiler and select the Frame By Frame Graph.
7. Determine the frame where the movie pauses, display the frame, and view the image.
8. Close the Macromedia Flash Player window.

Optimize a movie.

1. Select the frame on the mountains layer with the large image.
2. Replace the image with the mountains-sm bitmap symbol in the Library panel.
3. Center the image below the heading.
4. Save the movie.
5. Use the Publish Preview feature to view the movie in a browser.
6. Close the browser.

Change HTML publish settings.

1. Display the HTML tab in the Publish Settings dialog box.
2. Change width to **100%** and height to **40%**.
3. Click OK to close the dialog box.
4. Use the Publish Preview feature to view the movie in a browser.
5. Close the browser.
6. Save your work.

Edit an HTML document.

1. Open a text editor.
2. Open the skillsdemoF.html file.
3. Insert a blank line above the </BODY> tag.
4. Type **
** and move to the next line.
5. Type ** <font color="blue">Beautiful Northern Arizona</font> **.
6. Save your work.
7. Display skillsdemoF.html in your browser.

8. Close the browser.
9. Close the text editor.

Create a local Web site.

1. Create a folder on your hard drive and name it **sedonaWeb**.
2. Copy skillsdemoF.html and skillsdemoF.swf to the sedonaWeb folder.
3. Start Macromedia Dreamweaver.
4. Create a new site and name it **Sedona**.
5. Select the Local Root folder icon and navigate to the sedonaWeb folder.
6. Select the folder and close the Site Definition for Site Sedona dialog box.
7. Display the Site panel and verify that the Sedona site and the Local view are displayed.

Create a remote site and transfer files.

1. Display the Edit Sites dialog box.
2. Select to edit the Sedona site.
3. Choose Remote Info and display the FTP dialog box.
4. Complete the FTP dialog box, close it, then close the Edit Sites dialog box.
5. Connect to the remote site.
6. Display the remote view.

Change a Macromedia Flash animation and upload it to the server.

1. Display the skillsdemoF.fla file in Macromedia Flash.

2. Insert a new layer and move it below the mountains layer.
3. Rename the new layer **background**.
4. Select Frame 1 on the background layer.
5. Display the Library panel.
6. Drag the g_background graphic symbol to the center of the stage.
7. Save your work, then publish the movie.
8. Copy the newly published Macromedia Shockwave file to the sedonaWeb folder.

FIGURE F-20
Completed Skills Review

9. Display the Macromedia Dreamweaver Site panel.
10. Select the Local view, select skillsdemoF.swf, then use the Put command to upload it to the server.
11. Open the Web site in your browser.
12. Compare the last frame of your movie to Figure F-20.

The Ultimate Tours travel company has asked you to create a Web site, a GIF animation, and a JPEG image using movies you created in previous units.

1. Open ultimatetoursE.fla (the file you created in Unit E Project Builder 1) and save it as **ultimatetoursF.fla**. (*Hint*: If you did not create ultimatetoursE.fla in Unit E, see your instructor.)
2. Use the Publish Settings dialog box to publish the movie using the default setting for the Flash and HTML formats.
3. Use the Publish Preview feature to display the movie in the browser.
4. Display the GIF format tab in the Publish Settings dialog box, and make a change in the dimensions.
5. Create a GIF animation that repeats two times.
6. Display the GIF animation in your browser.
7. Create a JPEG image of the last frame of the home scene.
8. Display the JPEG image in your browser.
9. Use the Bandwidth Profiler to display a frame-by-frame graph of the movie and to determine which frame may cause a pause in the movie at a 28.8K connection speed.
10. Make a change in the movie to help optimize it.
11. Make a change in the HTML publish settings, then display the movie in your browser.

12. Edit the HTML document and display the movie in your browser.
13. Use Macromedia Dreamweaver to create a local Web site with the ultimatetours files.
14. Create a remote site and upload the files to it.

15. Display the Web site in your browser.
16. Test the movie, then compare your JPEG image to Figure F-21.

FIGURE F-21
Completed Project Builder 1

This is a continuation of Project Builder 2 in Unit E, which is the development of a personal portfolio. If you have not completed the previous project, see your instructor. In this project, you will create a Web site, a GIF animation, and a JPEG image with the movies you have created.

1. Open portfolioE.fla (the file you created in Project Builder 2, Unit E) and save it as **portfolioF.fla**. (*Hint*: In this file, the Tahoma font is used. You can replace this font with Impact or any other appropriate font on your computer.)
2. Use the Publish Settings dialog box to publish the movie using the default settings for the Flash and HTML formats.
3. Use the Publish Preview feature to display the movie in the browser.
4. Display the GIF format tab in the Publish Settings dialog box and make a change in the dimensions.
5. Create a GIF animation that repeats three times.
6. Display the GIF animation in your browser.
7. Create a JPEG image of the first frame of the home scene.
8. Display the JPEG image in your browser.
9. Use the Bandwidth Profiler to display a frame-by-frame graph of the movie and to determine which frame may cause a pause in the movie at a 28.8K connection speed.

10. Make a change in the movie to help optimize it.
11. Make a change in the HTML publish settings, then display the movie in your browser.
12. Edit the HTML document and display the movie in your browser.
13. Use Macromedia Dreamweaver to create a local Web site with the portfolio files.

FIGURE F-22
Completed Project Builder 2

14. Create a remote site and upload the files to it.
15. Display the Web site in your browser.
16. Save your work, then compare your JPEG image to Figure F-22.

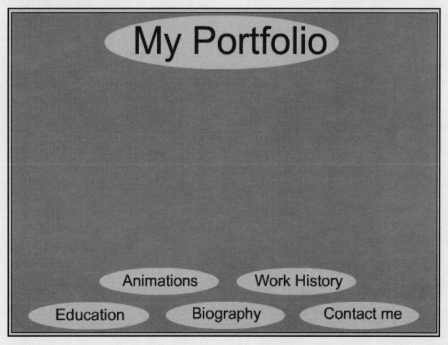

Figure F-23 shows the homepage of a Web site. Study the figure and complete the following questions. For each question, indicate how you determined your answer.

1. Connect to the Internet, and go to *www.course.com*. Navigate to the page for this book, click the Student Online Companion, then click the link for this unit.
2. Open a document in a word processor or open a new Macromedia Flash movie, save the file as **dpuUnitF**, then answer the following questions. (*Hint*: Use the Text Tool in Macromedia Flash.)
   - What seems to be the purpose of this site?
   - Who would be the target audience?
   - How might the Bandwidth Profiler be used when developing this site?
   - Assuming there is a pause in the playing of a Flash movie on the site, what suggestions would you make to eliminate the pause?
   - What would be the value of creating a GIF animation from one of the animations on the site?
   - What would be the value of creating a JPEG image from one of the animations on the site?

- What would be the value of using Macromedia Dreamweaver to create the Web site?

- What suggestions would you make to improve on the design, and why?

FIGURE F-23
Design Project

Your group can assign elements of the project to individual members, or you can work collectively to create the finished product.

Your group has been asked to test a previously developed Macromedia Flash movie, optimize the movie, and publish it. Then create a remote Web site and upload the files to the site. Figure F-24 shows an image from Unit D. Your group may choose a different unit.

1. Open a previously developed movie.
2. Use the Publish Settings dialog box to publish the movie using the default setting for the Flash and HTML formats.
3. Use the Publish Preview feature to display the movie in the browser.
4. Display the GIF format tab in the Publish Settings dialog box, and make a change in the dimensions.
5. Create a GIF animation that repeats two times.
6. Display the GIF animation in your browser.
7. Create a JPEG image of the first frame of the home scene.
8. Display the JPEG image in your browser.
9. Use the Bandwidth Profiler to display a frame-by-frame graph of the movie and to determine which frame may cause a pause in the movie at a 56K connection speed.

10. Make a change in the movie to help optimize it.
11. Make a change in the HTML publish settings, then display the movie in your browser.
12. Edit the HTML document and display the movie in your browser.

FIGURE F-24
Completed Group Project

13. Use Macromedia Dreamweaver to create a local Web site with the files.
14. Create a remote site and upload the files to it.
15. Display the Web site in your browser.

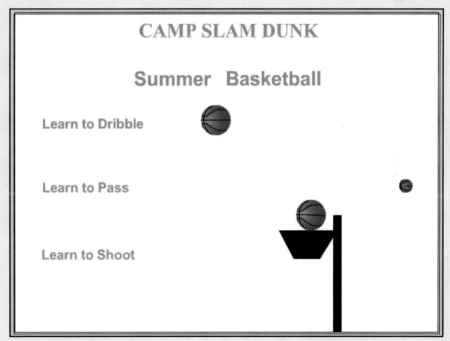

UNIT G

IMPORTING AND MODIFYING GRAPHICS

1. Understand and import graphics.

2. Break apart bitmaps and use bitmap fills.

3. Trace bitmap graphics.

4. Use imported graphics in a movie.

UNIT G
IMPORTING AND MODIFYING GRAPHICS

Introduction

Within your movies, you may often find yourself wanting to use a logo or image that originated in another application. In previous units, you learned to create images using the drawing tools on the toolbox. However, you are not limited to just what you can draw within your movie. You can import and even animate bitmap and vector graphics that have been created or modified in other applications.

Importing vector images from an application such as Macromedia Freehand or Adobe Illustrator is easy—the vector images are treated almost the same as if you created them in Macromedia Flash. While importing bitmap images is easy, working with them can be more difficult.

Using bitmaps can increase the file size of your movies dramatically, resulting in slower download times. Therefore, it is most efficient to use vector images or to create images directly within Macromedia Flash.

In this unit, you will practice importing graphics that have been created outside of the Macromedia Flash environment. For those who are "illustration-challenged," bringing in graphics from other applications can often help to make up for less-than-perfect drawing skills. You can import a wide variety of vector and bitmap graphics, and even video. Once the graphics are inside your Library, you can trace them, break them apart, use them to fill an object, optimize them, and animate them.

Tools You'll Use

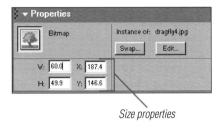

Size properties

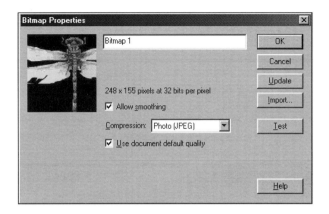

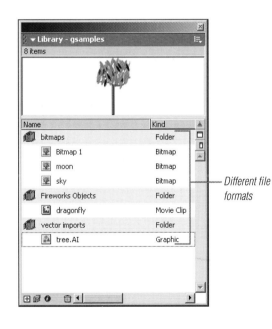

Different file formats

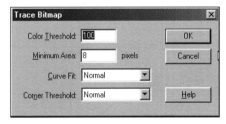

UNDERSTAND AND IMPORT GRAPHICS

What You'll Do

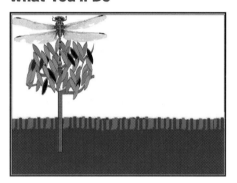

▶ *In this lesson, you will import graphics from several different drawing and image-editing programs.*

Understanding the Formats

Because Macromedia Flash is a vector-based application, all images and motion within the application are calculated according to mathematical formulas. This vector-based format results in smaller file size, as well as a robust ability to resize movies without a notable loss in quality.

When you introduce bitmapped images to the equation, some of the vector-based benefits change dramatically. A bitmap or raster image is based on pixels, not on a math formula. Importing multiple bitmaps will increase the file size of your movie and decrease flexibility in terms of resizing the movie.

Considering Adobe Illustrator import issues

Importing Adobe Illustrator files into Macromedia Flash is a tricky business, and the more complex the file, the trickier it gets. Generally, you will receive an error message when importing an Illustrator file with any level of complexity. Most of the time, despite the error message, the file will still import with full functionality.

You can avoid the error message by saving an Illustrator file as version 7, without blends, 8-bit, no document thumbnails, no document fonts included and using post-script level two. While these files will import without the error message, you might lose pertinent elements of your image.

You cannot import Illustrator 9 or 10 files into Macromedia Flash MX. However, you can export files from Illustrator 9 and 10 to SWF format. For earlier versions of Illustrator, a free plug-in provides the same export to SWF functionality. The plug-in is called Flash Writer, which you can download from the Macromedia Web site, *www.macromedia.com/software/flash/download/flashwriter/*.

You have the ability to import both vector and bitmap images from applications such as Macromedia Fireworks, Macromedia Freehand, Adobe Illustrator, Adobe Photoshop, and Adobe ImageReady. In many cases, you can retain features such as layers, transparency, and animation.

Importing Different Graphic Formats: Overview

There are several ways of getting external graphics into your movie. Generally, the best way to use a graphic in your movie is to **import** it by clicking the Import command on the File menu, and then navigating to the graphic of your choice. Figure G-1 displays some of the Import options, including the selected PNG option. Once you import a

graphic, you will see it on the stage or inside the Library panel. If the original graphic has layers in it, Macromedia Flash might create new layers in your document, depending on the file type and what you specify when you import the graphic. Macromedia Flash will automatically place the additional layers on the stage or inside a movie clip symbol, when applicable.

For some file formats, you can also cut and paste across applications, although with less flexibility than importing provides. If you are importing large numbers of graphics, you can import a batch of images, all of which will automatically use the same settings, enabling you to choose your import preferences once.

FIGURE G-1
Import dialog box

Using Macromedia Fireworks PNG files

You can import Macromedia Fireworks PNG files as flattened images or as editable objects. If you choose to import a flattened image, Macromedia Flash will automatically bitmap the image. To import a PNG file as a bitmap, choose the Import into new layer in current scene option. Macromedia Flash will create a new layer in your movie that contains the flattened layers from the original PNG file. You can also choose the Import as a single flattened bitmap option to add the image to the current layer.

When you insert a PNG file as an editable object, it retains its vector format as well as its layers and transparency features. If you click the Import as movie clip and retain layers option, all the features of the PNG file will appear inside a movie clip symbol that is stored in the Library. This will include layers, animation, and transparency, where applicable. Figure G-2 shows the dialog box in which these settings appear.

Importing Macromedia Freehand Files

When importing Macromedia Freehand files, you can preserve layers, text blocks, symbols, and pages, as well as choose certain pages within a document to import. Macromedia Flash will automatically convert cyan, magenta, yellow, and black (CMYK) files to red, green, and blue (RGB) files. Remember to place all Macromedia Freehand objects on their own layers when you want to preserve layers. As you import the file, choose the Layers option, which will preserve your objects and your layers. If you import a Macromedia Freehand file with overlapping objects on one layer, Macromedia Flash will treat the file as if it had overlapping objects. However, in Macromedia Freehand, each object remains intact, even when overlapped. In Macromedia Flash, selection and groups of elements are based on color. If two shapes of the same color are overlapped, they will become one shape. Keep the following points in mind as you import files from Macromedia Freehand to Macromedia Flash:

- Macromedia Flash will support only up to eight colors in a gradient fill.
- Macromedia Flash will import blends in separate paths; the more paths you have, the greater the file size.
- Macromedia Flash will import both CMYK and Grayscale Macromedia Freehand images as RGB, which in some cases might increase the file size.

FIGURE G-2
Fireworks PNG Import Settings dialog box

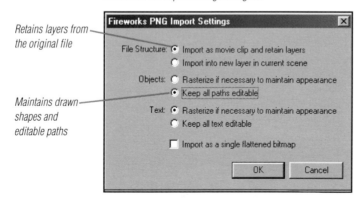

Retains layers from the original file

Maintains drawn shapes and editable paths

Importing Adobe Illustrator Files

Similar to Macromedia Freehand files, most Illustrator files are vector-based. However, importing Illustrator files can be problematic, as noted earlier in the Considering Adobe Illustrator import issues sidebar. You should remember to ungroup any grouped elements in the Illustrator file before starting to import. In Illustrator, you again have the ability to preserve layers on import. You can use layers in two ways: first with each layer as a keyframe, and second with each layer as its own layer in Macromedia Flash. Figure G-3 shows the importing while preserving layers option.

Importing Bitmaps from Adobe Photoshop/Adobe ImageReady

Macromedia Flash allows you to use and modify imported bitmaps in a variety of ways. You can control the size, compression, and anti-aliasing of an imported bitmap. You can also use a bitmap as a fill or convert a bitmap to a vector by tracing it or breaking it apart.

When using Photoshop or ImageReady, you must have QuickTime 4.0 or later installed on your computer in order to use the following file types: .psd, .pic, .pct, or .tif. QuickTime must be installed on your computer in the recommended or complete method; otherwise, you can import Photoshop/ImageReady documents only if they are saved in a .gif, .jpg, or .png format. When importing a flattened bitmap format, such as a .gif or .jpg, it is a good idea to compress the bitmap before you import it.

Once you import a bitmap, it becomes an element in the Library. To edit the graphic from the Library panel, double-click the object to open the Bitmap Properties dialog box. Inside these properties, you can compress the image even more and allow for smoothing (anti-aliasing) on the image.

If an instance of a bitmap symbol is on the stage, you can right-click (Win) or [control] click (Mac) it to open the Properties panel. The properties here will let you numerically change the size of the bitmap as well as swap it for another image and edit the bitmap in an outside application.

FIGURE G-3

Adobe Illustrator Import dialog box

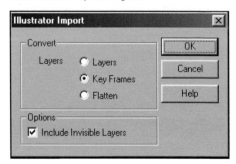

Import a layered PNG file as a movie clip symbol

1. Open a new movie, save it as **gsamples.fla**, then make sure its size is 550 × 400 pixels.

2. Make sure that the Library panel is open.

   | TIP   You can also open the Library panel by pressing F11.

3. Click File on the menu bar, click Import, then navigate to the folder where your data files are stored for this unit.

4. Click the Files of type list arrow (Win) or Show list arrow (Mac), click PNG File (*.png) (if necessary), click dragonfly.png, then click Open.

5. In the Fireworks PNG Import Settings dialog box, verify that the Import as a single flattened bitmap check box is deselected, then select the Import as movie clip and retain layers option in the File Structure section.

   | TIP   If you click the Import into new layer in current scene option instead, the PNG file will be flattened into a single layer.

6. Select the Keep all paths editable option in the Objects section.

7. Select the Keep all text editable option in the Text section, click OK, then compare your stage and Library panel to Figure G-4.

   The dragonfly appears on the stage and a new folder appears in the Library, which contains the dragonfly movie clip.

8. Rename Layer 1 **dragonfly**, then save your work.

You imported a Fireworks PNG file as a movie clip in the Library panel.

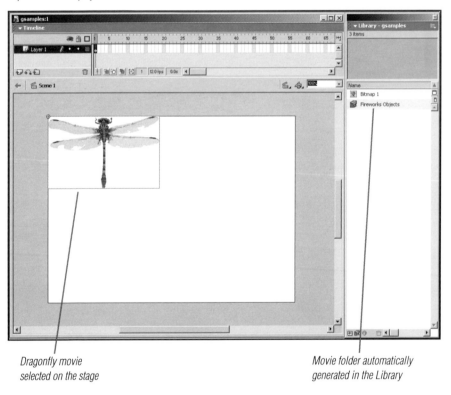

Dragonfly movie selected on the stage

Movie folder automatically generated in the Library

FIGURE G-5

Tree on the stage after importing

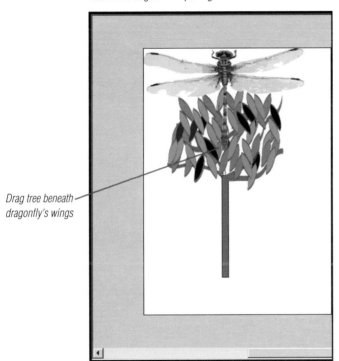

Drag tree beneath dragonfly's wings

1. Click File on the menu bar, then click Import to Library.

   TIP The Import to Library option imports the graphic into the Library panel as a symbol, but not to the stage.

2. Click the Files of type list arrow (Win) or Show list arrow (Mac), click Adobe Illustrator (*.eps, *.ai), click tree.AI, then click Open.

3. Select the Layers option in the Layers section of the Illustrator Import dialog box (if necessary) to convert each layer in the original graphic to a layer in the symbol.

   TIP If you select the Keyframes option instead of Layers, the layers will import as separate keyframes. This option might be useful if you are importing an animation.

4. Make sure the Include Invisible Layers option is selected, then click OK.

   A new graphic symbol, tree.AI, appears in the Library panel.

5. Insert a new layer, rename it **tree1**, then drag it beneath the dragonfly layer.

6. Drag the tree.AI graphic symbol from the Library panel to the left side of the stage beneath the dragonfly, as shown in Figure G-5.

7. Save your work.

You imported an Illustrator file with layers intact to the Library panel and dragged the symbol to the stage.

Import an Adobe Photoshop file saved in JPG format

1. Click File on the menu bar, then click Import to Library.

2. Click the Files of type list arrow (Win) or Show list arrow (Mac), click JPEG Image (*.jpg), click grass.jpg, then click Open.

   The JPG file imports as a flattened bitmap image into the Library panel.

3. Insert a new layer, move it to the bottom of the timeline, then rename it **grass**.

4. Drag the grass graphic symbol from the Library panel to the location shown in Figure G-6.

5. Save your work.

You imported a JPG file to the Library panel and dragged it to the stage.

FIGURE G-6

Grass on the stage after importing

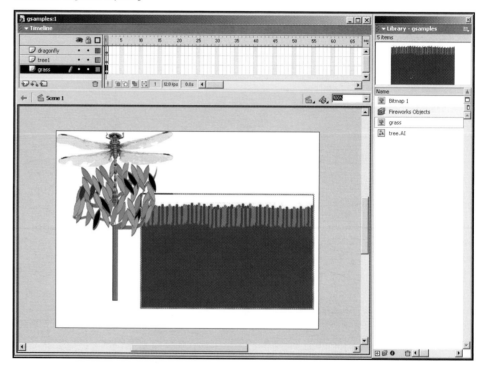

FIGURE G-7
Bitmap Properties dialog box

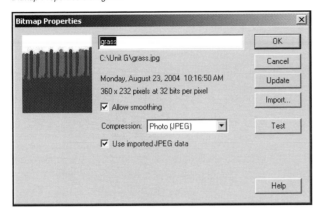

1. Right-click (Win) or [control] click (Mac) the grass bitmap symbol in the Library panel, then click Properties to open the Bitmap Properties dialog box.

2. Verify that the Allow smoothing option is checked and that Photo (JPEG) is selected for Compression, as shown in Figure G-7.

3. Click Test to see what the result of the compression will be, then click OK.

   The new file size and compression information is displayed at the bottom of the dialog box before you close it.

4. Verify that the Arrow Tool is selected on the toolbox, click the grass object on the stage, then open the Property inspector, if necessary.

5. Double-click the W: text box, type **550**, double-click the H: text box, type **158**, then press [Enter] (Win) or [return] (Mac).

6. Move the grass so it is centered and flush to the bottom of the stage, as shown in Figure G-8.

7. Save your work.

You compressed a bitmap file and changed the size of an instance of the bitmap.

FIGURE G-8
Grass resized and centered on the stage

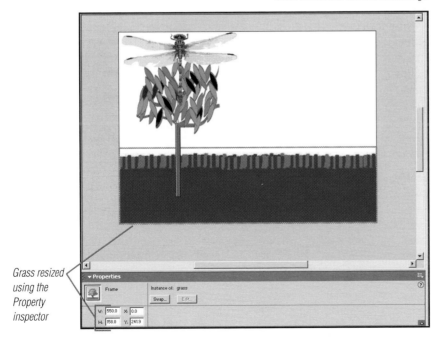

Grass resized
using the
Property
inspector

BREAK APART BITMAPS AND USE BITMAP FILLS

What You'll Do

In this lesson, you will break apart bitmap images and manipulate bitmap fill images to create new effects.

Breaking Apart Bitmaps

Breaking apart a bitmap image allows increased flexibility in how you can use it within a movie. If you are planning to use unmanipulated photographs or images, there is no need to break apart a bitmap image. Once you do break apart a bitmap image, you can click different areas of the image to manipulate them separately from the image as a whole, including changing color, cropping, and scaling. You can also sample a bitmap image you break apart with the Eyedropper Tool on the toolbox, and then use the image as a fill for a drawn shape or as the fill for text.

Breaking apart an image effectively makes each area of color a discrete element that you can manipulate separately from the rest of the image. When selected, a stage-level object appears as a series of pixels, whereas a symbol is selected with a blue outline surrounding it. A **stage-level object** is a vector object that you draw directly on the stage, unlike a symbol, which you place on the stage from the Library panel. You manipulate an image that you break apart the same as you would a stage-level object.

QUICKTIP

Introducing bitmaps will always increase the file size of your movie, resulting in slower download times for your end users.

Using Bitmap Fills

Figure G-9 shows different bitmap fill effects. You can apply a bitmap fill to any drawn shape. If necessary, Macromedia

Flash will tile the bitmap to fill the shape. You can use the Fill Transform Tool to change the size, shape, rotation, and skew of your fill, which allows you to position the original image exactly as you want it in the new shape.

In addition to filling shapes with a bitmap, you can also apply your images as a fill by using the Paintbrush Tool. This process involves breaking apart the image, selecting it with the Eyedropper Tool, and then choosing a paintbrush and brush size. When you begin painting, you will see your image as a fill. You can also use the Fill Transform Tool with the paintbrush fill.

Selecting a Bitmap Fill with the Color Mixer Panel

If the bitmap image you want to use for a fill is not on the stage, you can use the Color Mixer to select it. The process is similar to clicking a new color in the color picker, but instead of choosing a solid color or gradient, you choose Bitmap, and then select the bitmap of your choice. If you select a bitmap fill through the Color Mixer, you do not have to break apart the bitmap. Figure G-10 shows the Color Mixer panel with a bitmap fill selected.

FIGURE G-9
Different bitmap fill effects

Bitmap fill with
the paintbrush

Bitmap fill
in a circle

Bitmap fill in text

FIGURE G-10
Bitmap fill selected in Color Mixer panel

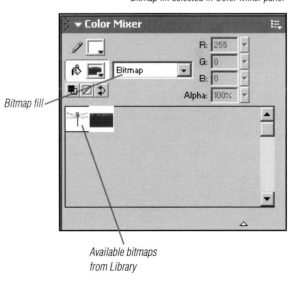

Bitmap fill

Available bitmaps
from Library

Break apart a bitmap

1. Click File on the menu bar, then click Import to Library.

2. Click the Files of type list arrow (Win) or Show list arrow (Mac), click JPEG Image (*.jpg), click moon, then click Open.

3. Insert a new layer, move it to the bottom of the timeline, then rename it **moon**.

4. Drag the moon graphic symbol from the Library panel to the top right corner of the stage, as shown in Figure G-11.

5. Click Modify on the menu bar, click Break Apart, then compare your image to Figure G-12.

6. Click any gray area around the stage to deselect the moon object.

7. Click the Lasso Tool on the toolbox, then click the Magic Wand Properties Tool in the Options section of the toolbox.

8. Click the Smoothing list arrow, choose Pixels, then click OK.

9. Click the Magic Wand Tool in the Options section of the toolbox, then click any part of the black background of the moon object, as shown in Figure G-13.

10. Click Edit on the menu bar, then click Cut.

    The selected black area no longer appears on the stage.

11. Save your work.

You broke apart and edited a bitmap image.

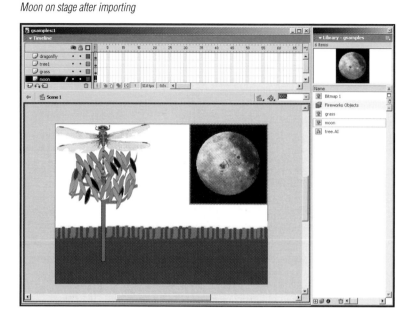

FIGURE G-12
Moon pixels after being broken apart

Individual pixels appear as a grid

FIGURE G-13
Selecting the black background with the Magic Wand Tool

Black background selected

Importing and Modifying Graphics

FIGURE G-14
Selecting a bitmap Fill with the Eyedropper Tool

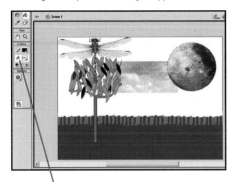

Bitmap displayed
for fill color

FIGURE G-15
Filling a shape with a bitmap

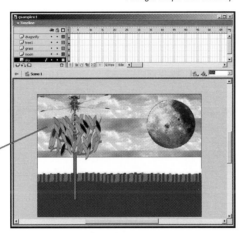

Sky bitmap tiles to
fill the rectangle

Use and edit a bitmap fill

1. Click File on the menu bar, then click Import to Library.

2. Click the Files of type list arrow (Win) or Show list arrow (Mac), click JPEG Image (*.jpg), click sky, then click Open.

3. Insert a new layer, move it to the bottom of the timeline, then rename it **sky**.

4. Drag the sky graphic symbol from the Library panel to the center of the stage covered by the tree.

5. Click Modify on the menu bar, then click Break Apart.

6. Click the Eyedropper Tool on the toolbox, click the sky object on the stage, then compare your screen to Figure G-14.

   > TIP The Eyedropper Tool lets you select a fill from an existing object so you can apply it to another object.

7. Click Edit on the menu bar, then click Cut to remove the graphic from the stage.

8. Click the Rectangle Tool on the toolbox, then using Figure G-15 as a guide, draw a rectangle over the top half of the stage.

   The rectangle fills with a tiling bitmap of the sky.

   > TIP To change the size or skew, or to move the bitmap fill image, click the Fill Transform Tool on the toolbox, then click one of the images in the fill.

9. Save your work.

You applied a bitmap fill to a shape.

Using the Lasso Tool and the Magic Wand Tool

The Lasso Tool lets you select an irregularly shaped part of a graphic, which you can then move, scale, rotate, or reshape. The Magic Wand Tool option extends the Lasso Tool so you can select areas of similar color in a bitmap you have broken apart. With the Magic Wand Properties Tool, you can specify a color similarity threshold for the Magic Wand Tool (a higher number means more matching colors will be selected) and the type of smoothing that will be applied to the selection.

TRACE BITMAP GRAPHICS

What You'll Do

 In this lesson, you will trace a bitmap graphic to create vectors and special effects.

Understanding Tracing

Tracing is an outstanding feature for the illustration-challenged, or if you need to convert a bitmap image into a vector image for animation purposes. When you apply the trace functions, you turn a pure bitmap into vector paths and fills with varying degrees of detail. If you keep all the detail in an image, you end up with very detailed, intricate vector paths, which tend to increase file size. If you remove some of the detail, you can turn a photograph into a more abstract-looking drawing, which usually requires less file size. Once traced, you can remove the original image from the Library panel and work with only the traced paths and shapes, thereby reducing the movie's file size. The traced shapes act just like shapes you have drawn, with fills, lines, and strokes that you can manipulate and change. Tracing allows an image to act as a graphic drawn directly in Macromedia Flash, which is why you are able to select paths based on color and to use paths to manipulate the shape of an object.

QUICKTIP

Tracing bitmaps can often take a long time, especially if it is a detailed trace or a large image.

One of the challenges with using the trace feature comes when you try to animate a traced object. Tracing creates paths and shapes, but every piece of the original image remains on one layer. To animate or tween between pieces of the shape, you often have to isolate parts of the image onto their own layers. Figure G-16 shows the before and after effects of tracing an image. In this example, you can see how tracing makes the original photograph appear more abstract. Figure G-17 shows the traced image cut up for animation.

Using the Trace Settings

It is possible to trace an image using very detailed or less detailed settings. Your traced image will look more like the original graphic if you retain more detail. If you want the traced object to look more abstract, use less detail. However, the greater the detail, the greater the file size.

In Figure G-18, three different trace effects are created by adjusting the trace values.

There are four options that affect how detailed the trace will appear: Color Threshold, Minimum Area, Curve Fit, and Corner Threshold. Color Threshold compares two side-by-side pixels; if the difference is less than the color threshold, the two are considered the same color. Color Threshold options include integers between 1 and 500. Minimum Area sets the number of surrounding pixels to consider, with options between 1 and 1000. Curve Fit determines how smoothly outlines are drawn. Corner Threshold works with sharp edges to retain them or smooth them out. Figure G-19 shows the Trace Settings dialog box.

QUICKTIP

You can no longer trace an image once you break it apart.

FIGURE G-16

Before and after tracing a bitmap

FIGURE G-17

Dividing a traced image by color

Sections of the moon selected by color and moved

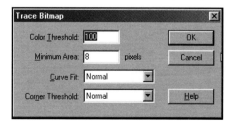

FIGURE G-18

Three different effects with different trace settings

FIGURE G-19

Trace Bitmap dialog box

Trace a bitmap image

1. Click the Arrow Tool on the toolbox, then click the grass object on the stage, as shown in Figure G-20.

2. Click Modify on the menu bar, then click Trace Bitmap.

3. Verify that **100** appears in the Color Threshold text box and **10** appears in the Minimum Area text box, then accept the default **Normal** settings for Curve Fit and Corner Threshold.

4. Click OK, then compare your image to Figure G-21.

(continued)

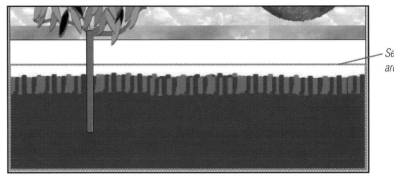

Selection box
around grass

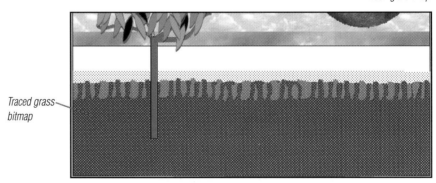

Traced grass
bitmap

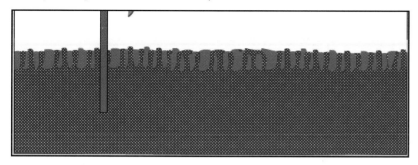

5. Click a gray area around the stage to dese-lect the traced image, click any dark green area of the traced image, then compare your image to Figure G-22.

6. Click the Free Transform Tool on the toolbox, then drag the top of the bounding box up approximately 10 pixels until the double arrow pointer is positioned in the middle of the white space, as shown in Figure G-23. ⊞

7. Click a gray area around the stage to dese-lect the grass.

8. Save your work.

You traced a bitmap and manipulated its shape.

FIGURE G-23

Resizing the dark-green section of the grass

Drag handle upwards until pointer is centered in white space

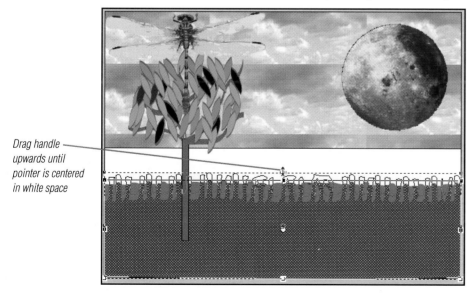

USE IMPORTED GRAPHICS IN A MOVIE

What You'll Do

In this lesson, you will optimize your Library of imported graphics and manipulate instances of symbols on the stage.

Mixing Graphic Formats

In the previous lessons, you combined importing graphics, filling with bitmaps, tracing bitmaps, and manipulating imported images. You can use all of these techniques in tandem to create a cohesive Macromedia Flash movie without having to be an artist or an illustration expert. Tracing also allows a way to tie together different photo styles without ruining the integrity of the movie.

In your sample file, the sky is a bitmap fill from a JPG file, the grass is an imported and traced Photoshop file, the dragonfly is a Macromedia Fireworks file, and the trees are Illustrator files. All of these combine to create a scene in the forest. Depending on the effect you are trying to achieve, you might use one or more of these techniques to create your own movies.

Optimizing Your Library

Because all the library elements have to be saved with the movie, make sure you do not have any extraneous bitmaps or imported images in the Library panel. If you broke apart an image, it is still necessary to keep the original image inside the Library. When an image is traced, the original image can be removed from the Library panel. If you import any images that you do not use, you should remove them from the Library panel before publishing. If you don't manipulate an imported image at all, it is still required to be in the Library panel. Taking the time to clean up your Library will result in a better-optimized Macromedia Flash movie.

A well-optimized movie means that you are not using any symbols gratuitously

Cropping images before importing

It is always a good idea to crop images prior to importing them into the Library. It is best to import only what you will use to help keep the file size down. If you are using an image more than once, and one version is cropped and the second version is not, then you would need to import the entire image and crop one instance of it.

and that all symbols have been optimized. Generally, it is also a good idea to group your symbols into folders in the Library panel. Grouping is commonly done by symbol type, as displayed in Figure G-24, or by the piece of the movie with which a symbol is associated.

Importing Idiosyncrasies

In addition to the applications mentioned above, you can also import graphics that are from AutoCAD, MacPaint, Silicon Graphics Image, and QuickTime. Table G-1, on the following page, details the file formats, applications, and platforms that

Macromedia Flash supports for importing. All the file formats have slightly different behavior when imported. Many of these files rely on QuickTime 5 or higher for support. Generally, if Macromedia Flash does not know what to do with a bitmap file or if QuickTime is not installed, it will import even a complex layered file as one single, flattened layer.

Animating Imported Graphics

One of the most powerful features and benefits to Macromedia Flash is its ability to animate. You can animate any type of imported graphic, from moving a photograph across a

scene to separating the pieces of a PNG file and animating them.

Once the images are inside Macromedia Flash, you can manipulate them the way you would any other object by utilizing Library elements, tweening animation, and other animation techniques to bring still images to life. Figure G-25 shows the tree image divided into layers by leaf color and animated inside a movie clip symbol.

FIGURE G-24
A well-organized Library

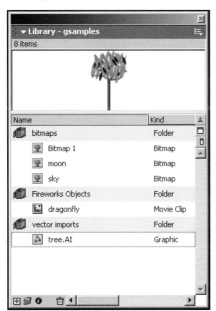

FIGURE G-25
Animating imported Library elements

Tree leaves split into layers and animated based on color

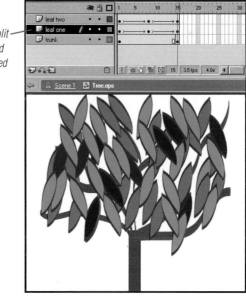

TABLE G-1: File Formats for Imported Graphics

file type	extension	supported on Windows/Macintosh	file type	extension	supported on Windows/Macintosh
Adobe Illustrator (version 8 or earlier)	.eps, .ai	Windows Macintosh	Photoshop	.psd	Windows Macintosh
AutoCAD DXF	.dxf	Windows Macintosh	PICT	.pic, .pct	Windows Macintosh
Bitmap	.bmp	Windows Macintosh	PNG	.png	Windows Macintosh
Enhanced Windows Metafile	.emf	Windows Windows	QuickTime Image	.qtif	Windows Macintosh
Macromedia FreeHand	.fh7, .fh8, .fh9, .fh10	Windows Macintosh	Silicon Graphics Image	.sgi	Windows Macintosh
GIF and animated GIF	.gif	Windows Macintosh	TGA	.tga	Windows Macintosh
JPEG	.jpg	Windows Macintosh	TIFF	.tif	Windows Macintosh
MacPaint	.pntg	Windows Macintosh	Windows Metafile	.wmf	Windows Macintosh

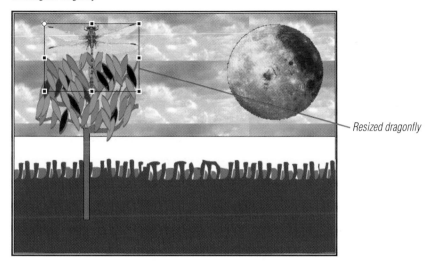

Resized dragonfly

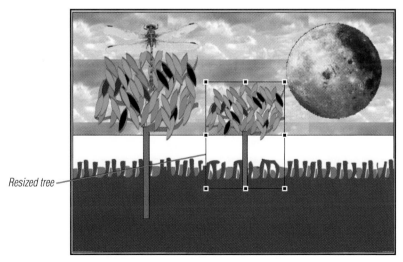

Resized tree

Using the images in combination to build a scene

1. Right-click (Win) or [control] click (Mac) the grass bitmap symbol in the Library panel, click Delete, then click the Delete button to confirm the deletion.

   TIP Deleting traced bitmaps is a good way to optimize the Library.

2. Click the Free Transform Tool on the toolbox, click the dragonfly, click a corner sizing handle, then drag the dragonfly to the size shown in Figure G-26. ⊞

3. Center the dragonfly over the tree.

4. Insert a new layer above the grass layer in the timeline, then rename it **tree2**. 🗂

5. Drag the tree symbol from the Library panel to the middle of the stage on the tree2 layer.

6. Click the Free Transform Tool on the toolbox, click a corner sizing handle on the tree, then drag to the size shown in Figure G-27. ⊞

   TIP Use the arrow keys to position the tree, if necessary.

7. Save your work, then close gsamples.fla.

You used traced images, bitmap fills, and imported PNG files to build a still scene that you can animate.

Understand and import graphics.

1. Create a new movie with a size of 550 × 400 pixels and no background color, then save it as **skillsdemoG.fla**.
2. Make sure the Library panel is open.
3. Import to the Library the Freehand file logo.FH10 with the following settings: under Mapping, select **Scenes** for Pages and **Flatten** for Layers; under Pages, select **All**; and under Options, select all three options.
4. Import to the Library roses.jpg.
5. Import to the Library mountain.jpg.
6. Import to the Library nightsky.jpg.
7. Rename Layer 1 **roses** and drag the roses symbol to the upper-right corner of the stage.
8. Create a layer named **logo** and drag the logo symbol to the upper-left corner of the stage.
9. Create a layer named **mountain** and drag the mountain symbol to the bottom-center of the stage.
10. Use either the Free Transform Tool or the Property inspector to change the size of the mountain to the width of the stage, 550 pixels. If necessary, move the mountain image so it is centered and flush with the bottom of the stage.
11. Save your work.

Break apart bitmaps and use bitmap fills.

1. Break apart the roses image.
2. Click the roses image with the Eyedropper Tool, then delete the image.
3. Create a rectangle behind the logo that spans the width of the stage. (*Hint*: Use the Rectangle Tool.)
4. Create a new layer above the mountain layer named **more roses**.
5. Paint a line of roses along the bottom of the mountain image. (*Hint*: Use the Brush Tool.)
6. Save your work.

Trace bitmap graphics.

1. Trace the mountain image, using settings of **100** for Color Threshold, **10** for Minimum Area, and **Normal** for Curve Fit and Corner Threshold.

2. Deselect the image.

3. Select the nightsky image as a bitmap fill, then use the Paint Bucket Tool to change the blue sky and clouds in the background of the mountain to stars. (*Hint*: You can either move the nightsky image to the stage and break it apart to create the bitmap fill, or try using the Color Mixer.)

4. Use the Free Transform Tool to make the peak approximately 20 pixels higher. (*Hint*: First select the peak with the Arrow Tool, then click the Free Transform Tool.)

5. Save your work.

Use imported graphics.

1. Delete the image you traced (mountain) from the Library panel to decrease file size.

2. Compare your movie to Figure G-28, then save your work.

FIGURE G-28
Completed Skills Review

Ultimate Tours is rolling out a new "summer in December" promotion in the coming months and wants a Macromedia Flash Web site to showcase a series of tours to Florida, Bermuda, and the Caribbean. The Web site should use bright, "tropical" colors and have a family appeal. Though you will eventually animate this site, Ultimate Tours first would like to see still pictures of what you are planning to do.

1. Open a new movie and save it as **ultimatetoursG.fla**.
2. Set the movie properties, including the size and background color if desired.
3. Create the following text elements on separate layers:
   - A primary headline **Ultimate Tours Presents...** with an appropriate font and treatment.
   - A subheading **Our new "summer in December" tour packages!** in a smaller font size.
4. Import to the Library the following JPG files (alternately, you can create your own images, obtain images from your computer or the Internet, or create images from scanned media):
   grtravel1.jpg
   gtravel2.jpg
   gtravel3.jpg
   gtravel4.jpg
   gtravel5.jpg
   gtravel6.jpg

5. Move three of the images to the stage to create an appealing vacation collage, arranging and resizing the images as appropriate. (*Hint*: Some of the sample files have a white background. If you want to include one of these images and your stage has a different background color, try breaking the image apart, then using the Magic Wand Tool to erase the background of the image.)
6. Trace one of the images on the stage to create an artistic effect and reduce file size, then delete the traced image from the Library panel.

FIGURE G-29
Completed Project Builder 1

7. Create three round or square buttons using an image from the Library panel as a bitmap fill. Resize or skew the bitmap fill as appropriate.
8. Apply a bitmap fill to some or all the letters in the title. (Hint: To add a bitmap fill to text, you must first convert the characters to shapes by breaking apart the text two times.)
9. Save your work, then compare your image to Figure G-29.

To showcase your broad range of skills, you want to add some Web-related work to your portfolio. This will allow you to display Web sites and artwork you previously created. First, you will need to take screen captures of the Web sites you have built and scan any artwork or design work that is in print. Try to create at least four samples of your work. Using an image editor, make all of these images into JPEGS.

1. Open portfolioF.fla and save it as **portfolioG.fla**. (*Hint*: If you did not create portfolioF.fla, see your instructor. In this file, the Tw Cen MT font is used. You can replace this font with Arial or any other appropriate font on your computer.)
2. Add a scene to the movie and label that scene **samples**.
3. Import to the Library at least four samples of your work in a variety of file formats if necessary.
4. Place the samples on the stage. Make sure each image is on its own layer.
5. Resize the images so you can fit all four of them on the stage at one time
6. Add a sentence below each image describing the image.
7. Save your work, then compare your movie to Figure G-30.

FIGURE G-30
Completed Project Builder 2

Samples of My Work

Website for an intranet. Used Photoshop, Flash and Dreamweaver to create it.

Website for a contracting company. Used Photoshop, Flash and Dreamweaver to create it.

Logo Development work for Ultimate Tours.

Website for online courses offered through the colleges for a company.

Importing and Modifying Graphics

Figure G-31 shows the homepage of the Bose Web site. Study the figure and complete the following. For each question, indicate how you determined your answer.

1. Connect to the Internet and go to *www.course.com*. Navigate to the page for this book, click the Student Online Companion, then click the link for this unit.
2. Open a document in a word processor or open a new Macromedia Flash movie, save the file as **dpuUnitG**, then answer the following questions. (*Hint*: Use the Text Tool in Macromedia Flash.)
   - Are photographs used well in this Web site, why or why not?
   - Could the goals and intent of the Web site be accomplished without the use of photographs?
   - Do the images contribute to the design of the site? If so, how?
   - Do you think the illustrations were traced or drawn by hand? How can you tell?
   - Can you guess what file format the logo was before it was brought into Macromedia Flash? Or, do you think it was recreated in the application?
   - Do you think the graphics in this site should be changed in any way? How?
   - Who do you think is the target audience for this Web site?

FIGURE G-31
Design Project

Importing and Modifying Graphics

Your group can assign elements of the project to individual members, or work collectively to create the finished product.

Your group has been asked to create several sample designs for the homepage of a new student art, poetry, and fiction anthology called AnthoArt. This Web site will showcase artwork that includes painting, woodcuts, and photography, as well as writing (including poetry and fiction). Your group must present the site's homepage and needs to use the artist's work to build it. The homepage should be a collage of work from contributing students.

1. Open a new movie and save it as **anthoartG.fla**.
2. Set the movie properties, including the size and background color if desired.
3. Import to the Library panel the following JPG files (alternately, you can create your own images, obtain images from your computer or the Internet, or create images from scanned media):
   gantho1.jpg
   gantho2.jpg
   gantho3.jpg
   gantho4.jpg
   gantho5.jpg

4. Using a combination of tracing and breaking apart images, create a collage on the stage from at least four images.
5. Create a title of **AnthoArt**, using a bitmap fill for some or all of the letters.
6. Create an enter button, using one of the images as a bitmap fill.
7. Save your work, then compare your movie image to Figure G-32.

FIGURE G-32
Completed Group Project

BUILDING COMPLEX ANIMATIONS

1. Plan for complex movies and animations.

2. Create an animated graphic symbol.

3. Create a movie clip symbol.

4. Animate buttons with movie clip symbols.

UNIT H
BUILDING COMPLEX ANIMATIONS

Introduction

As your movies become more complex and you begin utilizing more advanced features of Macromedia Flash, planning your work is critical. Part of the planning process is figuring out how to develop a clean timeline, with objects that are easy to recognize and manipulate, and how to optimize file size by reusing symbols as much as possible.

Creating animated graphic symbols and movie clip symbols can help meet both goals. A well-built movie consists of many small pieces of animation put together and often, of movies nested within movies. While the concept of movies within

movies might sound confusing, it is actually very logical from a file management, media management, and animation perspective. Building scenes with 40 layers and 200 keyframes can be unwieldy. The alternative is to split the many animations on the stage into smaller, reusable pieces, and then insert these smaller pieces as needed. When added up, you probably have an equal number of keyframes and layers, but they are never visible in a scene at the same time. Creating animated graphic symbols and movie clip symbols also allows you greater flexibility in adding ActionScript to elements, as well as with bringing elements on and off the stage.

Tools You'll Use

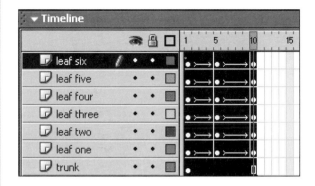

— *Movie clips*

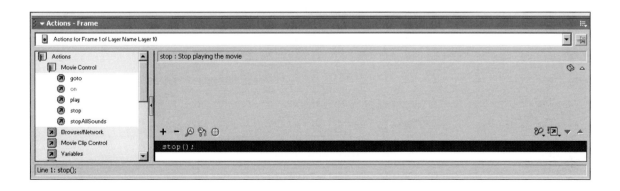

PLAN FOR COMPLEX MOVIES AND ANIMATIONS

What You'll Do

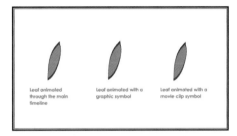

Leaf animated through the main timeline

Leaf animated with a graphic symbol

Leaf animated with a movie clip symbol

In this lesson, you will work with and compare animated graphic and movie clip symbols.

Making Effective Use of Symbols and the Library Panel

It is important to sketch out in advance what you are trying to accomplish in a movie. In addition to making development work easier, planning ahead will also allow you to organize your Library panel with more accuracy. Consider the following questions as you plan your next project:

- Are there any repeated elements on the stage? If yes, you should make them into graphic symbols. Graphic symbols should include any still element that is used on the stage more than once. Graphic symbols might also be elements that you want to be able to tween. Keep in mind a graphic symbol can contain other graphic symbols.
- Are there any repeating or complex animations, or elements onscreen that animate while the rest of the scene is still? If so, make these animated graphic symbols or movie clip symbols.

- What kind of interactivity will your Macromedia Flash movie have? You can assign ActionScript to button symbols and to movie clip symbols, but not to graphic symbols. You should use button symbols for any element that is acting as navigation or an element that you want to be clickable. Button symbols can contain both graphic and movie clip symbols inside them.

Remember, your Library panel should house all of the building blocks for your movies. In order to build a logical Library panel, you should have a solid plan in place for the different elements you expect to use.

Understanding Animated Graphic Symbols

Just as you can create a graphic symbol from multiple objects on the stage, you can convert an entire multiple-frame, multiple-layer animation into a single **animated graphic symbol** that you can store in the Library panel. Creating a single animated graphic symbol removes all of the associated keyframes, layers, and tweening of the animation from your timeline, which results in a much cleaner timeline. Animated graphic symbols can also reduce file size if you expect to use the animation in more than one place in a movie.

Compare the two timelines in Figure H-1. On the left is a tree animated through the main timeline; each individual leaf on the tree has its own layer. On the right is a timeline for a movie with the same animation, but with the leaves grouped into an animated graphic symbol and appearing on a single layer.

An animated graphic symbol remains tied to the timeline of the movie in which you place the symbol. This means there must be enough frames on the timeline for the animation to run, and that if the movie stops, so does the animation.

Understanding Movie Clip Symbols

A **movie clip symbol** is a more robust way to store complex animations in the Library panel: essentially a movie within a movie. The biggest difference between a movie clip symbol and an animated graphic symbol is

FIGURE H-1
Comparing timelines

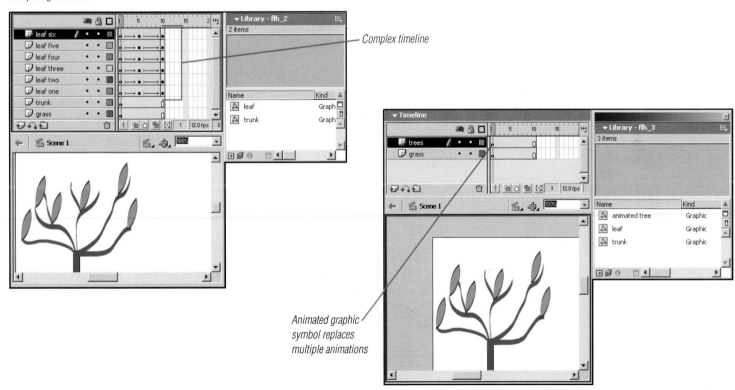

Complex timeline

Animated graphic symbol replaces multiple animations

that the movie clip symbol retains its own independent timeline when you insert an instance of the symbol into a movie. Even if the main timeline stops, the movie clip keeps going, endlessly repeating like a film loop.

Consider Figure H-2: This scene looks like a drawing of a still living room. However, if it were animated, the fire could be crackling and the candles flickering. Each one of these animated elements might reside in a movie clip symbol. That way, when placed on the stage in a scene, each of the movie clip symbols would move according to its own independent timeline, as well as only taking up one layer and, potentially, only one keyframe on the timeline. Not only does this help to organize the different pieces of a movie, it also allows you to isolate animated elements and have animations repeat at their own pace.

FIGURE H-2

Using movie clip symbols

You could create one movie clip symbol of a flickering flame, and use it to animate all three candles

The fire could be its own movie clip symbol, continuously crackling and moving as fires do

FIGURE H-3

Adding an animated graphic symbol to the stage

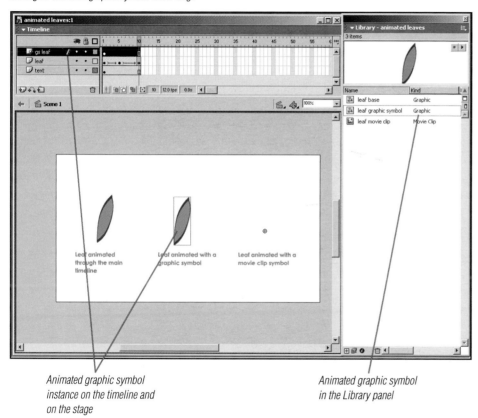

Animated graphic symbol
instance on the timeline and
on the stage

Animated graphic symbol
in the Library panel

1. Open flh_1.fla, then save it as **animated_leaves.fla**.

2. Make sure that the Library panel is open.

3. Click Control on the menu bar, then click Play to watch the leaf animate on the stage.

   The motion tween in the leaf layer of the timeline causes the leaf to move.

   > TIP You can also press [Enter] (Win) or [return] (Mac) to play the animation.

4. Insert a new layer above the leaf layer, then rename it **gs leaf**.

5. Drag the leaf graphic symbol from the Library panel to the stage above the text, as shown in Figure H-3.

   The animated graphic symbol version of the leaf still takes up 10 frames on the time-line, but the symbol's motion tween does not display because it is saved as part of the symbol.

6. Click Control on the menu bar, then click Play to animate the leaves.

7. Save your work.

You moved an instance of an animated graphic symbol to the stage and compared it to an animation created through the main timeline.

Work with a movie clip symbol

1. Insert a new layer above the gs leaf layer, rename it **mc leaf**, then drag the leaf movie clip symbol from the Library panel to the stage above the text, as shown in Figure H-4. ✛

2. Click Control on the menu bar, then click Play to animate the leaves.

   The movie clip symbol version of the leaf does not move because movie clips on the stage play only when you export the movie.

3. Click Control on the menu bar, then click Test Movie to export the movie.

   All three leaves animate in place continually.

   | TIP You can also press [Ctrl][Enter] (Win) or [command][return] (Mac) to test the movie.

4. Click File on the menu bar, then click Close to close the preview window.

5. Insert a new layer above the mc leaf layer, then rename it **action**. ✛

(continued)

FIGURE H-4
Adding a movie clip symbol to the stage

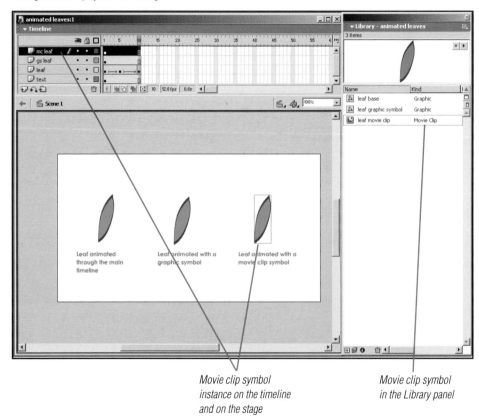

Movie clip symbol instance on the timeline and on the stage

Movie clip symbol in the Library panel

6. Click Window on the menu bar, click Actions, click Frame 1 on the actions layer, then double-click stop in the Actions panel, as shown in Figure H-5.

> TIP   If a stop action is not visible in the Actions panel, click Actions, then click Movie Control to expand the Actions menu.

7. Click Control on the menu bar, then click Test Movie.

Only the movie clip symbol moves because it has an independent timeline; the stop action stopped the main timeline, upon which the other two instances of the leaf are dependent.

8. Click File on the menu bar, then click Close to close the preview window.

9. Save your work, then close the movie.

You inserted an instance of a graphic symbol and a movie clip symbol to the stage and compared them to an animated graphic symbol.

FIGURE H-5

Inserting a stop action with the Actions panel

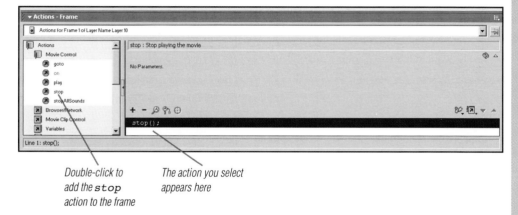

Double-click to add the stop action to the frame

The action you select appears here

CREATE AN ANIMATED GRAPHIC SYMBOL

What You'll Do

 In this lesson, you will convert an animation on the timeline into an animated graphic symbol.

Using Graphic Symbols for Animations

Most of the time, you will want to use movie clip symbols instead of animated graphic symbols to store animations. However, there are some situations where creating an animated graphic symbol is useful, such as a sequential animation you want to play only one time, rather than repeat continuously as a movie plays. Or, you might want an animation to synchronize with other elements on the stage, and since animated graphic symbols use the main timeline, it can be easier to achieve this effect. Also, you can preview animated graphic symbols you place on the stage right from the Macromedia Flash editing environment by dragging the playhead back and forth across the timeline (also called scrubbing), which makes them easier to test within Macromedia Flash than

movie clip symbols, which play only when you export the movie.

You create an animated graphic symbol in the same way you create a static graphic symbol, by choosing the Graphic option in the Create New Symbol dialog box. An animated graphic symbol looks the same as a static graphic symbol in the Library panel, but when you select the animated graphic symbol or a movie clip symbol, it displays with Stop and Play buttons in the Library panel that you can use for testing, as shown in Figure H-6.

Copying Frames and Layers from the Timeline

Despite good preliminary planning, you may end up drawing and animating objects in a scene and decide later that the animation would be better placed inside an animated graphic or movie clip symbol. Fortunately, it is easy to copy frames and layers from the main timeline and paste them into a new symbol.

To move multiple layers and frames from within a scene to a symbol, first select the layers and keyframes that you want to copy. To select multiple frames in one or more layers, click and hold in the first frame you want to select, then drag to the last frame.

Figure H-7 shows a selection across multiple frames and layers. Once you select the keyframes, click Edit on the menu bar and then click Cut Frames. Create or open the symbol, then place your cursor in a frame, click Edit on the menu bar, then click Paste Frames. Macromedia Flash pastes each individual layer from the original scene into the symbol, and even maintains the layer names.

Note that you cannot copy sound or interactivity in an animation from the main timeline to an animated graphic symbol. If you want to include sound or interactivity with an animation that you are using in the Library panel, you should create a movie clip symbol.

FIGURE H-6

Stop and Play buttons in the Library panel

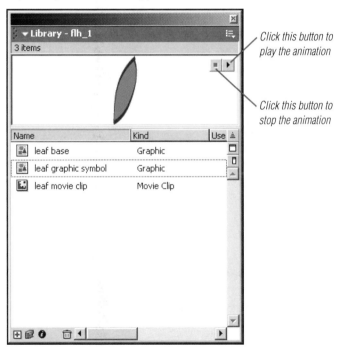

Click this button to play the animation

Click this button to stop the animation

FIGURE H-7

Multiple frames and layers selected

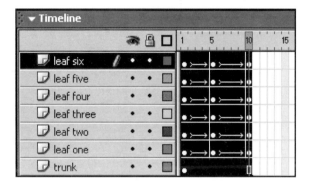

Delete objects from the timeline

1. Open flh_2.fla, then save it as **animated_trees.fla**.

2. Make sure that the Library panel is open.

3. Click Control on the menu bar, then click Play.

   The leaves animate on six separate layers.

4. Select the leaf and trunk layer frames on the timeline, as shown in Figure H-8.

   > **TIP** You can press and hold [Shift], then click one or more layer names to select all frames in the layers.

5. Click Edit on the menu bar, then click Cut Frames.

   The tree is no longer visible on the stage.

6. Save your work.

You selected the frames of the layers on the timeline that made up the tree.

Move frames to create an animated graphic symbol

1. Click Insert on the menu bar, then click New Symbol.

2. Type **animated tree** in the Name text box, click the Graphic option (if necessary), as shown in Figure H-9, then click OK.

   You are now in the graphic object-editing environment.

3. Click Frame 1 on Layer 1, click Edit on the menu bar, then click Paste Frames.

   The tree trunk and leaves appear on the stage.

   (continued)

FIGURE H-8

Selecting frames in the main timeline

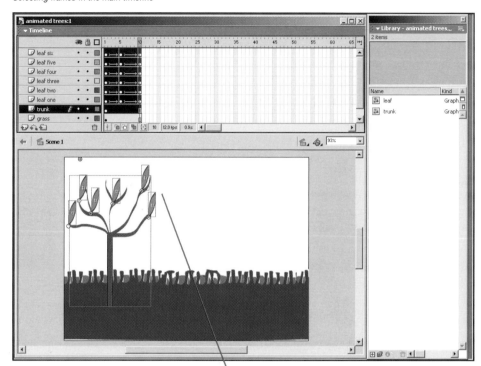

Selecting the frames in the timeline also selects the elements on the stage

FIGURE H-9

The Create New Symbol dialog box

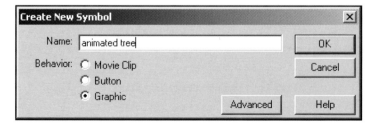

FIGURE H-10

Moving an instance of the tree symbol to the stage

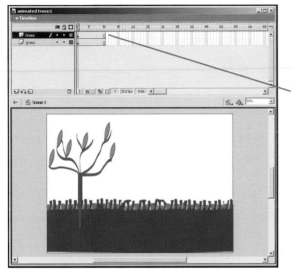

The tree symbol takes up only one layer on the timeline

FIGURE H-11

Resizing the second instance of the tree symbol

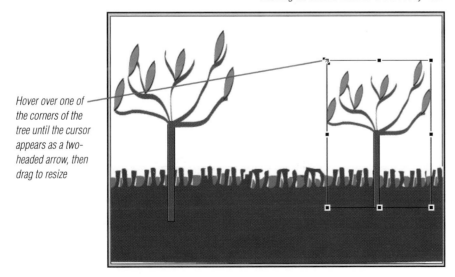

Hover over one of the corners of the tree until the cursor appears as a two-headed arrow, then drag to resize

4. Click the Scene identifier icon on the Information bar to return to Scene 1. 🎬 Scene 1

5. Click the leaf six layer, right-click (Win) or [control] click (Mac), then click Delete Layer.

   TIP   You can also click the Delete Layer icon on the bottom of the timeline. 🗑

6. Repeat Step 5 for the remaining leaf layers and the trunk layer.

7. Save your work.

You pasted frames from the main timeline and converted them into an animated graphic symbol.

Move an animated graphic symbol to the stage

1. Insert a new layer above the grass layer, then rename it **trees**. ➕

2. Click Frame 1 on the trees layer, then drag the animated tree graphic symbol from the Library panel to the left side of the stage, as shown in Figure H-10.

3. Click Control on the menu bar, then click Play.

4. Drag another instance of the animated tree graphic symbol from the Library panel to the right side of the stage.

5. Click the Free Transform Tool on the toolbox, click a corner sizing handle on the tree, then drag to the size shown in Figure H-11. ⊞

6. Click Control on the menu bar, then click Play to watch the leaves animate on the stage.

7. Save your work, then close the movie.

You created two instances of an animated graphic symbol on the stage.

CREATE A MOVIE CLIP SYMBOL

What You'll Do

In this lesson, you will create a movie clip symbol and nest movie clips symbols within one another.

Using Movie Clip Symbols for Animations

Movie clip symbols are usually the most efficient choice for creating and storing complex animations. The main advantage of movie clip symbols is that they maintain their own independent timeline, which is especially useful for animating continuous or looping actions. Movie clip symbols require only one layer and one frame in the main movie, regardless of the complexity of the animation, which can make it easier to work with the timeline.

Movie clip symbols offer many other sophisticated features not available with animated graphic symbols. For example, you can add sound and associate ActionScript statements to movie clip symbols, or create an animation for a movie clip in the main timeline (such as a motion tween) while the movie clip continues to play its own animation on its independent timeline. In addition, you can use movie clip symbols to animate a button.

To start building a movie clip symbol, create a new symbol and then choose Movie Clip in the Create New Symbol dialog box. You can create the movie clip animation from scratch, or cut and copy frames and layers from the main timeline, as you did with the animated graphic symbol in the previous lesson.

> **QUICKTIP**
>
> While you're working in editing mode, you can see only a static image of the first frame of a movie clip symbol on the stage. To view the full animation, you must export the movie.

Nesting Movie Clips

A movie clip symbol is often made up of many other movie clips, a process called **nesting**. You can nest as many movie clip symbols inside another movie clip as you like. You can also place a symbol, graphic, or button inside of a movie clip symbol. Figure H-12 shows a diagram of nesting.

Nesting movie clips creates a **parent-child relationship** that will become increasingly important as you enhance the interactivity of your movies and begin to deploy more sophisticated ActionScript statements. When you insert a movie clip inside another movie clip, the inserted clip is considered the child and the original clip the parent. These relationships are hierarchical, similar to folders that contain files on your computer or in your file cabinet. Keep in mind that if you place an instance of a parent clip into a scene and change it,

you will also affect the nested child clip. Any time you change the instance of a parent clip, the associated child clips update automatically.

The Movie Explorer panel, shown in Figure H-13, allows you to inspect the nesting structure of your entire movie. This is a useful reference to print out as you work on a movie, so you can easily view the movie's structure and see which elements are nested inside each other. You can also apply a filter to view just the

elements you want. To access the Movie Explorer, click Window on the menu bar and then click Movie Explorer. Click the expand or collapse branch icons to tailor your view of nested symbols.

The Options menu lets you perform a variety of actions on the elements listed in the Movie Explorer. For example, you can go to the element on the stage and timeline, find the element in the Library panel, or open all panels relevant to the element so you can edit it.

FIGURE H-12
Diagram of a nested movie clip animation

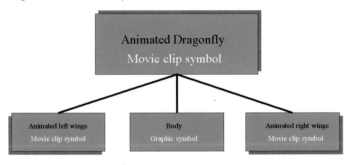

FIGURE H-13
Movie Explorer panel

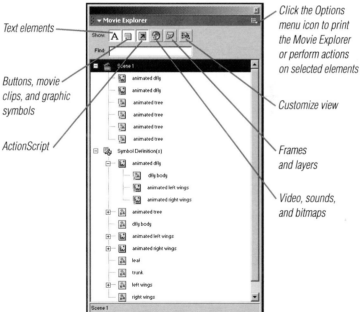

Text elements

Buttons, movie clips, and graphic symbols

ActionScript

Click the Options menu icon to print the Movie Explorer or perform actions on selected elements

Customize view

Frames and layers

Video, sounds, and bitmaps

Create a movie clip symbol

1. Open flh_3.fla, then save it as **dragonfly.fla**.

2. Make sure that the Library panel is open, then notice the symbols.

   The Library panel contains the dfly body, left wings, and right wings graphic symbols, as well as the animated left wings movie clip symbol. These symbols will form the basis of your movie clip.

3. Click the animated left wings movie clip symbol in the Library panel, then click the Play button. ▶

   The wings appear to flutter. Next, you will create another movie clip symbol to animate a set of right wings for the dragonfly.

4. Click Insert on the menu bar, then click New Symbol.

5. Type **animated right wings** in the Name text box, click the Movie Clip option, then click OK.

6. Click Frame 1 on Layer 1 on the timeline, then drag the right wings graphic symbol from the Library panel to the center of the stage, so that the round cross hair is above the centering cross hair.

7. Insert new keyframes in Frames 5 and 10 on the timeline.

8. Click Frame 5 on Layer 1, open the Property inspector (if necessary), click the wings object on the stage, double-click the W: text box, type **47**, as shown in Figure H-14, then close the Property inspector.

   (continued)

FIGURE H-14
Resizing the wings

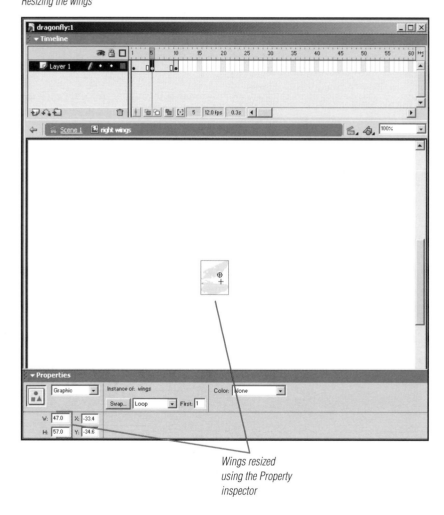

Wings resized
using the Property
inspector

FIGURE H-15
Animated timeline

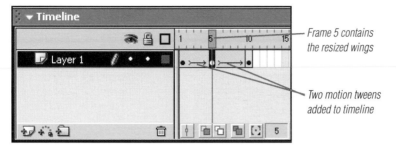

Frame 5 contains
the resized wings

Two motion tweens
added to timeline

FIGURE H-16
Assembled animated dragonfly

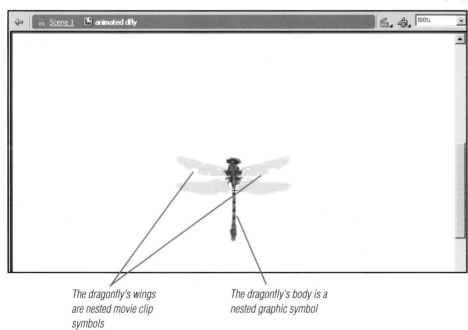

The dragonfly's wings
are nested movie clip
symbols

The dragonfly's body is a
nested graphic symbol

9. Click Frame 1 on Layer 1, click Insert on the menu bar, then click Create Motion Tween.

10. Click Frame 5 on Layer 1, click Insert on the menu bar, click Create Motion Tween, then compare your timeline to Figure H-15.

11. Click the Scene identifier icon on the Information bar to return to Scene 1, then save your work. 🎬 Scene 1

You created a movie clip symbol.

Nest movie clip symbols

1. Click Insert on the menu bar, then click New Symbol.

2. Type **animated dfly** in the Name text box, click the Movie Clip option (if necessary), then click OK.

3. Drag the dfly body graphic symbol from the Library panel to the center of the stage.

4. Drag the animated left wings movie clip symbol from the Library panel to the stage, then attach it to the upper left side of the dragonfly's body.

5. Repeat Step 4, but drag the animated right wings to the upper right side of the body.

6. Compare your image to Figure H-16, click the Scene identifier icon on the Information bar, then save your work. 🎬 Scene 1

You nested two movie clips inside a new movie clip symbol.

Move the movie clip symbol to the stage and enhance animation

1. Insert a new layer above the trees layer, then rename it **dragonfly**.

2. Click Frame 1 on the dragonfly layer, then drag the animated dfly movie clip symbol from the Library panel on top of the left tree on the stage, as shown in Figure H-17.

3. Insert a keyframe in Frame 40 on all the layers on the timeline.

4. Click Frame 1 on the dragonfly layer, then click the Add Motion Guide icon on the bottom of the timeline.

   A new motion guide layer appears above the dragonfly layer.

5. Click Insert on the main menu, then click Create Motion Tween.

   The motion tween appears on the dragonfly layer.

6. Click Frame 1 on the guide: dragonfly layer, click the Pencil Tool on the toolbox, click the Smooth Tool option in the Options section of the toolbox, then draw a path between the trees, as shown in Figure H-18.

   | TIP   The currently selected Stroke color determines the color of the motion path.

   (continued)

FIGURE H-17
Animated dragonfly instance placed on the stage

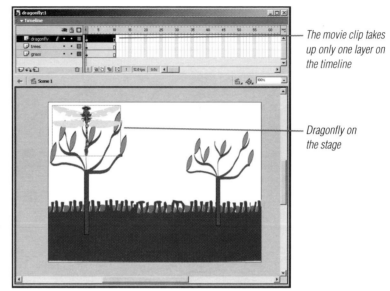

The movie clip takes up only one layer on the timeline

Dragonfly on the stage

FIGURE H-18
Motion guide path for the dragonfly

The color of your motion guide path may vary

Moving the dragonfly to the end of the motion guide path

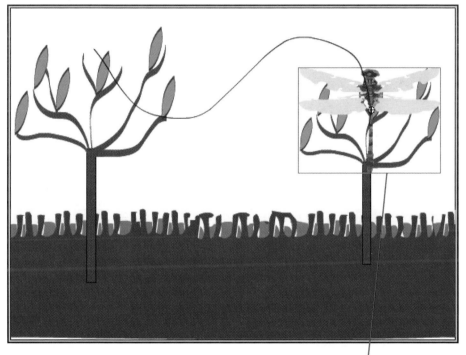

Drag the dragonfly to
the end of the path

7. Click Frame 1 on the dragonfly layer, open the Property inspector, verify that the Snap option is selected, then close the Property inspector.

8. Click Frame 1 on the dragonfly layer, click the Arrow Tool on the toolbox, click the dragonfly on the stage, then drag the dragonfly to the start of the path, if necessary.

9. Click Frame 40 on the dragonfly layer, then drag the dragonfly to the end of the path, as shown in Figure H-19.

10. Click Control on the menu bar, then click Test Movie to preview the movie.

The dragonfly moves between the trees, its wings fluttering at the same time.

11. Click File on the menu bar, click Close to close the preview window, then save your work.

You moved a movie clip from the Library panel to the stage and then animated the instance of the movie clip.

ANIMATE BUTTONS WITH MOVIE CLIP SYMBOLS

What You'll Do

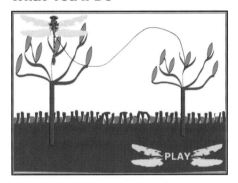

 In this lesson, you will create an animated button and put together a short interactive movie using ActionScript.

Understanding Animated Buttons

As you learned in a previous lesson, a button symbol does not have the standard timeline, but instead has four states associated with it. You can animate a button by nesting a movie clip symbol inside any one of the three visible states of the button, Up, Over, or Down, although Up and Over are most common.

Depending on the state in which you nest the symbol, you will have different results. If you nest the animation inside the Up state, the movie/button will continue to animate as long as the button is visible on the stage in the main timeline. If you nest the movie inside the Over state, the animation will be visible only when the user's mouse is over the button. If the animation is nested inside the Down state, the user will see only a brief flicker of animation as they click the mouse. The first two are the most common and both have obvious interface benefits as well—if your users

see something animated, they are more inclined to interact with it and discover it is actually a button.

Building an Animated Button Symbol

To build an animated button symbol, you need at least two symbols in the Library panel. First, you need to create a movie clip symbol with the animation. In building this animation, make sure you design it to repeat cleanly, especially if you plan to use it in the Up state of a button. Once you have built the movie clip symbol, you need to create a button symbol in which to nest the animation. Remember, because movie clips have independent timelines, the clip will run continually while the button symbol is on the stage, even if the main movie pauses or stops. Figure H-20 shows the Information bar for a movie clip symbol nested inside of a button.

As with a movie clip, you must export the movie in order to see the animation of a button. The Enable Button option will not play the movie clip—you will see only a static view of the first frame of the clip.

Creating an Interactive Movie

Adding interactivity to a movie simply means you are asking your user to be involved in the movie in some way other than watching it. It can be as simple as adding a button for a user to click or giving them a choice to make. Interactivity can also be complex, in the case of a game where a user must assemble a puzzle, as shown in Figure H-21. Because adding interactivity means you are forcing the user to become involved in your movie, you are more likely hold your users' interest.

You can also create complex interactions by using ActionScript in combination with movie clip symbols. With ActionScript, you can set up movie clips to play, pause, or perform other actions based on user input such as clicking the mouse or hitting a key on the keyboard, similar to the interactions you can create with a button. You can also use ActionScript to instruct movie clips to perform actions without waiting for user input and to jump to specific frames on the timeline of a movie clip symbol.

FIGURE H-20

Movie clip symbol nested inside a button

FIGURE H-21

Interactive game created with symbols, buttons, and ActionScript

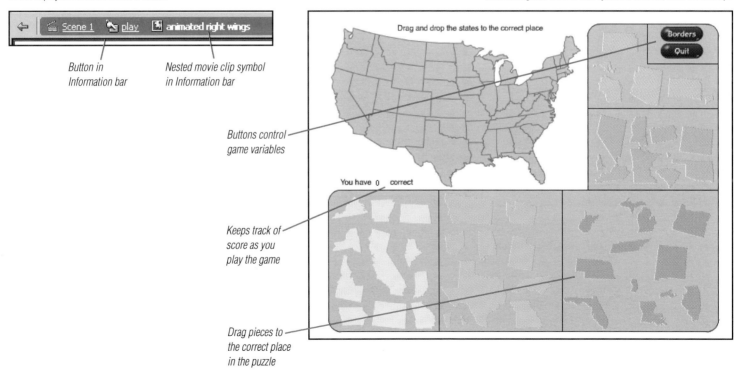

Button in
Information bar

Nested movie clip symbol
in Information bar

Buttons control
game variables

Keeps track of
score as you
play the game

Drag pieces to
the correct place
in the puzzle

Create an animated button

1. Click Insert on the menu bar, then click New Symbol.

2. Type **play** in the Name text box, click the Button option, then click OK.

3. Click the Up frame on Layer 1, click the Text Tool on the toolbox, then open the Property inspector, if necessary. A

4. Click the font list arrow, click Verdana, click the font size list arrow, then drag the slider to **24**.

5. Click the Text (fill) color button, click the top black color swatch in the top row, then click the Bold icon. ▪️

6. Click the Text Tool pointer in the center of the stage, then type **PLAY**. ⁺A

7. Click the Arrow Tool in the toolbox, then drag the animated left wings movie clip symbol from the Library panel to the left of the word "PLAY," then drag the animated right wings movie clip symbol from the Library panel to the right side of the word, as shown in Figure H-22. ▸

(continued)

Adding the animated wings to the text

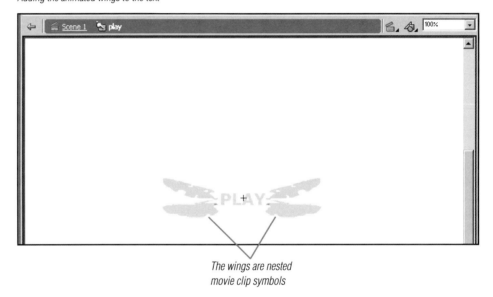

The wings are nested
movie clip symbols

FIGURE H-23
Setting the Hit area

8. Click the Arrow Tool on the toolbox, click the word "PLAY" on the stage, click the Text (fill) color button on the Property inspector, then click the left wing on the stage with the eyedropper pointer.

   The text and the wings are now the same color.

9. Insert a keyframe in the Hit frame of the button, click the Rectangle Tool on the toolbox, then draw a box around both sets of wings and the text, as shown in Figure H-23.

   TIP Remember that the Hit state is invisible on the stage, but defines the clickable area of a button.

10. Click the Scene identifier icon on the Information bar, then save your work. 🔖 **Scene 1**

You placed an animation inside a button symbol.

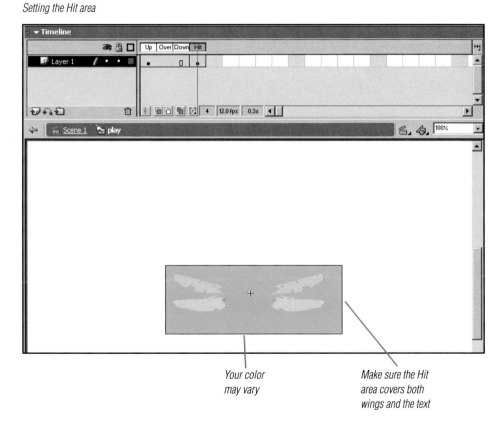

*Your color
may vary*

*Make sure the Hit
area covers both
wings and the text*

Place the animated button on the stage

1. Make sure that the Library panel is open.

2. Insert a new layer above the Guide: dragonfly layer, then rename it **button**.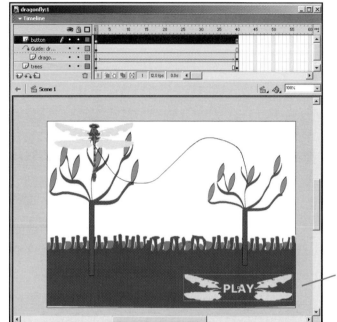

3. Drag the play button symbol from the Library panel underneath the right tree, as shown in Figure H-24.

4. Insert a new layer above the button layer, then rename it **actions**.

5. Click Frame 1 on the actions layer, click Window on the menu bar, click Actions, then double-click stop, as shown in Figure H-25.

   TIP If stop action is not visible, click Actions, then click Movie Control to expand the Actions menu.

6. Click Control on the menu bar, then click Test Movie.

   The wings flutter on the animated button. Notice that while the dragonfly's wings also move, the dragonfly does not fly on the motion guide, nor do the leaves on the trees animate. This is because both the dragonfly's motion and the leaves are dependent on the main timeline, which is stopped on Frame 1.

7. Click File on the menu bar, click Close to close the preview window, then save your work.

8. Minimize the Actions panel.

You placed an animated button on the stage and added a stop action.

FIGURE H-24
Placing the button on the stage

The animated button is made up of text and two movie clip symbols

FIGURE H-25
Adding a stop action

Double-click stop to add the action to the frame

Add a button action

1. Click the Play button on the stage to select it.

2. Open the Actions panel, if necessary, then double-click the goto action.

3. Click gotoAndPlay(1); in the Script pane, if necessary.

4. Type **2** in the Frame: text box, then compare your Actions panel to Figure H-26.

5. Insert a blank keyframe in Frame 40 on the actions layer.

6. Double-click stop in the Actions panel.

7. Click Control on the menu bar, then click Test Movie.

8. Click the Play button.

   Notice that the movie plays to the end—the leaves on the trees animate and the dragonfly flies on the motion guide.

9. Click File on the menu bar, then click Close to close the preview window.

10. Save your work, then close the movie.

You added actions to the movie, creating interactivity.

FIGURE H-26

Adding the button navigation in the Actions panel

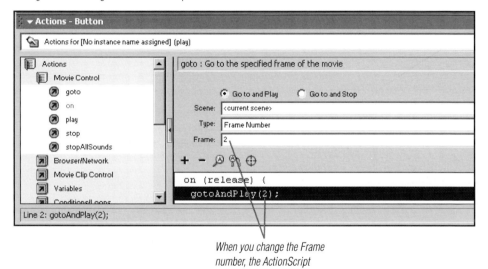

When you change the Frame number, the ActionScript automatically updates

Plan for complex movies and animations, and create an animated graphic symbol.

1. Open flh_4.fla, then save it as **skillsdemoH.fla**.
2. Play the animation in the main timeline.
3. Cut all the frames from the two layers on the main timeline. (*Hint*: Use the Cut Frames command on the Edit menu.)
4. Create a new graphic symbol named **TV**.
5. Paste the frames you cut into the new graphic symbol.
6. Return to Scene 1 and delete the TV screen layer.
7. Click Frame 1 on the TV set layer, then drag the TV animated graphic symbol from the Library panel to the top center of the stage.
8. Play the animation, then save your work.

Create a movie clip symbol.

1. Create a new movie clip symbol named **clock**.
2. Rename Layer 1 on the timeline of the new movie clip **clock face**.
3. Drag the clock face graphic symbol from the Library panel to the exact center of the stage. (*Hint*: Use the arrow keys to move the clock face symbol so the cross hairs in the center of the face line up with the cross hairs on the stage.)
4. Insert a new layer above the clock face layer, then rename it **clock hands**.
5. Drag the clock hands graphic symbol from the Library panel to the exact center of the stage, again using the cross hairs to line up elements.
6. Insert keyframes in Frame 10 and Frame 20 of the clock hands layer, and in Frame 20 of the clock face layer.
7. Click Frame 10 of the clock hands layer, and then use the Free Transform Tool to move the hands about halfway around the clock, so that the time reads 9:30.
8. Create two motion tweens in the clock hands layer, first from Frame 1 to Frame 10, then from Frame 10 to Frame 20. Use the Property inspector to set the Rotate option to CW (clockwise) for both tweens.
9. Test the animation using the Play button in the preview area at the top of the Library panel, then return to Scene 1. (*Hint*: Select the clock movie clip symbol in the Library panel.)

Animate buttons with movie clip symbols.

1. Create a new button symbol named **change channels**.
2. Insert the clock movie clip symbol in the Up state of the button.
3. Insert a keyframe in the Over state of the button, then add the text **Time to Change Channels** to the right of the clock movie clip symbol with the following properties: Font: Verdana, Font Size: 16 pt, Color: black. (*Hint*: Insert new lines after "to" and "Change".)
4. Insert a keyframe in the Hit state of the button, then create a hit area that encompasses the clock and text. (*Hint*: Use the Rectangle Tool on the toolbox to create the hit area.)

5. Return to Scene 1, insert a new layer above the TV set layer, then rename it **button**.

6. In Frame 1 on the button layer, drag the change channels button symbol from the Library panel to the stage, directly beneath the TV.

7. Insert a new layer above the button layer, rename it **actions**, then insert a stop action in Frame 1.

8. Add a goto action to the button on the stage, and specify **2** as the frame to go to.

9. Test your movie and click the button to see the animation.

10. Save your work.

FIGURE H-27
Completed Skills Review

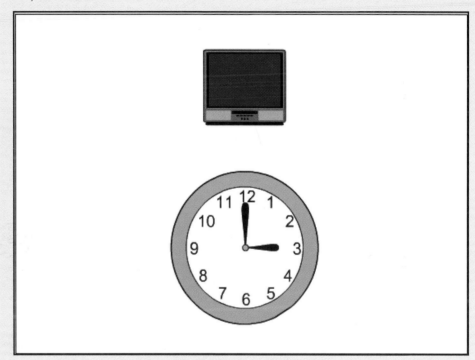

Ultimate Tours has decided they want to add animation to the opening page of their "summer in December" Web site, which is promoting a series of tours to Florida, Bermuda, and the Caribbean. They would like the animation to draw attention to the company name and to the navigation buttons, so visitors will click to find out more information about specific tours. Though the site is still at an early stage, they would like to see some prototypes of potential animations.

1. Open ultimatetoursG.fla (the file you created in Unit G Project Builder 1) and save it as **utlimatetoursH.fla**. (*Hint*: If you did not create ultimatetoursG.fla, see your instructor.)
2. On paper, plan how you might add animations to this page that will fulfill the criteria Ultimate Tours has established.
3. Build the animation you have planned for emphasizing the company name. For example, you might convert the text of the company name ("Ultimate Tours") to a graphic symbol, then create a movie clip symbol in which the text dissolves and reappears (using a text tween), changes color, rotates, or moves across the screen.

4. Build the animation you have planned for encouraging visitors to click the navigation buttons. For example, you might create an animation of an orange ball representing the sun rolling across the sand image already in the button. Then create one sample button, inserting the animation into the Up state.
5. Save your work, then compare your image to Figure H-28.

FIGURE H-28
Completed Project Builder 1

To add some pizzazz to your existing portfolio, you want to change the navigation on your homepage. Your goal is to have visitors mouse over the navigation buttons and see an animation that, hopefully, will better entice employers and potential clients with your skills. The animation should be fairly subtle and elegant, and showcase your animation skill.

1. Open portfolioG.fla and save it as **portfolioH.fla**. (*Hint*: If you did not create

portfolioG.fla, see your instructor. In this file, the Trebuchet font is used. You can replace this font with Arial or any other appropriate font on your computer.)

2. Insert a new movie clip symbol named **animated button.**

3. Inside the movie clip symbol create an animation that would be appropriate for the mouse-over of your primary navigation buttons in the portfolio.

4. Open each of your button symbols and place the animation in the Over state. (*Hint*:

Your new animation should integrate with existing work, or you should update all button states to reflect the new style.)

5. If necessary, add appropriate goto actions from the buttons to the areas of your portfolio that you have built, such as the samples section.

6. Save your work, then compare your movie to Figure H-29.

FIGURE H-29
Completed Project Builder 2

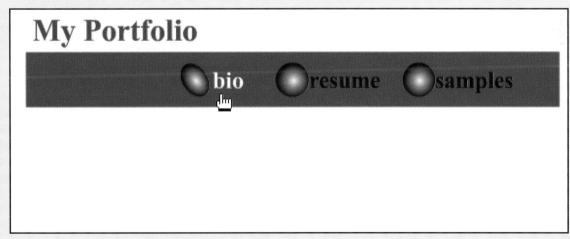

Figure H-30 shows a birthday card created in Flash. Study the figure and complete the following. For each question, indicate how you determined your answer.

1. Connect to the Internet, and go to *www.course.com*. Navigate to the page for this book, click the Student Online Companion, then click the link for this unit.
2. Open a document in a word processor or open a new Macromedia Flash movie, save the file as **dpuUnitH**, then answer the following questions. (*Hint*: Use the Text Tool in Macromedia Flash.)

- Without seeing the source file in this movie, make a list of objects you believe to be in the Library panel and why you think they should be stored there.
- Do you think all the images in this work were drawn in Macromedia Flash?
- What in this scene could be animated?
- Would you use animated graphic symbols or movie clip symbols to create the animations?
- Are there any animated graphic symbols or movie clip symbols you could create once and use in multiple places?

- Suppose you want to create an animation sequence where one jester strums his lute, some text appears and then dissolves, the other jester bangs his tambourine, more text appears and dissolves, then both jesters play simultaneously while the words "Happy Birthday" float across the screen. Plan a strategy for creating this animation that will streamline the timeline, reuse symbols to conserve file size, and allow you to easily set up the timing of the sequence so the text appears at the appropriate time.

FIGURE H-30
Design Project

Your group can assign elements of the project to individual members, or work collectively to create the finished product.

Your group has been asked to create a short interactive movie on ocean life for the local elementary school, which is planning a visit to an oceanographic institute. This project should be colorful, interactive, and full of images, in order to appeal to 7–12-year-old children.

The opening page of the site should show some images of sea creatures which, when clicked, lead to more information. You must include at least three clickable objects on this opening page.

1. Obtain some images of fish, coral, and other ocean creatures from your computer, the Internet, or from scanned media.
2. Open a new movie and save it as **ocean_life.fla**.
3. Set the movie properties including the size and background color, if desired.
4. Create animated movie clips for at least three life forms. Try to use as many different types of animation as you can think of for these movie clips. For example, you might use motion tweening to move, resize, or rotate objects, or fade them in or out.
5. Create buttons for the life forms, using your animated movies in the Up state and also designating a Hit state. (*Hint*: Be creative about the appearance of the buttons—use different shapes and sizes, or try cropping and making the images themselves clickable.)
6. Place the three buttons in the scene.
7. Add some explanatory text.
8. Save your work and compare your image to Figure H-31.

FIGURE H-31
Completed Group Project

USING BASIC ACTIONSCRIPT

1. Work with actions.

2. Work with targets and movie clip symbols.

3. Create interactive movie clip symbols.

4. Define variables.

UNIT I
USING BASIC ACTIONSCRIPT

Introduction

In an earlier unit, you began working with ActionScript, the built-in scripting language for Macromedia Flash. In this unit, you will explore more of the ways in which ActionScript can take your movies to the next level of interactivity and sophistication. For example, you can create ActionScript that changes the appearance of objects in a movie based on the actions a user takes. Or, you can create a form that captures user data and displays it elsewhere in your site.

You can add actions to a frame, button, or movie clip symbol. Since ActionScript is a type of programming language, using exact syntax—spelling action names correctly and including the necessary parameters—is essential. The Actions panel, in which you add ActionScript to frames and objects, helps ensure that your ActionScript follows the required syntax and runs efficiently. The Actions panel includes a normal mode, in which you create ActionScript by selecting actions from a list, and an expert mode, in which you can write your ActionScript directly.

Tools You'll Use

Normal mode

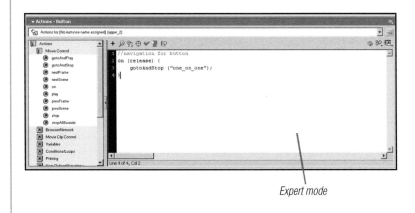

Expert mode

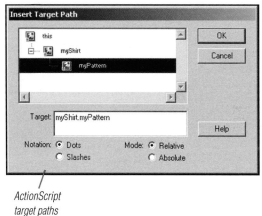

ActionScript
target paths

Input text field

WORK WITH ACTIONS

What You'll Do

In this lesson, you will use ActionScript and frame labels to create navigation to specific frames on the timeline, and you will work in expert mode in the Actions panel.

Referencing the Timeline in Actions

One of the most common uses of ActionScript is to create navigation buttons that jump between frames on a user action, such as a click of the mouse. Referencing a specific frame allows you to break your movies out of the sequential movement of the timeline. You can use either a frame number or frame label to reference the timeline in actions. A **frame label** is simply a text name for a keyframe. Frame labels have an advantage over frame numbers, in that adding or deleting frames won't disrupt any navigation or frame references you have already included in actions, since the label remains attached to the frame even if the frame moves.

You add a label to a frame using the Frame Property inspector. A small red flag appears in labeled frames, as shown in Figure I-1. The label appears to the right of the frame, space permitting, and also when you hover over the frame with the mouse. Because frame labels are exported with the final movie, you should try to keep them short to minimize file size.

Using the Actions Panel in Expert Mode

In previous units, you have used the Actions panel in normal mode. You can also display the Actions panel in expert mode, which allows you to write ActionScript directly in the Script pane. Figure I-2 shows the Actions panel in expert mode.

> **QUICKTIP**
>
> To switch to expert mode, click the View Options icon on the Actions panel, then select Expert Mode. To add actions, click in the Script pane and begin typing.

You can still select action names from the Actions toolbox, but the parameters and text fields for the actions do not appear in the area above the Script pane. You can copy and paste actions in the Script pane in expert mode, which means you can create ActionScript for one object and easily move it to another object, or write your ActionScript in a text editor and then paste it into the Script pane.

There are certain syntax rules you must follow when writing ActionScript. You must use exact case for action names; for example, when typing the `gotoAndPlay` action, be sure to capitalize the "A" and "P." A semicolon (;) terminates an ActionScript statement. Functions or parameters for an action are enclosed in parentheses. Text strings appear between quotation marks. To group actions, you enclose them in braces—{}.

After you are done entering actions, you should click the Check Syntax button above the Script pane to check the code and display errors in an output window.

If you need help while working in expert mode, you can display code hints. Code hints give the syntax or possible parameters for an action in a pop-up window as you are entering the action. To see a code hint, type the action statement, then type an opening parenthesis. To dismiss the code hint, type a closing parenthesis or press [Esc]. You can turn off code hints displaying when you type by clicking Edit on the menu bar,

clicking Preferences, then deselecting the Code Hints check box on the ActionScript Editor tab.

QUICK**TIP**

You can add a comment to your ActionScript by placing a slash and asterisk (/*) at the beginning and an asterisk and slash (*/) at the end of one or more lines of text. Any text between the set of symbols will be ignored when the ActionScript runs. If your comment is only a single line, you can alternatively place two slashes (//) at the beginning of the line, and that line will be ignored when the ActionScript runs.

FIGURE I-1
A frame label

FIGURE I-2
Actions panel in expert mode

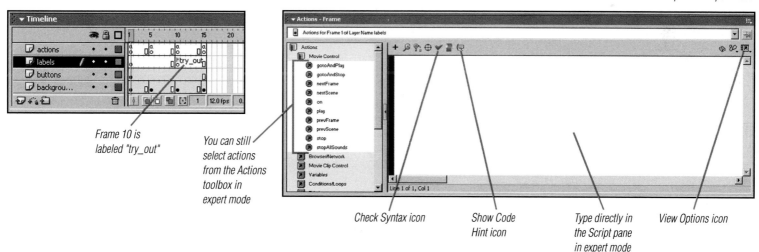

Frame 10 is
labeled "try_out"

You can still
select actions
from the Actions
toolbox in
expert mode

Check Syntax icon

Show Code
Hint icon

Type directly in
the Script pane
in expert mode

View Options icon

Create a frame label

1. Open fli_1.fla, then save it as **sale.fla**.

2. Drag the playhead through the timeline to see the scenes in the movie.

   There are four different screens, in Frames 1, 5, 10, and 15. There are also four stop actions in the corresponding frames in the actions layer, which stop the movie after each screen displays.

3. Insert a new layer above the buttons layer, then rename it **labels**.

4. Insert a keyframe in Frame 10 on the labels layer.

5. Open the Property inspector, click Frame 10 on the labels layer, click the Frame Label text box on the left side of the Property inspector, type **try_out** for the frame label, press [Enter] (Win) or [return] (Mac), then compare your Property inspector to Figure I-3.

6. Repeat Steps 4 and 5 for Frame 15 on the labels layer, but name the label **one_on_one**.

   The label name doesn't appear on the timeline because the timeline currently ends at Frame 15.

7. Save your work.

You created frame labels.

FIGURE I-3
Creating a frame label

Type frame label here

Adding comments to a frame

You can add a comment to a frame, instead of a label, by prefacing the text you enter with two slashes: //. Space permitting, comments appear on the timeline with two green slashes to the right of the frame. You cannot reference comments in actions; however, because Macromedia Flash does not export comments with the final movie, comments can be of any length.

FIGURE I-4

Adding a `goto` *action that references a frame label*

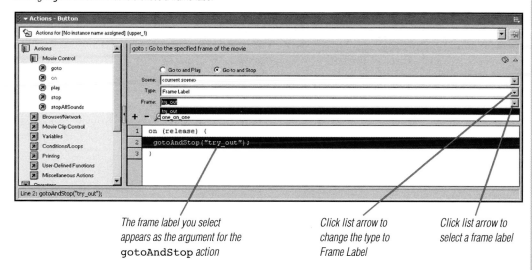

The frame label you select
appears as the argument for the
`gotoAndStop` *action*

*Click list arrow to
change the type to
Frame Label*

*Click list arrow to
select a frame label*

Use frame labels with actions

1. Click the Try Out button on the stage to select it, close the Property inspector, then open the Actions panel.

   TIP   You can also press [F9] to open the Actions panel.

2. Click the View Options icon on the Actions panel, then click Normal Mode.

3. Double-click `goto` in the Movie Control folder in the Actions toolbox, then click the Go to and Stop at the top of the Script pane.

4. Click the Type list arrow, then click Frame Label.

5. Click the Frame list arrow, then click try_out, as shown in Figure I-4.

6. Test the scene, then click the Try Out button.

   The movie jumps to the shoes product frame.

   TIP   You can also press [Ctrl][Alt][Enter] (Win) or [command][option][return] (Mac) to test the scene.

7. Close the test window, then save your work.

You created navigation by referencing an action to a frame label.

Getting help on ActionScript

If you're not sure what an action does, or need some guidance on which parameters to use, the Reference panel can provide more information. To display the Reference panel, highlight an action in the Actions toolbox, then click the Reference icon. An explanation of the action, along with details about its usage and parameters, appears in a separate panel. You can navigate through this panel to show information about other actions in the same way you navigate the Actions panel.

Work in expert mode in the Actions panel

1. Click the Consultant button on the stage.

2. Click the View Options icon on the Actions panel, then click Expert Mode. 🔳

   The Script pane enlarges, and new icons for working in expert mode appear above the panel.

   > TIP You can also press [Ctrl][Shift][E] (Win) or [command][Shift][E] (Mac) to switch to expert mode.

3. Click the View Options icon, then click View Line Numbers if it does not already have a check mark next to it. 🔳

   > TIP You can press [Ctrl][Shift][L] (Win) or [command][Shift][L] (Mac) to toggle the display of line numbers.

4. Type **//navigation for button** in the Script pane.

   This comment will be ignored when the ActionScript runs. Comments that explain the intent of your ActionScript can help when troubleshooting, and are especially important if you are working collaboratively on a movie.

5. Press [Enter] (Win) or [return] (Mac) to insert a new line, then type **on (**

   The code hint list appears, displaying the options for the action.

   > TIP You can also click the Show Code Hint button to display the code hint list. 🔲

   (continued)

FIGURE I-5

Adding an on (release) *action in expert mode*

FIGURE I-6

Adding a `gotoAndStop` *action in expert mode*

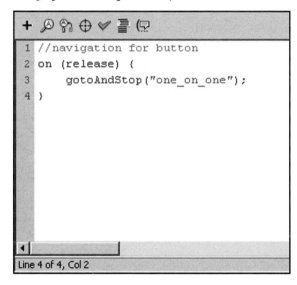

```
1  //navigation for button
2  on (release) {
3      gotoAndStop("one_on_one");
4  }
```

Line 4 of 4, Col 2

6. Double-click release to select it, type **)** to end the function, press [Spacebar], then type **{** as shown in Figure I-5.

7. Press [Enter] (Win) or [return] (Mac) to move to line 3, then type **gotoAndStop (**

   A code hint appears, displaying the syntax for the action.

   > TIP   Be sure to use exact case when typing actions.

8. Immediately after the opening parenthesis, type **"one_on_one");**

   The quotation marks indicate that one_on_one is a frame label to which you want the button to lead when clicked. The semicolon indicates the end of a line of code.

9. Press [Enter] (Win) or [return] (Mac) to move to Line 4, type **}** then compare your Script pane to Figure I-6.

10. Test the scene, then click the Consultant button.

    The movie jumps to the consultation frame.

11. Close the test window, save your work, then close the file.

You created navigation in expert mode using a frame label.

WORK WITH TARGETS AND MOVIE CLIP SYMBOLS

What You'll Do

In this lesson, you will use ActionScript to control movie clip timelines.

Working with Movie Clips

Most large Macromedia Flash documents include many movie clip symbols. Using movie clips helps you better manage your document by breaking down complex tasks into smaller components, and also lets you reuse content and reduce file size. Another advantage to movie clips is you can use actions with them, allowing you greater control over the objects on the stage.

You can set up the actions you associate with movie clips to run when a user performs an action, to run automatically when the movie plays, or to run when a condition is met, such as if the movie clip has been dropped on top of another movie clip. Some common uses of ActionScript with movie clip symbols include creating actions that run a specific frame within the movie clip symbol's timeline, and making a movie clip draggable, so users can move it in games, shopping carts, or simulations.

QUICKTIP

The ActionScript that you associate with movie clips will run only when you test or publish your movie.

Referencing Movie Clip Symbols as ActionScript Targets

To control movie clip symbols and their timelines with ActionScript, you must target the movie clips, or refer to them by path and name. Since actions are associated with specific instances of objects, you cannot just use the movie clip symbol name that appears in the Library panel. Instead, you must use the Property inspector to create an instance name for the movie clip to which you want to refer. You can target movie clip symbols at any level, even movie clips nested inside other movie clips.

In normal mode, the `with` action lets you target a movie clip on which to perform other actions. You can specify the movie clip symbol either by typing a path and name directly using dot syntax, which is explained below, or by clicking the Insert a target path icon. The Insert Target Path dialog box, shown in Figure I-7, displays movie clip symbol names hierarchically. You can click the plus sign next to a name to see nested movie clips.

In expert mode, you use what Macromedia Flash refers to as **dot syntax** to create targets. A dot (.) identifies the hierarchical nature of the path to a movie clip symbol, similar to the way slashes are used to create a path name to a file in some operating systems. For example, "dragonfly.left_wings", as shown in the ActionScript statement in Figure I-8, refers to a movie clip symbol named left_wings nested within the symbol dragonfly. You can also use dot syntax in an ActionScript statement to set actions and variables for a movie clip. For example, "`square._x = 150`" sets the X-axis position of a movie clip symbol named square to 150.

There are also two special terms, `_root` and `_parent`, which you can use when creating target paths with dot syntax. `_root` refers to the main timeline. You can use it to create an absolute path, or a path that works downward from the top level of a movie. `_parent` refers to the movie clip in which the current clip is nested. You can use it to create a relative path, or a path that works backward through the hierarchy. (`_parent` essentially means "go up one level from where I currently am.") Relative paths are helpful when writing ActionScript you intend to reuse for multiple objects.

FIGURE I-7
Insert Target Path dialog box

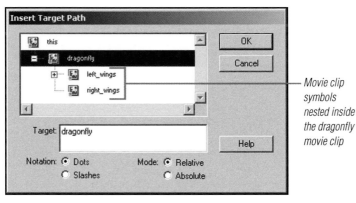

Movie clip symbols nested inside the dragonfly movie clip

FIGURE I-8
ActionScript statement using dot syntax

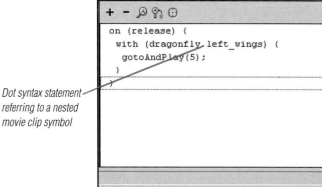

Dot syntax statement referring to a nested movie clip symbol

Use ActionScript to control the timeline of a movie clip symbol

1. Open fli_2.fla, then save it as **shirt.fla**.

2. Click the Arrow Tool on the toolbox (if necessary), then double-click the yellow shirt on the stage to open the shirt_color movie clip symbol. ▶

   This movie clip symbol has a layer that changes the color of the shirt, a layer that includes actions to stop the clip after each frame, and a layer that includes a nested movie clip to change the pattern of the shirt.

3. Drag the playhead along the movie clip timeline to see how the shirt changes color, then click the Scene identifier icon on the Information bar to return to Scene 1. 🎬 Scene 1

4. Click the shirt_color movie clip symbol to select it, open the Property inspector, click the Instance Name text box, type **myShirt** for the instance name, press [Enter] (Win) or [return] (Mac), as shown in Figure I-9, then close the Property inspector.

5. Click the red button on the stage (under the words "Click to Pick a Color"), then open the Actions panel, if necessary.

   (continued)

FIGURE I-9
Naming a movie clip symbol instance

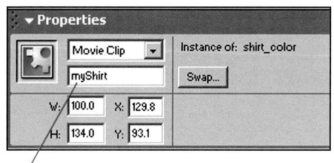

Type the name
in this field

FIGURE I-10

Movie clip symbol instance name in Insert Target Path dialog box

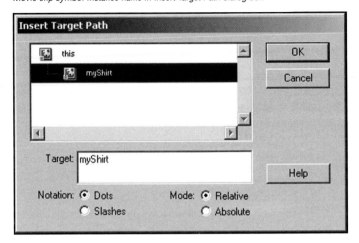

6. Click the View Options icon, then click Normal Mode to switch to normal mode. 🔲

   > TIP   You can also press [Ctrl][Shift][N] (Win) or [command][Shift][N] (Mac) to switch to normal mode.

7. Double-click `on` in the Movie Control folder on the Actions toolbox.

8. Click the Variables folder on the Actions toolbox, to open the folder, then double-click `with`.

9. Click the Insert a target path icon to open the Insert Target Path dialog box, click the myShirt movie clip symbol, as shown in Figure I-10, then click OK. ⊕

10. Double-click `play` in the Movie Control folder on the Actions toolbox, then compare your image to Figure I-11.

11. Test the scene, then click the red button repeatedly.

    Each time you click the button, the shirt color changes.

12. Close the test window, then save your work.

You used ActionScript to control the timeline of a movie clip symbol.

FIGURE I-11

ActionScript to change the color of the shirt on button press

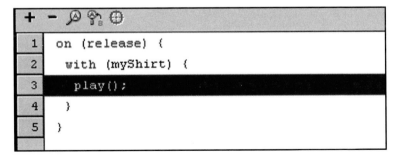

```
1  on (release) {
2    with (myShirt) {
3      play();
4    }
5  }
```

Use ActionScript to control the timeline of a nested movie clip symbol

1. Verify that the Arrow Tool is selected, double-click the shirt on the stage, double-click the shirt again to open the pattern_shirt nested movie clip symbol, then compare your image to Figure I-12.

   The pattern_shirt movie clip symbol is a nested movie clip symbol that changes the pattern of the shirt. It includes two frame labels, "circles" and "stars".

2. Drag the playhead along the movie clip symbol timeline to see how the shirt changes.

3. Click the shirt_color movie clip on the Information bar, click the shirt_color movie clip symbol on the stage, open the Property inspector, click the Instance Name text box, type **myPattern** for the instance name, press [Enter] (Win) or [return] (Mac), then close the Property inspector.

   TIP The Property inspector changes the settings for the currently selected object. To select a nested movie clip, the parent movie clip must be open.

4. Click the Scene identifier icon on the Information bar to return to Scene 1.

   ⛋ Scene 1

5. Click the Stars button on the stage (under the word "Patterns"), then open the Actions panel, if necessary.

   (continued)

FIGURE I-12

Timeline of a nested movie clip symbol

The timeline includes two frame labels, "circles" and "stars"

Information bar shows nested movie clip

FIGURE I-13

Nested movie clip symbol in the Insert Target Path dialog box

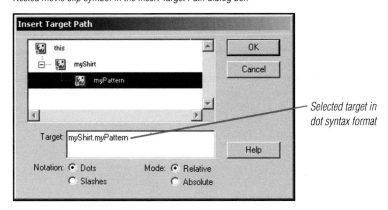

Selected target in
dot syntax format

6. Double-click **on** in the Movie Control folder on the Actions toolbox.

7. Double-click **with** in the Variables folder on the Actions toolbox.

8. Click the Insert a target path icon, click the + sign (Win) or triangle (Mac) to expand the myShirt path, click the myPattern movie clip symbol, as shown in Figure I-13, then click OK. ⊕

   Flash inserts a path to the nested movie clip symbol in dot syntax format (myShirt.myPattern) as the argument for the **with** action.

9. Double-click **goto** in the Movie Control folder on the Actions toolbox, click the Type list arrow, click Frame Label, click the Frame text box, type **stars**, then compare your Actions panel to Figure I-14.

10. Test the scene, then click the Stars button.

    The shirt pattern changes.

11. Close the test window, then save your work.

You used ActionScript to control the timeline of a nested movie clip symbol.

FIGURE I-14

Referencing a frame label in the nested movie clip symbol in the `gotoAndPlay` *action*

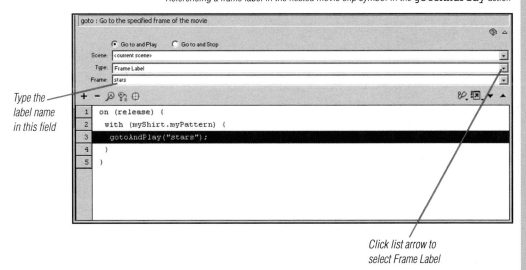

Type the
label name
in this field

Click list arrow to
select Frame Label

Copy ActionScript between objects in expert mode

1. Click the View Options icon in the Actions panel, then click Expert Mode. 🔁
2. Click and drag to select all the ActionScript for changing the pattern to stars, as shown in Figure I-15.
3. Right-click (Win) or [control] click (Mac) the selection, then click Copy.
4. Click the Circles button on the stage.
5. Click in the Script pane, right-click (Win) or [control] [click] (Mac), then click Paste.

(continued)

FIGURE I-15

Selecting the ActionScript to copy

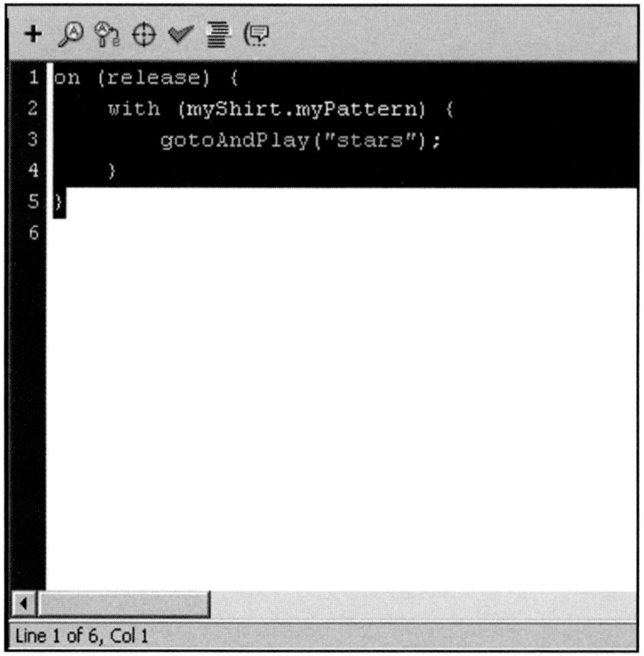

```
1 on (release) {
2     with (myShirt.myPattern) {
3         gotoAndPlay("stars");
4     }
5 }
6
```

Line 1 of 6, Col 1

6. Double-click the word "stars" in the Script pane to highlight it, then type **circles**, as shown in Figure I-16.

7. Test the scene, then click the Stars button and Circles button.

   The shirt pattern changes.

8. Close the test window, save your work, then close the file.

You copied and edited ActionScript in expert mode.

FIGURE I-16

Editing the copied ActionScript

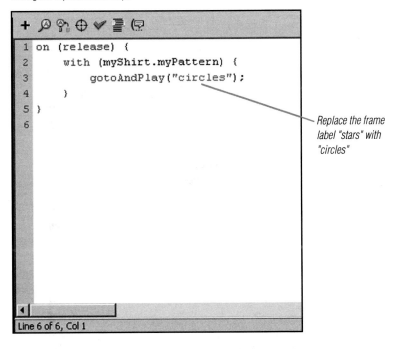

```
1  on (release) {
2      with (myShirt.myPattern) {
3          gotoAndPlay("circles");
4      }
5  }
6
```

Line 6 of 6, Col 1

Replace the frame label "stars" with "circles"

CREATE INTERACTIVE MOVIE CLIP SYMBOLS

What You'll Do

 In this lesson, you will use ActionScript to make a movie clip draggable and change the properties of a movie clip based on user actions.

Understanding Interactive Movie Clips

Using ActionScript with movie clip symbols offers many opportunities for creating a richer user experience. With the `startDrag` and `stopDrag` actions, you can make a movie clip draggable while a movie is playing; that is, you can allow a user to click the movie clip and then move it to another location on the screen. You have probably seen draggable movie clips in games created with Macromedia Flash, as shown in Figure I-17, or in user interface features such as scroll bars and sliders in Web applications created with Macromedia Flash.

Another action, `_droptarget`, extends the draggable movie clip feature by allowing Macromedia Flash to determine if a movie clip has collided with (been placed on top of) another movie clip or a specified area on the stage. Macromedia Flash can then take another set of actions based on where the user has dragged the clip.

ActionScript statements can also change the properties of movie clip symbols as a movie is playing. You can control such properties as position, rotation, color, size, and whether the movie clip is visible or hidden. Actions that change movie clip properties are often used in combination with actions that test for user input or interactions. For example, you can create ActionScript that makes a movie clip disappear when it is dragged onto another movie clip.

Creating Conditional Actions

If-then statements are familiar to anyone who has had minimal programming exposure. ActionScript includes an if action that can test whether certain conditions have been met and, if so, can perform other actions. Such conditional statements offer many possibilities for building more interactive and involving movies. You should enclose all the actions you want Macromedia Flash to carry out in braces following the if action. If the conditions are not met, the actions in the braces are ignored, and Macromedia Flash jumps to the next action.

When creating conditions in ActionScript, you must use two equals signs (==). A single equals sign (=) sets a variable to a specific value. For example, x=9 in ActionScript sets a variable named x to the value 9, where x==9 is a conditional statement that checks if the variable x has a value of 9, and if so, performs another action. Figure I-18 shows an example of a conditional statement.

QUICKTIP

ActionScript includes many other actions for creating conditional statements and loops, such as else, which lets you specify actions to run when an if statement is false, and do while, which lets you specify a set of actions to run continuously until a certain condition is met. See the Reference panel for more information.

FIGURE I-17
Draggable movie clips in a Macromedia Flash game

Each checker is a movie clip symbol, which you can drag to a square

FIGURE I-18
Example of a conditional ActionScript statement

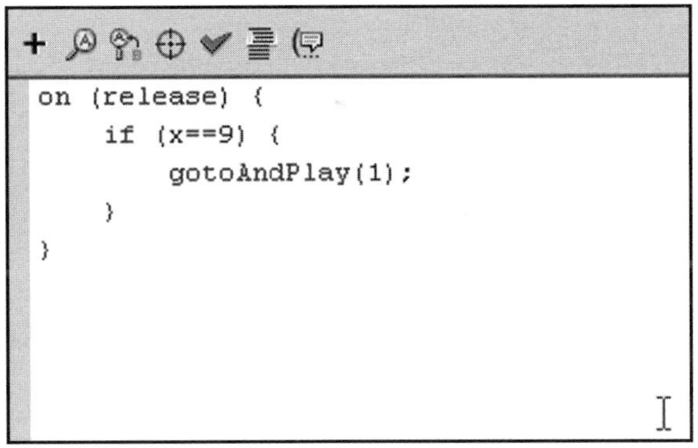

```
on (release) {
    if (x==9) {
        gotoAndPlay(1);
    }
}
```

Use ActionScript to make a movie clip symbol draggable

1. Open fli_3.fla, then save it as **shapes.fla**.

2. Drag the playhead through the timeline.

   This movie contains two frame labels, "start" and "play", which are associated with two separate screens. The actions layer contains stop actions that correspond to each screen. All the shapes on the "play" screen are movie clip symbols.

3. Click Frame 7 on the timeline to display the play screen, click the black square in the Start Bin, open the Actions panel, click the View Options icon, then click Normal Mode.

4. Double-click on in the Movie Control folder in the Actions panel, click the Press check box to select it, click the Release check box to deselect it, if necessary, then compare your image to Figure I-19.

5. Double-click startDrag in the Movie Clip Control folder on the Actions toolbox.

6. Click the next line in the ActionScript (the one with the closing brace), then double-click on in the Movie Control folder in the Actions panel.

   Macromedia Flash inserts the on (release) action after the closing brace, indicating the start of a new action.

   (continued)

FIGURE I-19

Adding an on (press) *action in the Actions panel*

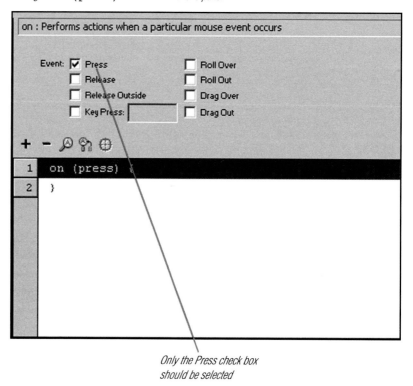

Only the Press check box should be selected

FIGURE I-20

ActionScript to make the movie clip draggable

```
+ - 🔍 📑 ⊕
1  on (press) {
2    startDrag("");
3  }
4  on (release) {
5    stopDrag();
6  }
```

7. Double-click `stopDrag` in the Movie Control folder on the Actions toolbox, then compare your image to Figure I-20.

8. Test the scene, click the Start button, then drag and drop the square around the screen.

9. Close the test window, then save your work.

> TIP To make the other two movie clip symbols draggable, you could switch to expert mode and cut and paste between Script panes. The same ActionScript will work for all three symbols.

You made a movie clip symbol draggable.

Create a conditional action

1. Double-click the yellow square in the Drop Bin to open the square movie clip, then drag the playhead along the movie clip timeline.

   This movie clip symbol has two states: one with the square filled in, and one with just an outline. In the steps below, you'll create a conditional statement that moves the movie clip to Frame 2 when a user drops the square from the Start Bin onto the square in the Drop Bin.

2. Click the Scene identifier icon on the Information bar to return to Scene 1, then close the Actions panel. 🎬 Scene 1

3. Click the yellow square to select it, open the Property inspector, then click the Instance Name text box.

4. Type **targetSquare** for the instance name, press [Enter] (Win) or [return] (Mac), then close the Property inspector.

(continued)

5. Click the black square to select it, open the Actions panel, click the View Options icon, then click Expert Mode.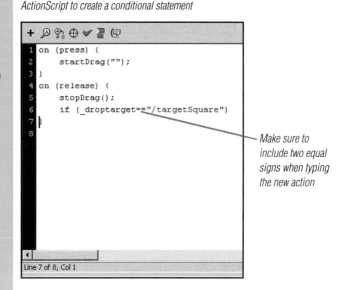

6. Click the end of Line 5 in the Script pane (after the semicolon), press [Enter] (Win) or [return] (Mac) to create a new line, then type the following ActionScript, as shown in Figure I-21:

   if (_droptarget=="/targetSquare")

   This line of ActionScript creates a condition. It tells Macromedia Flash that if the square from the Start Bin is placed on top of the square in the Drop Bin, then perform the next set of actions enclosed in braces.

7. Press [Enter] (Win) or [return] (Mac) to create a new line, then type the following ActionScript, as shown in Figure I-22:

   {_root.targetSquare.gotoAndPlay (2)}

   This line of ActionScript tells Macromedia Flash to play Frame 2 of the targetSquare movie clip.

8. Test the scene, click the Start button, then drag and drop the black square from the Start Bin onto the yellow square in the Drop Bin.

   Macromedia Flash plays the second frame of the targetSquare movie clip, which changes the square in the Drop Bin to just an outline.

9. Close the test window, then save your work.

You created a conditional ActionScript statement that plays a specified frame in a movie clip symbol when two movie clips collide.

FIGURE I-21
ActionScript to create a conditional statement

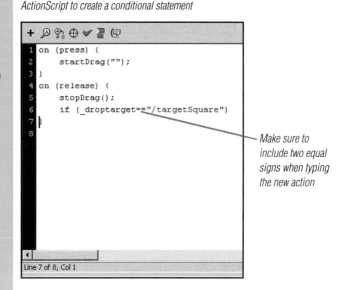

```
1  on (press) {
2      startDrag("");
3  }
4  on (release) {
5      stopDrag();
6      if (_droptarget=="/targetSquare")
7  }
8
```
Line 7 of 8, Col 1

Make sure to include two equal signs when typing the new action

FIGURE I-22

Actions to execute if the conditional statement is true

```
1  on (press) {
2      startDrag("");
3  }
4  on (release) {
5      stopDrag();
6      if (_droptarget=="/targetSquare")
7      {_root.targetSquare.gotoAndPlay (2)}
8  }
9
```
Line 7 of 9, Col 38

Make sure to use exact case when typing the new action

FIGURE I-23

ActionScript to hide the square

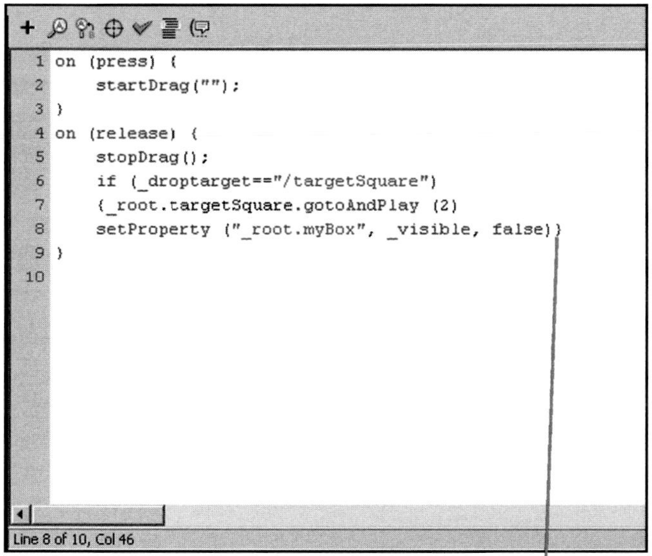

```
 1  on (press) {
 2      startDrag("");
 3  }
 4  on (release) {
 5      stopDrag();
 6      if (_droptarget=="/targetSquare")
 7      {_root.targetSquare.gotoAndPlay (2)
 8      setProperty ("_root.myBox", _visible, false)}
 9  }
10
```

Line 8 of 10, Col 46

*Make sure to type the
new action inside the
closing curly brace*

Understanding the / (slash) in the `_droptarget` action

`_droptarget` was first introduced in Macromedia Flash Version 4.0, before dot syntax was available, and when only slash syntax was supported. The slash in "/targetSquare" is the equivalent of `_root` in dot syntax: it tells Macromedia Flash where the movie clip is relative to the main timeline. Other actions may also require paths that use slash syntax; be sure to check the Reference panel when using a new action. Macromedia Flash includes an `eval` action with which you can convert dot syntax paths to slash syntax in an ActionScript statement.

Use ActionScript to change the properties of a movie clip symbol

1. Click the black square in the Start Bin, open the Property inspector, name the movie clip symbol **myBox**, then close the Property inspector.

    You must name the square so you can reference it in ActionScript.

2. Verify that the black square is still selected, then open the Actions panel, if necessary.

3. Click the Script pane between the closing parenthesis and closing brace at the end of Line 7, then press [Enter] (Win) or [return] (Mac) to create a new line.

    The closing brace should move to Line 8.

4. Before the closing brace on Line 8, type the following ActionScript, as shown in Figure I-23:

    setProperty ("_root.myBox," _visible, false)

5. Test the scene, click the Start button, then drag and drop the square from the Start Bin onto the square in the Drop Bin.

    The square becomes invisible.

6. Close the test window, save your work, then close shapes.fla.

You created an ActionScript statement that hides a movie clip symbol when a condition is met.

DEFINE VARIABLES

What You'll Do

 In this lesson, you will use ActionScript with interactive text and number variables.

Understanding Variables

A **variable** is a container that holds information. Variables are dynamic; that is, the information they contain changes depending on an action a user takes or another aspect of how the movie plays. A Macromedia Flash game that keeps track of scores is an example of using variables, as is a form in which a user enters credit card information while making an online purchase.

You create variables in ActionScript with the `setvar` action or by using an equals sign (=). You do not have to specify a data type for the variable when you create it, but it is good practice to give the variable an initial value so you can keep track of how it changes as you use it in expressions. To create a **string variable**, which is a sequence of characters including letters, numbers, and punctuation, place quotations marks around the string. For example, the ActionScript statement `myExam = "Pop Quiz"` sets the variable myExam to the string Pop Quiz. To create a **number variable**, just write the

number. For example, `myScore = 93` sets a variable named myScore to the number 93.

Macromedia Flash includes the following data types for variables: String, Number, Boolean, Object, Movieclip, Null, and Undefined. See the Macromedia Flash Help system for a full explanation of each type.

> **QUICK**TIP
>
> To ensure your ActionScript will run correctly, do not include spaces in variable names.

Using Text Fields to Collect User Information

One of the most powerful uses of variables is to collect and work with information from users. To do this, you create input and dynamic text fields.

An **input text field** takes information entered by a user and stores it as a variable. To create an input box, first create a text box with the Text Tool on the toolbox, then open the Property inspector. You then change the field type and assign a variable name, as shown as Figure I-24. You can also set other properties, such as whether the input box appears with a border, or the maximum number of characters allotted for user input.

A **dynamic text field** displays information derived from variables. You use the Text and Property inspector to create a dynamic text field. If you want exactly what a user has typed to appear in the dynamic text field (for example, a name to appear on a series of pages), assign the dynamic text field the same name as the input text field. If you want to manipulate variables using ActionScript before populating the dynamic text field, assign the field a unique name.

Understanding Expressions

Expressions are formulas for manipulating or evaluating the information in variables. This can range from string expressions that concatenate (join together) user and system-derived text (as in a paragraph that inserts a user's name right in the text) to numeric expressions that perform mathematical calculations like addition, subtraction, or incrementing a value. Macromedia Flash also lets you enter logical expressions that perform true/false comparisons on numbers and strings, with which you can create conditional statements and branching.

Note that some expressions have different results depending on whether they are performed on string or number variables. For example, the comparison operators >, >=, <, and <= determine alphabetical order when used with string variables, and the mathematical operator + concatenates strings.

The Operators and Functions folders on the Actions toolbox contain operators and functions you can use to build expressions in ActionScript, as shown in Figure I-25.

FIGURE I-24
Using the Property inspector to create an input text field

FIGURE I-25
Folders with actions to create expressions

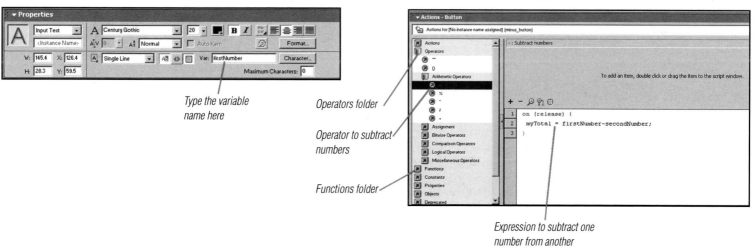

Type the variable name here

Operators folder

Operator to subtract numbers

Functions folder

Expression to subtract one number from another

Create an input text box

1. Open fli_4.fla, then save it as **math.fla**.

2. Click Frame 1 on the background layer.

3. Click the Text Tool on the toolbox, then open the Property inspector. 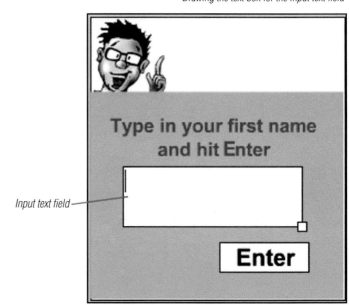A

4. Click the Text type list arrow, click Input Text, click the Font list arrow, drag the slider to **Arial**, click the Font Size list arrow, drag the slider to **18**, click the Text (fill) color box, type **#990000** for the color, click the Bold icon, then click the Show Border Around Text icon, as shown in Figure I-26.

5. Draw a text box in the empty area between the red text and the Enter button, as shown in Figure I-27.

6. Click the Variable text box in the Property inspector, type **myname**, then press [Enter] (Win) or [return] (Mac).

   TIP   Close the Property inspector or the Actions panel, if necessary.

7. Test the scene.

   A white input text box appears.

8. Close the test window, then save your work.

You created an input text box in which users can type their name.

FIGURE I-26
Creating the input text field

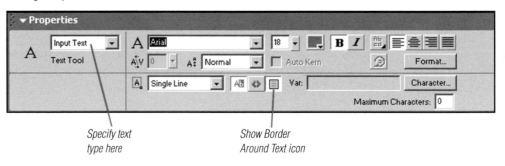

Specify text
type here

Show Border
Around Text icon

FIGURE I-27
Drawing the text box for the input text field

Input text field

Type in your first name
and hit Enter

Enter

FIGURE I-28
Drawing the text box for the dynamic text field

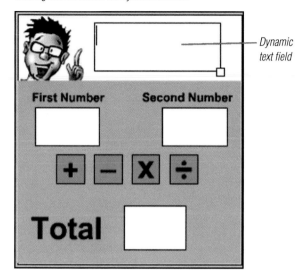

Dynamic
text field

First Number   Second Number

Total

FIGURE I-29
Creating the dynamic text field

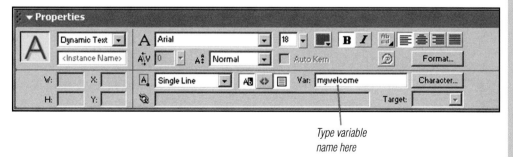

Type variable
name here

Create a dynamic text box

1. Click Frame 5 on the background layer.

2. Click the Text Tool on the toolbox, draw a text box in the white area of the stage to the right of the cartoon character, as shown in Figure I-28, then open the Property inspector. **A**

3. Click the Text type list arrow, click Dynamic Text, click the Variable text box, type **mywelcome**, then press [Enter] (Win) or [return] (Mac), as shown in Figure I-29.

4. Close the Property inspector, then save your work.

You created a dynamic text box to hold the name the user enters.

Use ActionScript to collect and modify string variables

1. Click Frame 1 on the buttons layer, click the Arrow Tool on the toolbox, click the Enter button on the stage, then open the Actions panel. ➤

2. If necessary, click the View Options icon, then click Expert Mode. ▣▪

3. In the Script pane, click at the end of Line 2, press [Enter] (Win) or [return] (Mac) to create a new blank line after Line 2 but before the closing brace, then type the following line of ActionScript, as shown in Figure I-30:
   mywelcome = "Hello, " + myname;

   When the user presses the Enter button, this ActionScript tells Macromedia Flash to take the name the user has entered in the myname input field, preface it with the word "Hello", then place the text string in the mywelcome dynamic text box.

4. Test the scene, click the name input field, type **Jesse**, then click Enter.

   The name "Jesse" appears in the dynamic text field, prefaced by the word "Hello".

5. Close the test window, then save your work.

You used ActionScript to modify a text variable and place it in a dynamic text box.

FIGURE I-30

ActionScript to populate the mywelcome dynamic text box

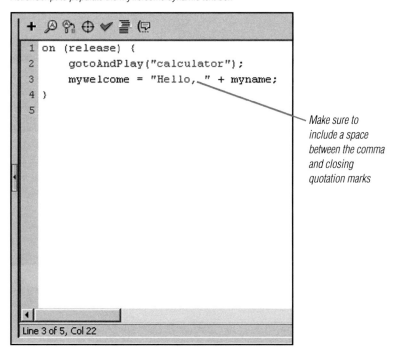

```
1  on (release) {
2      gotoAndPlay("calculator");
3      mywelcome = "Hello, " + myname;
4  }
5
```

Line 3 of 5, Col 22

Make sure to include a space between the comma and closing quotation marks

FIGURE I-31
ActionScript for subtraction operation

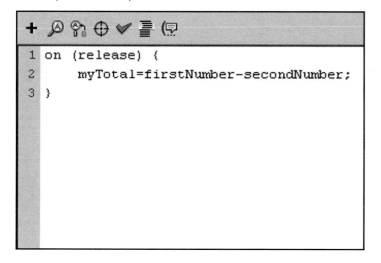

```
1 on (release) {
2     myTotal=firstNumber-secondNumber;
3 }
```

FIGURE I-32
The working formula

Hello, Jesse

First Number   Second Number
20   10

+ − X ÷

Total   10

Use ActionScript to collect and perform mathematical operations on numeric variables

1. Click Frame 5 on the timeline to display the second screen.

   This screen already contains two input text boxes (First Number and Second Number) and a dynamic text box (Total).

2. Click the Arrow Tool on the toolbox, click the subtraction button, then open the Actions panel, if necessary.

3. Type the three lines of ActionScript in the Script pane, as shown in Figure I-31.

   When the user presses the subtraction button, this ActionScript tells Macromedia Flash to subtract the number the user has typed in the secondNumber input field from the number in the firstNumber field, then to place the result in the myTotal dynamic text field.

   | TIP As you type the opening parenthesis after on, the code hint list appears, displaying options for the action.

4. Test the scene, click the Enter button, type **20** in the First Number box, type **10** in the Second Number Box, click the subtraction button, as shown in Figure I-32, then close the test window.

   (continued)

5. Click and drag to select all the actions in the Script pane (including the brace on Line 3), right-click (Win) or [control] click (Mac) the selection, then click Copy.

6. Click the multiplication button on the stage, right-click (Win) or [control] click (Mac) in the Script pane, click Edit on the menu bar, then click Paste.

7. Double-click the minus sign, type * (an asterisk), then compare your Script pane to Figure I-33.

8. Click the division button on the stage, click in the Script pane, right-click (Win) or [control] click (Mac), then click Paste.

9. Double-click the minus sign, then type / (forward slash).

   The forward slash is the division operator.

10. Test the scene, click the Enter button, then experiment with adding numbers in the input boxes and clicking the subtraction, multiplication, and division buttons.

11. Close the test window, then save your work.

You used ActionScript to create mathematical operations that work with variables.

FIGURE I-33
ActionScript for multiplication operation

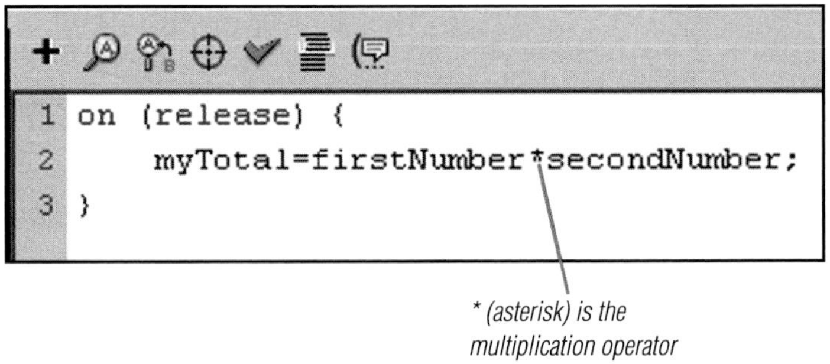

```
1  on (release) {
2      myTotal=firstNumber*secondNumber;
3  }
```

* (asterisk) is the multiplication operator

FIGURE I-34

ActionScript utilizing the Number function

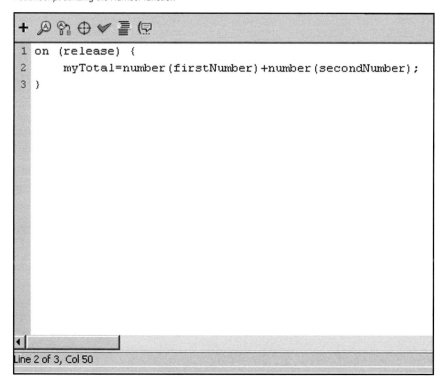

```
1  on (release) {
2      myTotal=number(firstNumber)+number(secondNumber);
3  }
```

Line 2 of 3, Col 50

1. Click the addition button on the stage, then open the Actions panel, if necessary.

2. Click in the Script pane, right-click (Win) or [control] click (Mac), then click Paste.

3. Edit the second line of the ActionScript to the following, as shown in Figure I-34:

   myTotal=number (firstNumber)+number (secondNumber);

   The number function indicates the variable in parentheses is a number, which ensures Macromedia Flash will perform an addition operation, rather than a concatenation.

4. Test the scene, click the Enter button, then experiment with typing numbers in the input boxes and clicking the plus sign.

5. Close the test window, save your work, then close math.fla.

   TIP Macromedia Flash also includes a string function that converts a variable or result of an expression to text.

You used the Number function to create an addition operation in ActionScript.

Work with actions.

1. Open fli_5.fla, then save it as **skillsdemo1.fla**.

2. Use the playhead to look at all the frames in the movie.
   (*Hint*: This movie includes three different screens, starting in Frames 1, 5, and 10. There are stop actions in Frames 4, 9, and 15.)

3. Use the Property inspector to label Frame 5 **seasonChange**. (*Hint*: You can create the frame label in any layer, but you must add the label to a keyframe.)

4. Click Frame 1 on the timeline, select the Start button, then use the Actions panel to create a link to the seasonChange frame when a user clicks the button. (*Hint*: Use the goto action to create the link.)

5. Test the scene, then save your work.

Work with targets and movie clip symbols.

1. Click Frame 5 on the timeline.

2. Double-click the tree on the stage, then move the playhead through the timeline of the movie clip symbol.
   The movie clip symbol animates the changing seasons.

3. Return to Scene 1, then use the Property inspector to name this instance of the movie clip **change**.

4. Select the green button to the right of the word "Seasons", then use the Actions panel to add actions that will play the movie clip when a user clicks the button. (*Hint*: If you are using normal mode in the Actions panel, you will have to use three actions: on, with, and play.)

5. Test the scene, click the Start button to move to the second screen, then click the green button repeatedly.
   (*Hint*: Each time you press the button, the season changes.)

6. Close the test window, then save your work.

Create interactive movie clip symbols.

1. Click Frame 10 on the timeline.

2. Select the scarf movie clip symbol, then use the Property inspector to name the instance **scarf**.

3. Select the winter movie clip symbol in the upper-right corner of the screen, then use the Property inspector to name the instance **winter_mc**.

4. Select the scarf movie clip symbol, then use the Actions panel to add startDrag and stopDrag actions that allow users to drag the scarf. (*Hint*: Be sure to include an on (press) action with the startDrag action, and an on (release) action with the stopDrag action.)

5. Use the Actions panel to add an if action to the scarf movie clip symbol that uses _droptarget to test whether the scarf has been placed on top of the movie clip instance named winter_mc. (*Hint*: Switch to expert mode to add this ActionScript.)

6. Use the Actions panel to add a setProperty action to the scarf movie clip symbol that turns the scarf invisible if it is dropped onto the winter_mc movie clip. (*Hint*: Remember to enclose the action in its own set of braces, within the closing brace of the on (release) action.)

7. Test the scene, then save your work.

Define variables.

1. Click Frame 1 on the title_screens layer.

2. Below the "All About Seasons" title, insert the text **What is your favorite season?**. Use these settings: color: black, font: Arial, size: 12, Bold.

3. Directly beneath the text, create an input text field with the variable name **mySeason**. Click the Show Border Around Text icon for the field. (*Hint*: Be sure to type the variable name in the "Var" field in the Property inspector, not the Instance Name field.)

4. Click Frame 5 on the title_screens layer.

5. Below the "All About Seasons" title, create a dynamic text field with the variable name **mySeasonText**. (*Hint*: You might want to select the Multiline option in Property inspector to ensure all the dynamic text displays.)

6. Click Frame 1 on the timeline, select the Start button, then use the Actions panel to create ActionScript which, upon a click of the button, populates the mySeasonText dynamic text field with the season the user has typed in the mySeason input field, prefaced with the words **My favorite season is**. (*Hint*: Switch to expert mode, if necessary. Be sure to insert the new action before the closing brace of the `on (release)` action, and to include a space at the end of the "My favorite season is" text.)

7. Test the scene, then save your work.

FIGURE I-35
Completed Skills Review

Ultimate Tours wants to add a page to their Web site that will provide price information for various tour packages, so visitors can sample packages and find one within their budget. Ultimate Tours would like the page to provide information on airfare, hotel, and estimated food costs, based on a destination chosen by the visitor. They would also like the page to have some visual interest beyond just a series of text and figures, in order to be engaging to the visitor.

1. Open ultimatetoursH.fla (the file you created in Unit H Project Builder 1) and save it as **utlimatetoursl.fla**. (*Hint*: If you did not create ultimatetoursH.fla, see your instructor.)

2. Create a new screen or scene with a title of **Package Rates** and a subheading of **Click a button below to see price estimates on selected packages**.

3. Insert two buttons on the page that include the text **Cozumel** and **St. Lucia**.

4. Insert a movie clip symbol on the page that includes three frames with a different image in each frame. You can use the images supplied with Project Builder 1 at the end of Unit G, or find your own images.

5. Label Frame 2 of the movie clip symbol **cozumel_graphic** and Frame 3 **stlucia_graphic**.

6. Add `stop` actions to each frame of the movie clip symbol.

7. Name the movie clip symbol instance **rates**.

8. Create three dynamic text fields on the Package Rates page with the variable names **myHotel**, **myAirfare**, and **myFood**. Format the text fields in any way you wish.

9. Use the Text tool on the toolbox to label the dynamic text fields **Hotel**, **Airfare**, and **Estimated Food Costs**.

10. Attach ActionScript to the two buttons you created which, upon a click of each button, sets the dynamic text field variables to different figures for each location (for example, **100** for hotel in Cozumel, **50** for hotel in St. Lucia, **200** for airfare to Cozumel, etc.) and also displays the appropriate image for the location in the rates movie clip symbol (that

is, either the frame labeled cozumel_graphic or the frame labeled stlucia_graphic). (*Hint*: To set a variable to a specific value in expert mode, just type the variable name, an equals sign, and the value. To set a variable to a specific value in normal mode, use the `set variable` action.)

11. Create a button that links the Ultimate Tours introductory page to the Package Rates page, and then a button that links the Package Rates page back to the introductory page. Use ActionScript and frame labels to create this navigation.

12. Save your work, then compare your image to Figure I-36.

FIGURE I-36
Completed Project Builder 1

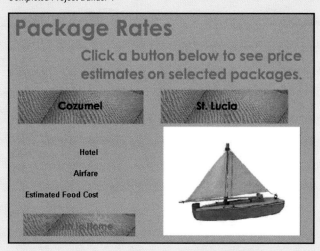

In a previous unit, you created a page for your portfolio Web site that contained thumbnail pictures of work samples. Another way to highlight your work might be to create a slide show, which would display a different sample each time the visitor clicks a button. Such a strategy could motivate the visitor to look at more samples, and would allow you to display a larger area of the sample without forcing the visitor to follow a link.

1. Open portfolioH.fla and save it as **portfolioI.fla**. (*Hint*: If you did not create portfolioH.fla, see your instructor.)
2. Create a series of screen shots with at least four samples of your work, or use the screen shots you created for Project Builder 2 at the end of Unit G.
3. Create a new page or scene with the title of **Portfolio Slide Show**.
4. Create a new movie clip symbol that includes a series of screens with a sample of your work and some explanatory text. Each sample and associated text should appear in a separate frame.
5. Add stop actions to each frame in the movie clip symbol.
6. Return to the scene and add the movie clip symbol in the center of the Portfolio Slide Show page. Use the Property inspector to name the instance of the movie clip symbol **samples**.

7. Add a button with the text **Click to view next slide** on the Portfolio Slide Show page. Program the Over and Down states for the button in any way you'd like.
8. Attach ActionScript to the button which, upon a click, will advance the samples movie clip one frame.

FIGURE I-37
Completed Project Builder 2

9. If desired, create navigation from your current samples page to the Portfolio page, and then back to the samples page from the Portfolio page. Use ActionScript and frame labels to create the navigation.
10. Save your work, then compare your movie to Figure I-37.

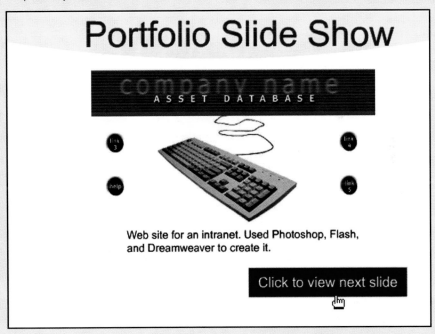

Figure I-38 shows a page from a Web site created using Macromedia Flash. Study the figure and complete the following. For each question, indicate how you determined your answer.

1. Connect to the Internet, and go to *www.course.com*. Navigate to the page for this book, click the Student Online Companion, then click the link for this unit.

2. Open a document in a word processor or open a new Macromedia Flash movie, save the file as **dpuUnitI**, then answer the following questions. (*Hint*: Use the Text Tool in Macromedia Flash.)

   ■ In this game, when the visitor moves the Winnie the Pooh image to a letter in the middle area of the screen, that letter disappears, and the corresponding letter in the word on the right side of the screen changes color. What are some of the actions that might have been used to create these effects? Which elements would the actions be attached to?

   ■ Which elements of the movie must be movie clip symbols? Would all the movie clips need instance names?

   ■ It would be time-consuming to reference each individual letter in each different word in the ActionScript you create to achieve the effects of this game. Can you think of another strategy you might use?

   ■ When the Next button in the lower-right portion of the screen is clicked, another word and set of letters appears. How would you create this navigation? Why?

   ■ Suppose you wanted the text "Good job" to appear for two seconds each time a visitor successfully "captured" a letter by dragging Winnie the Pooh. What are some of the ways you might go about creating this effect?

FIGURE I-38
Design Project

Your group can assign elements of the project to individual members, or work collectively to create the finished product.

Your group works in the multimedia department of a university. A professor has asked you to build an interactive study guide in Macromedia Flash that includes a series of test questions. The professor would like to see a prototype of a multiple choice style test question with two choices, similar to the following:

What is the periodic symbol of oxygen?

1. Ox
2. O

The professor would like you to build in feedback telling students whether the answer they supply is correct or incorrect. (In this case, the correct answer is choice 2, "O".)

1. Open a new movie and save it as **test_question.fla**.
2. Set the movie properties including the size and background color, if desired.
3. Use the Text tool on the toolbox to create a multiple choice style question of your own, or use the example above. The question should have two choices.
4. Create an input text field in which a student can type an answer.
5. Create a text label for the field that reads **Your answer:**
6. Create a Submit button near the input field.
7. Create two feedback screens. One screen should indicate an answer is correct, and the other that an answer is incorrect.
8. Attach ActionScript to the Submit button which, upon a click of the button, uses `if` actions to compare the letter the student has typed in the input text field with the correct answer, then sends the student to the appropriate "correct" or "incorrect" screen.
9. Create a Start Again button that uses ActionScript to return the student to the original question, and also sets the input text field to blank. Add the Start Again button to each of the feedback screens.
10. Save your work and compare your image to Figure I-39.

FIGURE I-39
Completed Group Project

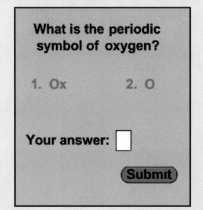

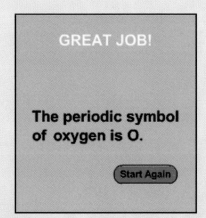

UNIT J

ADDING SOUNDS

1. Work with sounds.

2. Specify synchronization options.

3. Modify sounds.

4. Specify compression options.

5. Use ActionScript with sounds.

UNIT J
ADDING SOUNDS

Introduction

Like animation and interactivity, sound is an important tool you can use to express a message and make your site appealing and involving to visitors. In an earlier unit, you added sound to a button. In this unit, you will see that there is much more you can do with sound in Macromedia Flash. For example, you can set a short sound clip to play continuously, creating a musical backdrop for your movie. Or, you can synchronize sound with an animation or movie clip, perhaps providing a voice-over that explains what's happening on the screen.

Sound can add significantly to the size of published movies, so you should plan ahead and try to use sound strategically, only in places where it will have the most impact. Macromedia Flash includes a number of compression options that can help you achieve a balance between sound quality and file size in your movies. Effective and judicious use of sound is a key ingredient in making a Macromedia Flash site a truly multimedia experience.

Tools You'll Use

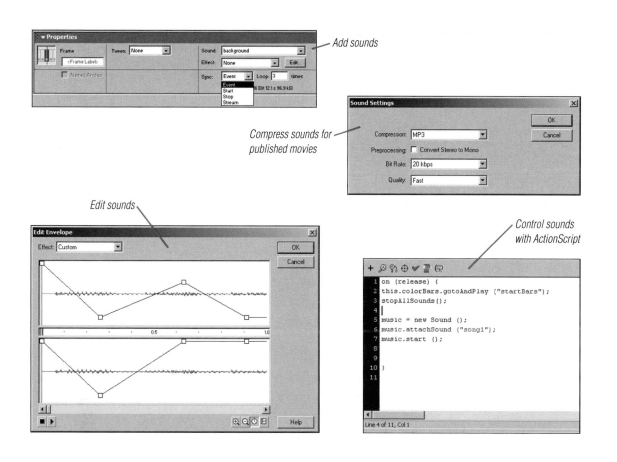

Add sounds

Compress sounds for
published movies

Edit sounds

Control sounds
with ActionScript

WORK WITH SOUNDS

What You'll Do

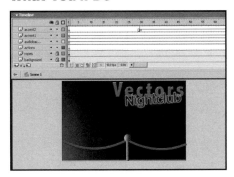

In this lesson, you will add background music to a movie and work with layering and looping sounds.

Importing Sound Files

Before you can add a sound to an object or the timeline in Macromedia Flash, you must import the file that contains the sound. Macromedia Flash stores sounds in the Library panel. Table J-1 shows the types of sound files you can import.

Adding a Sound to the Timeline

When you want a sound to play in the background, rather than tie it to a specific object on stage like a button, you can add an instance of the sound to a frame in the timeline. You can drag a sound from the Library panel to the stage to add the sound to the current keyframe, or you can add a sound through the Property inspector to the keyframe. Using the Property inspector is the recommended method, because it ensures that the sound appears in the keyframe you intend.

TABLE J-1: Sound Files that Macromedia Flash Imports		
sound type	**Windows**	**Mac**
Waveform Audio File (.wav)	Yes	Yes, requires QuickTime
Audio Interchange File (.aif)	Yes, requires QuickTime	Yes
MPEG-1 Audio level 3 (.mp3)	Yes	Yes
Sound only QuickTime movies (.mov)	Yes, requires QuickTime	Yes, requires QuickTime
System 7 sounds (.snd)	No	Yes, requires QuickTime
Sound Designer II (.sd2)	No	Yes, requires QuickTime
SunAU (.au)	Yes, requires QuickTime	Yes, requires QuickTime

Sounds are represented on the timeline by either a straight or waveform line, as shown in Figure J-1. The approximate duration of the sound is indicated by the number of frames the line occupies. However, the line will extend only to the last keyframe in the movie. The duration of the sound may be longer than the duration of the movie.

You can play multiple sounds at once by placing the sounds on different layers. For example, you might have background music that plays continuously, but then play accent sounds at various points to act as a supplement or counterpoint to the background. You can stagger where each sound begins by creating a keyframe at a later point in the timeline, and then adding the sound to this keyframe. You can also add multiple instances of the same sound to different layers.

Understanding Event Sounds

By default, sounds you add in Macromedia Flash are considered **event sounds**. Event sounds are like movie clip symbols in that they play independently of the timeline. The sound starts in the keyframe to which you add it, but can continue playing even after a movie ends. In addition, event sounds may play at a faster or slower rate than indicated by the frames on the timeline, depending on the speed of the computer on which the movie is played.

Event sounds have an advantage in that you can use them as many times as you like in a movie, with no increase in the file size of your published movie. However, when a movie is played over the Web, event sounds do not begin until the entire sound file is downloaded; this may cause a disconnection between sound and images for some visitors.

There is another type of sound in Macromedia Flash, called **streaming sound**. Streaming sounds are similar to animated graphic symbols because they are closely tied to the main timeline; whatever its length, a streaming sound stops at the end of the movie. Streaming sounds can also start playing as your computer downloads them. You will work with streaming sounds in the next lesson.

Looping Sounds

Looping lets you repeat a sound a specified number of times, useful in situations such as creating background music for a movie. If you want your audio to loop continuously, make sure you use a loop number large enough for the entire duration. For example, if you have a 30-second clip of music and you want it to loop for 10 minutes, you should enter 20 as the loop value.

FIGURE J-1
A sound on the timeline

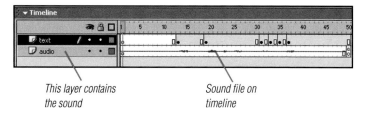

This layer contains
the sound

Sound file on
timeline

Add sound to a timeline

1. Open flj_1.fla, then save it as **nightclub.fla**.

2. Open the Library panel, click the Audio folder to open it (if necessary), then preview the accent1, accent2, and background sounds by clicking each sound, then clicking the Play button in the preview area at the top of the Library panel. ▶

3. Close the Library panel.

4. Insert a new layer above the actions layer, then rename it **audiobackground**. 🖝

5. Click Frame 1 on the audiobackground layer, open the Property inspector, click the Sound name list arrow, click background, then verify that Event appears in the Sync sound text box, as shown in Figure J-2.

   Macromedia Flash adds the sound file to the layer, as indicated by the line on the audiobackground layer.

   TIP   When you click the Sound name list arrow, a list appears of all sound files you have imported into the Library panel. The file already contains several sounds.

6. Test the scene.

   The background music sound clip plays, ending after about 13 seconds.

7. Close the test window, then save your work.

You added a sound to the timeline.

FIGURE J-2
Selecting a sound file in the Property inspector

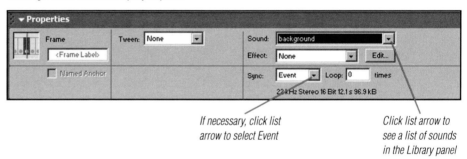

If necessary, click list arrow to select Event

Click list arrow to see a list of sounds in the Library panel

FIGURE J-3

A timeline with layered sounds

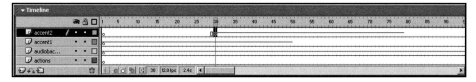

1. Insert a new layer above the audiobackground layer, then rename it **accent1**. ![icon]

2. Click Frame 1 on the accent1 layer, click the Sound name list arrow in the Property inspector, click accent1, then verify that Event appears in the Sync sound text box.

3. Insert a new layer above the accent1 layer, then rename it **accent2**. ![icon]

4. Insert a keyframe in Frame 30 on the accent2 layer.

5. Click the Sound name list arrow in the Property inspector, click accent2, then compare your image to Figure J-3.

6. Test the scene.

   All three sound files play simultaneously for a short time. However, since the sound clips are of different durations, they do not all play to the end of the movie.

7. Close the test window, then save your work.

You layered sounds.

Create a sound loop

1. Click Frame 1 on the audiobackground layer, double-click 0 in the Loop text box in the Property inspector, type **3**, press [Enter] (Win) or [return] (Mac), then compare your image to Figure J-4.

   The sound line in the audiobackground layer now stretches to the end of the movie, Frame 200.

2. Click Frame 1 on the accent1 layer, double-click 0 in the Loop text box in the Property inspector, type **5**, then press [Enter] (Win) or [return] (Mac).

3. Click Frame 30 on the accent2 layer, double-click 0 in the Loop text box in the Property inspector, type **4**, then press [Enter] (Win) or [return] (Mac).

   Since the accent2 sound starts in a later keyframe than the accent1 sound, you do not have to loop it as many times to have it play until the end of the movie.

   (continued)

FIGURE J-4

Specifying a number of loops for a sound

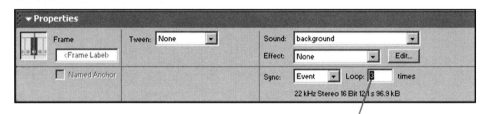

Specify loops in
this text box

4. Drag the playhead to Frame 200 in the timeline, as shown in Figure J-5.

All the sounds now extend at least through the end of the movie.

5. Test the scene until the sound stops playing.

The sound files play simultaneously until the end of the movie. (You can tell the movie has ended when the words "Vectors Nightclub" stop flashing.) Because the sounds are event sounds, they continue to play even after the movie ends, each stopping only when it reaches the number of loops you specified.

6. Close the test window, then save your work.

You looped three sounds so they play until the end of a movie.

FIGURE J-5

Sounds in timeline extend to end of movie

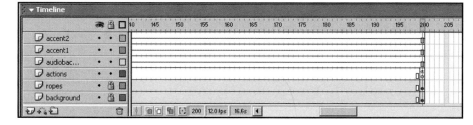

SPECIFY SYNCHRONIZATION OPTIONS

What You'll Do

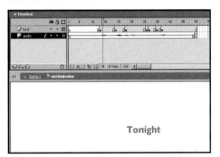

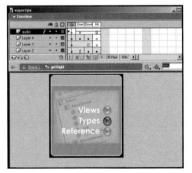

 In this lesson, you will synchronize a streaming sound with an animation, and you will set a button to play a sound in the Over state and stop playing the sound in the Up state.

Understanding Synchronization Options

As you've seen, Event is the default synchronization option in the Property inspector. You can also choose three other synchronization options: Start, Stop, and Stream, as shown in Figure J-6.

Understanding Streaming Sounds

Unlike event sounds, streaming sounds are tied to the timeline and the number of frames in the timeline. When you add a sound and set it to be streaming, Macromedia Flash breaks up the sound into individual sound clips and then associates each clip with a specific frame on the timeline. The frame rate of your movie determines the number of clips that Macromedia Flash creates. If the sound is longer than the number of frames on the timeline, it still stops at the end of the movie.

On the Web, streaming sounds will start to play as soon as a computer has downloaded a part of the sound file; this provides a usability advantage over event sounds. However, unlike event sounds, streaming sounds increase the file size of your movie each time they are looped or reused, which means you should use them only when necessary. It is especially recommended that you do not loop streaming sounds.

One important use of streaming sounds is to synchronize animation and audio, since the sounds can be better coordinated with the timeline during both development and playback. If the computer playing a movie is slow, Macromedia Flash will skip frames of an animation in order to maintain synchronization with a streaming sound. To avoid a jumbled or jerky playback, you should try to keep your animation simple when using streaming sound.

QUICKTIP

Once you set a sound to be streaming, you can preview the sound by dragging the playhead through the timeline.

Understanding the Start and Stop Synchronization Options

Start sounds act just like event sounds, but will not begin again if an instance of the sound is already playing. The Start option is often used with sounds associated with buttons or with movies that loop back to the beginning, in order to avoid overlapping sounds.

The Stop option lets you end an event sound at a specific keyframe. For example, you can start a sound in Frame 1 and then stop it playing in Frame 40, even if the sound is of a much longer duration. You must specify the name of the sound you want to stop in the Property inspector for the keyframe when using this option. If you want to stop multiple sounds, you must insert separate Stop options in keyframes on each sound layer. Macromedia Flash indicates a Stop option with a small square in the keyframe, as shown in Figure J-7.

QUICKTIP

You can stop a streaming sound at a specific frame by adding a keyframe in the sound's layer. Event sounds will continue to play through a keyframe unless it includes a Stop option.

FIGURE J-6

The Sync sound options in the Property inspector

Click this arrow to display the options

FIGURE J-7

A Stop option on the timeline

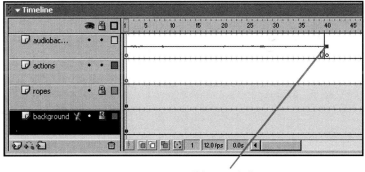

This square indicates Stop option

Set synchronization to the Stream option

1. Click Insert on the menu bar, then click New Symbol.

2. Type **wordanimation** in the Name text box, click the Movie Clip option, if necessary, then click OK.

3. Rename Layer 1 on the timeline **audio**.

4. Insert a keyframe in Frame 50 on the audio layer.

5. Open the Actions panel, verify that Normal mode is selected, double-click stop in the Movie Control folder in the Actions toolbox, as shown in Figure J-8, then close the Actions panel.

   Inserting a keyframe creates a movie clip of sufficient length for the sound to play, and adding a stop action to the keyframe stops the movie from repeating.

6. Click Frame 1 on the audio layer, click the Sound name list arrow, then click bitmaps_free_vo.

7. Click the Sync list arrow, click Stream, then compare your image to Figure J-9.

8. Drag the playhead through the timeline, starting at Frame 1.

   As you drag, the sound file plays, saying, "Tonight all bitmaps get in for free."

9. Save your work.

You set the synchronization of a sound to streaming.

FIGURE J-8

Adding a stop *action*

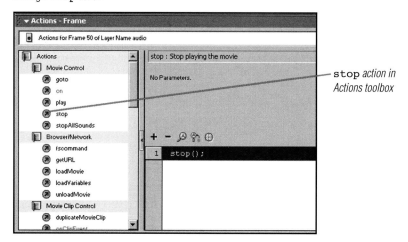

stop *action in Actions toolbox*

FIGURE J-9

The streaming sound in the timeline and Property inspector

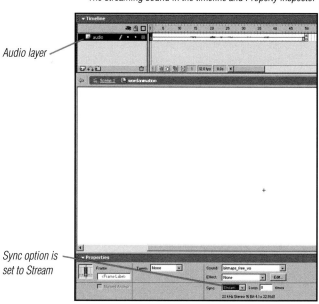

Audio layer

Sync option is set to Stream

Adding Sounds

FIGURE J-10

Property inspector for instance of the tonight graphic symbol

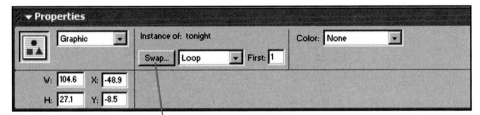

Click the Swap button
to open the Swap
Symbol dialog box

1. Insert a new layer above the audio layer in the wordanimation movie clip, then rename it **text**.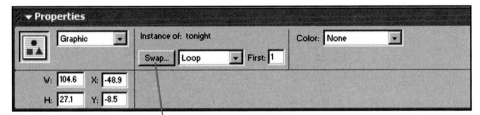

   You will add text that synchronizes text with spoken voice-over.

2. Insert a keyframe in Frame 13 on the text layer, open the Library panel, double-click the Text folder in the Library panel to open it (if necessary), then drag the tonight graphic symbol approximately to the middle of the stage.

   TIP   Scroll down the Library panel as necessary to view the Text folder symbols.

3. In the Property inspector, double-click the value in the X text box, type **–48.9**, double-click the value in the Y text box, type **–8.5**, then press [Enter] (Win) or [return] (Mac).

   The word "Tonight" appears centered on the stage.

4. Insert a keyframe in Frame 19 on the text layer, click the word "Tonight" on the stage to select it, then click the Swap button in the Property inspector as shown in Figure J-10, to open the Swap Symbol dialog box.

   TIP   The Swap Symbol dialog box lets you replace an object on the stage with a different object, keeping all other properties the same, including any actions you have assigned to the original object.

(continued)

5. Click the all graphic symbol in the Text folder, as shown in Figure J-11, then click OK.

Macromedia Flash replaces the instance of the tonight graphic symbol with an instance of the all graphic symbol. The X and Y coordinates change slightly in order to keep the word centered on the stage.

6. Insert a keyframe in Frame 23 on the text layer, click the word "all" on the stage to select it, click the Swap button in the Property inspector, click the bitmaps graphic symbol in the Text folder in the Swap Symbol dialog box, then click OK.

7. Insert a keyframe in Frame 31 on the text layer, click the word "Bitmaps" on the stage to select it, click the Swap button in the Property inspector, click the get graphic symbol in the Text folder in the Swap Symbol dialog box, then click OK.

8. Insert a keyframe in Frame 32 on the text layer, click the word "Get" on the stage to select it, click the Swap button in the Property inspector, click the in graphic symbol in the Text folder in the Swap Symbol dialog box, then click OK.

9. Insert a keyframe in Frame 35 on the text layer, click the word "in" on the stage to select it, click the Swap button in the Property inspector, click the for graphic symbol in the Text folder in the Swap Symbol dialog box, then click OK.

(continued)

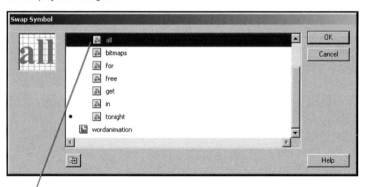

This list includes all symbols in the Library panel

The wordanimation movie clip symbol timeline

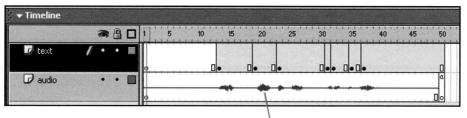

The keyframes containing
graphic symbols in the text layer
synchronize with the spoken
words in the audio layer

FIGURE J-13
Movie clip symbol on the stage

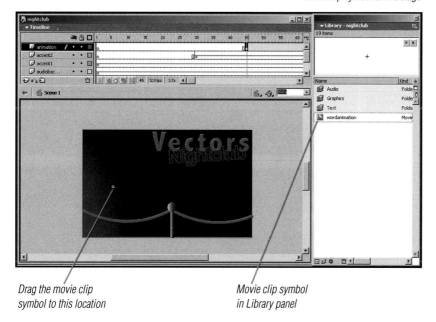

Drag the movie clip
symbol to this location

Movie clip symbol
in Library panel

10. Insert a keyframe in Frame 37 on the text
layer, click the word "for" on the stage to
select it, click the Swap button in the
Property inspector, click the free graphic
symbol in the Text folder in the Swap
Symbol dialog box, compare your timeline to
Figure J-12, then click OK.

11. Click the Scene identifier icon on the
Information bar to return to Scene 1.

Scene 1

*You created a text animation, then synchronized
the appearance of each word in the animation with
a voice-over saying the word.*

Add the synchronized animation to the stage

1. Insert a new layer above the accent2 layer,
then rename it **animation**.

2. Insert a keyframe in Frame 45 on the animation layer, then drag the wordanimation
movie clip symbol from the Library panel
to the left side of the stage, as shown in
Figure J-13.

3. Test the scene.

The words and streaming sounds appear
synchronized.

4. Close the test window, save your work, then
close nightclub.fla.

*You added an animation synchronized with sound
to the stage.*

Set synchronization to the Start option

1. Open flj_2.fla, then save it as **supertips.fla**.

2. Click the Arrow Tool on the toolbox, if necessary, then double-click the Views button to open it.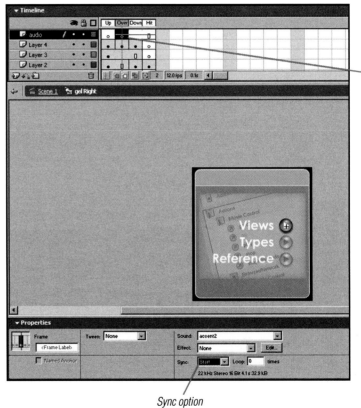

   The gelRight button symbol currently has four layers, which create the visual effects of the button.

3. Insert a new layer above Layer 4, then rename it **audio**.

4. Insert a keyframe in the Over frame on the audio layer.

5. Click the Sound name list arrow in the Property inspector, then click accent2.

   Macromedia Flash adds the sound file, as indicated by the straight line in the audio layer, which will start to play once you move the mouse pointer over the button, and continues even after you move off the button.

6. Click the Sync list arrow, click Start, then compare your image to Figure J-14.

7. Click the Scene identifier icon on the Information bar to return to Scene 1.

8. Test the scene, position the mouse pointer over a button, then move the mouse pointer off the button.

   The music starts playing when you hover over a button, and continues even if you move the mouse pointer away from the button.

9. Close the test window, then save your work.

You added sound to the Over state of a button.

FIGURE J-14

Inserting a start sound in the Over state of a button

Sound added to the Over frame

Sync option set to Start

FIGURE J-15

Inserting a Stop option in the Up state of a button

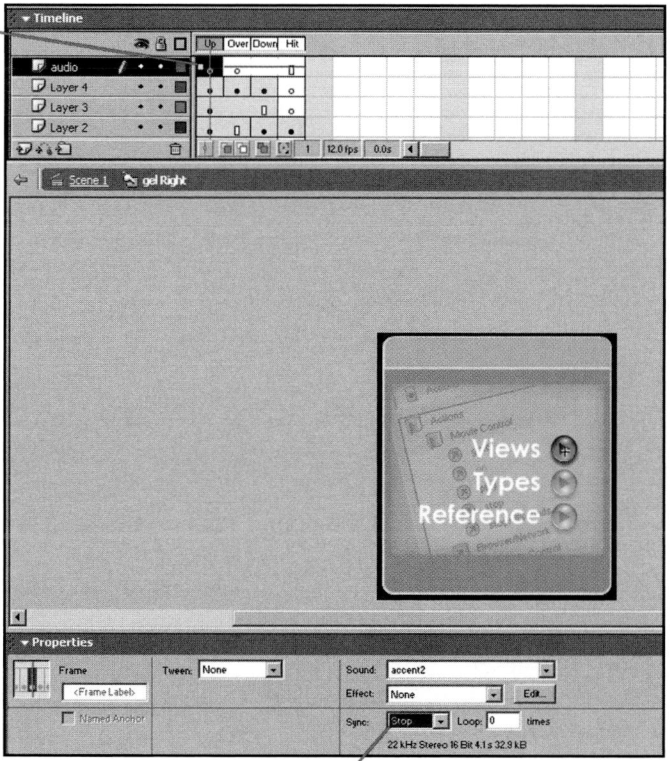

Square
indicates
Stop option
in Up frame

Sync option
set to Stop

1. Double-click the Views button on the stage to open it.

2. Click the Up frame on the audio layer.

3. Click the Sound name list arrow in the Property inspector, then click accent2.

4. Click the Sync list arrow, click Stop, then compare your image to Figure J-15.

5. Click the Scene identifier icon on the Information bar to return to Scene 1.

   Scene 1

6. Test the scene, position the mouse pointer over a button, then move the mouse pointer off the button.

   The music stops playing when you move the mouse pointer away from the button.

7. Close the test window, save your work, then close the file.

You directed a sound to stop when a button is in the Up state.

MODIFY SOUNDS

What You'll Do

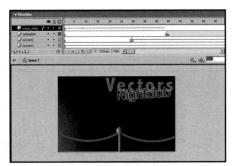

In this lesson, you will set and edit when one sound begins and create a custom sound effect for another sound.

Editing Sounds for Length

In most cases, you will want to edit and enhance sounds in a sound-editing program before you import them into Macromedia Flash. However, Macromedia Flash does include some basic editing features you can use on sounds you have already imported.

> **QUICKTIP**
>
> Popular sound-editing programs include, for Windows, ACID and Sound Forge (both available from Sonic Foundry), and, for Macintosh, Peak (available from BIAS).

You can trim the length of a sound file using the Edit Envelope dialog box, shown in Figure J-16. By moving the Time In and Time Out controls, you can set where the sound file will start and stop playing. Adjusting the controls lets you delete unwanted sounds and remove silent sections at the start and end of sounds, reducing the file size of the published movie.

You can preview the edits you make to a sound by clicking the Play icon at the bottom-left of the Edit Envelope dialog box. Other icons in this dialog box let you zoom the display of the sound in or out and set the units in the center of the dialog box to seconds or frames, which can help you determine the length of event sounds and make frame-by-frame adjustments to streaming sounds.

Changing Sound Effects

Macromedia Flash includes the following effects you can apply to sounds:

- Left Channel plays the sound only in the left channel or speaker.
- Right Channel plays the sound only in the right channel or speaker.
- Fade Left to Right gradually shifts the sound from the left channel to the right channel over the duration of the sound.
- Fade Right to Left gradually shifts the sound from the right channel to the left channel over the duration of the sound.

- Fade In ramps up the volume of the sound as it begins to play.
- Fade Out diminishes the volume of the sound as it ends.

You can set these options either in the Property inspector of the frame to which you have added the sound, or in the Edit Envelope dialog box for the sound.

An additional option—Custom—lets you create your own volume variations over the duration of a sound. By clicking the envelope line and then moving the envelope handles toward the top (to make the sound louder) or bottom (to make the sound lower), you can specify up to eight locations where you want the sound to fade in, fade out, or play at less than 100% volume. For stereo sounds, you can set different custom envelopes for the two channels. Figure J-17 shows a custom volume envelope.

FIGURE J-16

The Edit Envelope dialog box

Edit Envelope
Effect: None
OK
Cancel
Help
Envelope handles
Time In control
Time Out control
Units in seconds
Play or stop sound
Zoom in
Zoom out
Display units in seconds
Display units in frames

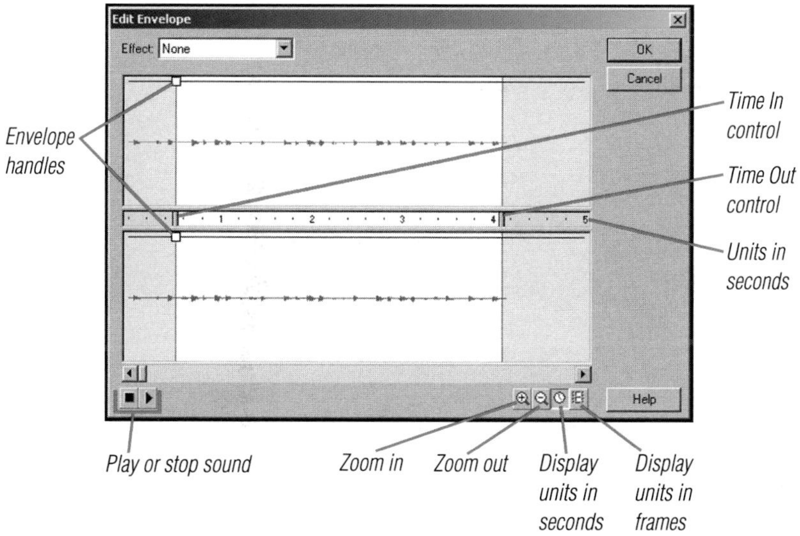

FIGURE J-17

A custom volume envelope

Edit Envelope
Effect: Custom
OK
Cancel
Help
0.5
1.0
Sound decreases in volume here
Sound increases in volume here

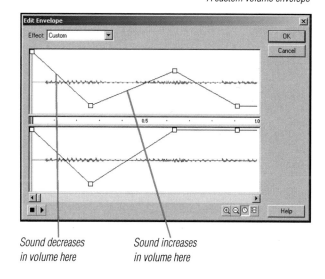

Edit a sound using the Time In control

1. Open nightclub.fla, then save it as **vectors.fla**.

2. Insert a new layer above the animation layer, then rename it **voice_intro**.

3. Click Frame 1 on the voice_intro layer, click the Sound name list arrow, click hello_vo, click the Sync list arrow, then click Stream.

4. Test the scene.

5. Close the test window, then click the Edit button in the Property inspector.

   You will edit the sound file so it plays only the words "Vectors Nightclub."

6. Click the Frames icon in the Edit Envelope dialog box, if necessary.

7. Click the Zoom Out icon repeatedly until you can see the entire sound with the frames shown in Figure J-18.

8. Click and drag the Time In control to Frame 30, then compare your image to Figure J-19.

   When you release the control, the frame markers that indicate where the sound plays are renumbered.

9. Click the Play button in the Edit Envelope dialog box.

   Only the last two words of the sound, "Vectors Nightclub," should play. If necessary, adjust the Time In control.

10. Click OK, then test the scene.

11. Close the test window, then save your work.

You changed the point at which a sound begins playing.

FIGURE J-18
Zooming the hello_vo sound in the Edit Envelope dialog box

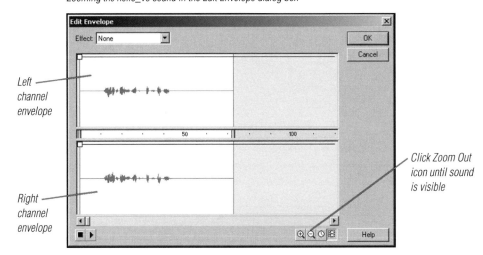

Left channel envelope

Right channel envelope

Click Zoom Out icon until sound is visible

FIGURE J-19
Trimming the length of a sound

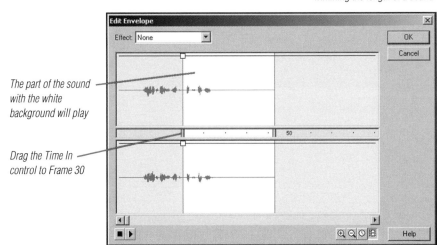

The part of the sound with the white background will play

Drag the Time In control to Frame 30

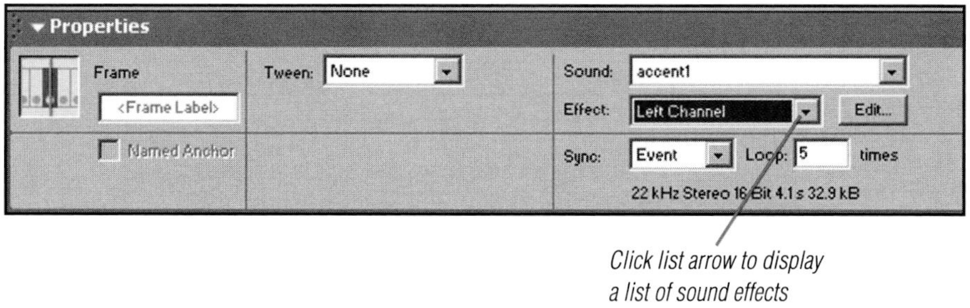

Set sound effects

1. Click Frame 1 on the accent1 layer.

2. Click the Effect list arrow in the Property inspector, then click Left Channel, as shown in Figure J-20.

3. Click Frame 30 on the accent2 layer, click the Effect list arrow in the Property inspector, then click Right Channel.

4. Test the scene.

   Each sound file plays only in the channel you specified. (Try using headphones to get the full effect.)

5. Close the test window, then save your work.

You created sound effects.

FIGURE J-20
Setting a sound effect in the Property inspector

*Click list arrow to display
a list of sound effects*

Edit envelopes to create custom volume effects

1. Click Frame 1 on the audiobackground layer.

2. Click the Effect list arrow in the Property inspector, then click Custom.

   TIP You can also select Custom using the list arrow in the Edit Envelope dialog box.

3. Click the Zoom Out icon, if necessary, until the frames display 5, 10, and so on, then drag the envelope handle for the left channel, and then the right channel, down to the lowest point to decrease the sound in both channels, then compare your dialog box to Figure J-21. 🔍

4. Click the left channel sound line on Frame 20.

   New envelope handles appear on Frame 20 for both the left and right channel envelope sound lines.

   (continued)

FIGURE J-21
Decreasing the volume of both channels

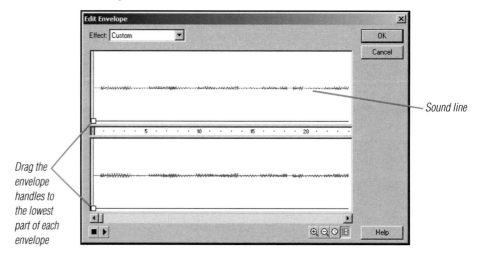

Sound line

Drag the envelope handles to the lowest part of each envelope

5. Drag the new handle on the left channel up to the highest point, as shown in Figure J-22.

6. Drag the new handle on the right channel up to its highest point.

7. Click the Play button in the Edit Envelope dialog box. ▶

   The music fades in gradually in both channels.

8. Click the Stop button, click OK in the Edit Envelope dialog box, then save your work. ■

You established a fade in effect for a sound file by creating a custom envelope.

FIGURE J-22
Increasing the volume of the left channel

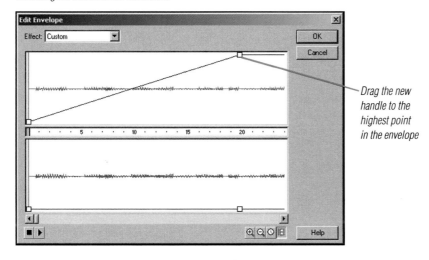

Drag the new handle to the highest point in the envelope

SPECIFY COMPRESSION OPTIONS

What You'll Do

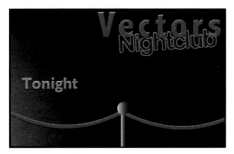

 In this lesson, you will compress sound files in order to reduce the size of a published movie.

Understanding Compression Options

Sounds can add greatly to the file size of published movies. Macromedia Flash includes a number of options that let you compress and reduce the sampling rate of sounds. Depending on the options you choose, there may be a trade-off in the quality and fidelity of the sounds. Be sure to thoroughly test your exported movies to make sure you are not sacrificing usability when selecting a sound compression option.

Macromedia Flash includes the following compression options:

- ADPCM (Adaptive Differential Pulse-Code Modulation)
  This option is best for short sounds, such as those used for buttons or accents. When you select this option, you can also set whether or not the sound is converted from stereo to mono (which will reduce file size), a sampling rate (a lower sampling rate degrades sound quality but reduces file size), and a number of bits

(again, a lower bit rate reduces both sound quality and file size).
- MP3 (MPEG-1 Audio Layer 3)
  This option is used primarily for music and longer streaming sounds, but can also be applied to speech. When you select this option, you can also set a bit rate (20 kbps or higher is recommended for music), whether or not to convert stereo to mono (only available if you are using a setting of 20 kbps or higher for the bit rate), and an option for compression speed/sound quality (the Fast option increases download speed for Web delivery, although it may result in poorer sound quality).
- Raw
  This option exports a sound with no compression. You can still set whether or not to convert stereo to mono and a sampling rate.
- Speech compression
  This option is best for voice-overs and other speech. It will not work well for music. You can also set a sampling rate when you choose this option.

By default, Macromedia Flash uses MP3 16-bit mono compression.

If you are using effects that shift sound between channels, such as Fade Right to Left, be sure to des-elect the Convert Stereo to Mono option when set-ting compression or the effect will not be heard when the movie plays.

Setting Compression Individually or Globally

You can set compression either for individ-ual sounds or globally for all sounds in your movie.

To set compression for an individual sound, select the sound in the Library panel and then open the Sound Properties dialog box, as shown in Figure J-23. You can select a compression and its associated options. You can also preview the sound using the options you have selected, update the sound if you have edited it in another pro-gram, and import another sound file and have the current compression settings applied to it.

To set compression globally, click File on the menu bar, click Publish Settings, then click the Flash tab, as shown in Figure J-24. The compression options you select will be applied to all sounds for which you have not set individual options. You can also choose to override all individual options, which is useful if you are creating different versions of your movie for intranet and Internet distribution.

All streaming sounds in a movie are exported using the highest compression setting specified either for an individual sound or in the Publish Settings dialog box. It is recommended that you decide on one com-pression option for all streaming sounds and set it in the Publish Settings dialog box.

FIGURE J-23
The Sound Properties dialog box

FIGURE J-24
The Flash tab of the Publish Settings dialog box

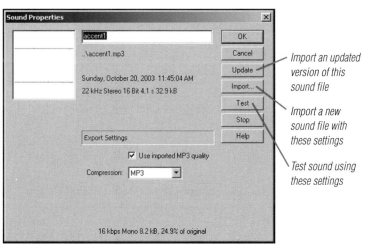

Import an updated version of this sound file

Import a new sound file with these settings

Test sound using these settings

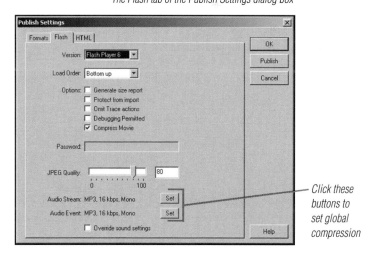

Click these buttons to set global compression

Set compression for a single sound file

1. Open the Library panel, click the hello_vo sound symbol in the Audio folder, click the Options menu icon at the top of the Library panel, then click Properties to open the Sound Properties dialog box. ▤

2. Click the Compression list arrow, click Speech, then compare your image to Figure J-25.

   The dialog box indicates the reduction in size as a percent.

3. Click the Test button.

   The sound clip plays, allowing you to determine if the quality is sufficient.

4. Click OK, then save your work.

You changed the compression option for a sound.

FIGURE J-25
Setting the speech compression option

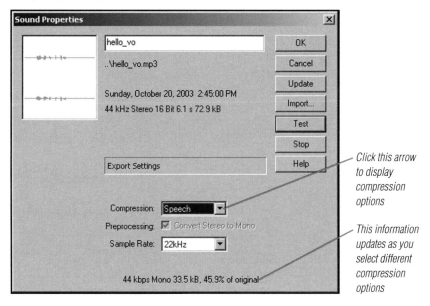

Click this arrow to display compression options

This information updates as you select different compression options

FIGURE J-26

Setting a global compression option for all streaming sounds

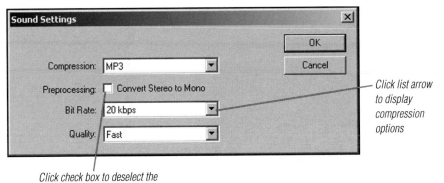

Click list arrow to display compression options

Click check box to deselect the option to convert stereo to mono

FIGURE J-27

Overriding individual settings

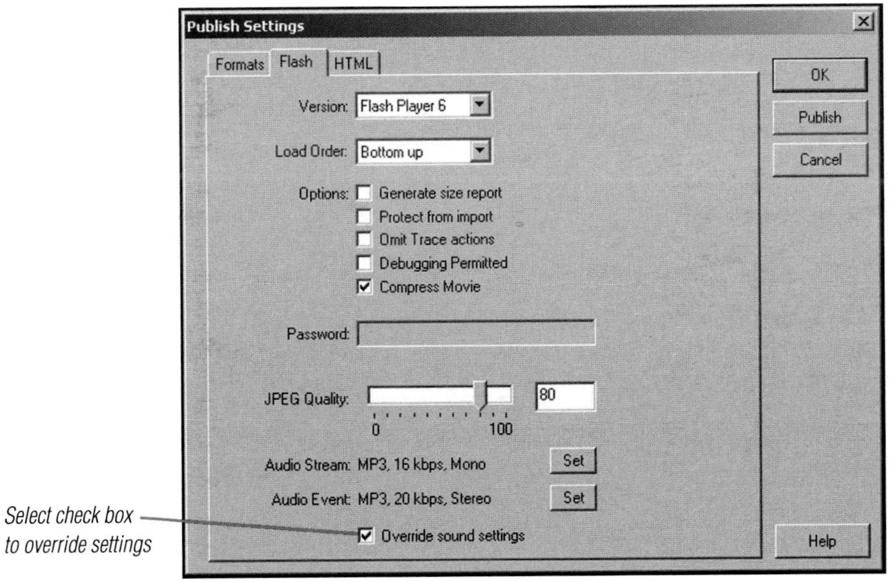

Select check box to override settings

Set global compression for sound files

1. Click File on the menu bar, click Publish Settings, then click the Flash tab in the dialog box.

2. Verify that Flash Player 6 is selected as the Version, that the Compress Movie check box is selected, then click the Audio Event Set button at the bottom of the dialog box.

3. Click the Bit Rate list arrow, then click 20 kbps.

4. Click the Convert Stereo to Mono check box to deselect it, accept the remaining default values, as shown in Figure J-26, then click OK.

5. Click the Override sound settings check box to select it, accept the remaining default values, as shown in Figure J-27, then click OK.

   The new compression settings take effect when you publish the file.

6. Save your work, then close the file.

You set the compression for all event sounds in your movie.

USE ACTIONSCRIPT WITH SOUNDS

What You'll Do

 In this lesson, you will use ActionScript to play and stop sounds.

Understanding ActionScript and Sound

ActionScript and sound are a powerful combination. You can use actions to set how and when sounds play in a movie, and to start or stop sounds in response to user interactions. You can also use actions to trigger an event such as navigating to a frame or scene based on when a sound ends.

To reference a sound from the Library panel in ActionScript, you must assign a **linkage identifier string** and create a **sound object**. Sounds you reference in ActionScript may never appear on the stage or be associated with a specific frame, which means they

will not be exported with the movie. You use the Linkage Properties dialog box, shown in Figure J-28, to make sure a sound in the Library panel will be exported for ActionScript, and also to assign a linkage identifier string, which is the name you will use to identify the sound in ActionScript. The identifier string may be the same as the sound name.

A sound object is a way for ActionScript to recognize and control a sound. Creating a sound object is similar to creating an instance of a sound on the stage, except it happens entirely in ActionScript. First, you create the object using the new Sound

Sound and Movie Clip Symbols

Another way to control sound through ActionScript is to embed the sound in a movie clip symbol. You must still create a sound object in ActionScript, but you specify the movie clip symbol instance name as part of the new Sound action, rather than using attachSound. For example, the following line of ActionScript creates a sound object called "music" and attaches a movie clip symbol named "Verdi" to it:

```
music = new Sound (verdi)
```

action, and then you attach a sound to the object using the `Sound.attachSound` action. You reference the sound using the linkage identifier string, as shown in Figure J-29.

Starting and Stopping Sounds with ActionScript

Once you have created a sound object and attached a sound to it, you can begin controlling the sound using ActionScript.

The `Sound.start` action starts a sound playing. When using this action, you substitute the name of a sound object for "Sound." For example, if you have a sound object named "BackgroundMusic," you would include the action `BackgroundMusic.start` to play the sound. `Sound.start` includes optional parameters that let you specify a sound offset (for example, if you want to start playing a sound that is 15 seconds long at the 10-second mark) and also the number of times to loop the sound.

The `stopAllSounds` action stops all sounds currently playing, regardless of whether the sound is event or streaming. It's a good idea to include a `stopAllSounds` action at the end of a movie, especially if the movie uses event sounds. If your movie uses sound jumps between scenes, you may also want to include a `stopAllSounds` action in the first frame of each scene to ensure that any sounds still playing from the previous scene will not overlap sounds in the new scene.

FIGURE J-28

The Linkage Properties dialog box

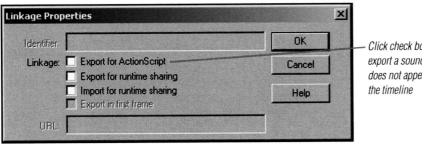

Click check box to export a sound that does not appear on the timeline

FIGURE J-29

Example of ActionScript to create a sound object

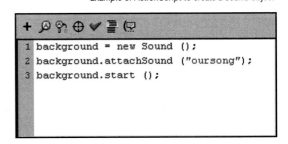

Link a sound file with a movie

1. Open flj_3.fla, then save it as **levels.fla**.

2. Open the Library panel, click the song1 audio file, click the Options menu icon at the top of the Library panel, then click Linkage to open the Linkage Properties dialog box. 🖃

3. Click the Export for ActionScript check box to select it, as shown in Figure J-30, then click OK.

   When you click the check box, Macromedia Flash adds the sound name to the Identifier field and automatically selects the Export in first frame check box.

   | TIP   The identifier is the name you will use to reference this sound clip in ActionScript.

4. Save your work.

You linked a sound with a movie without adding the sound to the timeline.

→ click the audio file
→ Options menu
→ Linkage
→ Export for ActionScript

FIGURE J-30

Using the Linkage Properties dialog box to export a sound and create an identifier string

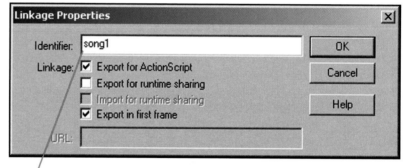

ActionScript indentifier
string for sound

FIGURE J-31

ActionScript to create a new sound object

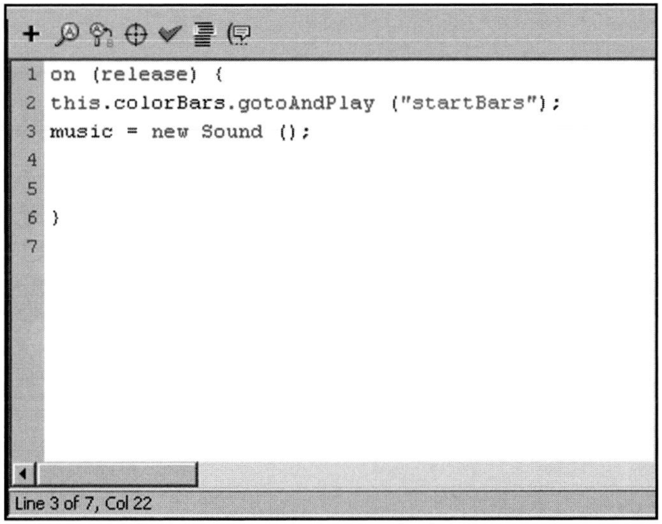

```
+  🔍 🔧 ⊕ ✔ ☰ ⊡
1 on (release) {
2 this.colorBars.gotoAndPlay ("startBars");
3 music = new Sound ();
4
5
6 }
7
```
Line 3 of 7, Col 22

FIGURE J-32

ActionScript to play a sound object

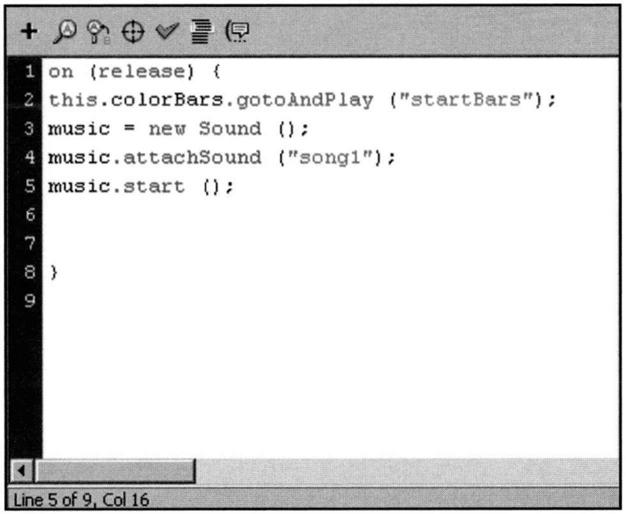

```
+  🔍 🔧 ⊕ ✔ ☰ ⊡
1 on (release) {
2 this.colorBars.gotoAndPlay ("startBars");
3 music = new Sound ();
4 music.attachSound ("song1");
5 music.start ();
6
7
8 }
9
```
Line 5 of 9, Col 16

1. Click the Arrow Tool on the toolbox (if necessary), click the start button to select it, then open the Actions panel. ▶

2. If the Actions panel is not in expert mode, click the View Options icon on the Actions panel, then click Expert Mode. 🔳

3. Click the View Options icon, then click View Line Numbers if it does not already have a check mark next to it. 🔳

4. Click the end of Line 2 in the Script pane (after the semicolon), press [Enter] (Win) or [return] (Mac) to create a new Line 3, then type **music = new Sound ();** as you refer to Figure J-31.

   This ActionScript statement creates a new sound object named "music."

5. Press [Enter] (Win) or [return] (Mac) to create a new Line 4, then type **music.attachSound ("song1");**

   This ActionScript statement attaches the sound with the linkage identifier song1 to the sound object.

6. Press [Enter] (Win) or [return] (Mac) to create a new Line 5, then type **music.start ();** as you refer to Figure J-32.

   This ActionScript statement plays the sound object.

   (continued)

Lesson 5   Use ActionScript with Sounds

7. Test the scene, click the start button, then click the mute button.

The sound file plays when you click start; when you click mute, the color bars stop playing, but the sound file does not.

8. Close the test window, then save your work.

You added actions to play a sound.

Stop sounds using ActionScript

1. Click the mute button on the stage to select it.

2. Click Line 4 in the Script pane of the Actions panel.

3. Double-click `stopAllSounds` in the Movie Control folder on the Actions toolbox, as shown in Figure J-33.

4. Click the start button on the stage to select it.

(continued)

FIGURE J-33

ActionScript to stop all sounds when Mute button is clicked

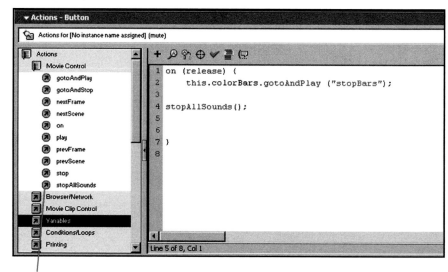

`stopAllSounds`
action in Movie Control folder

Adding Sounds

FIGURE J-34

ActionScript to stop currently playing sounds before starting sound

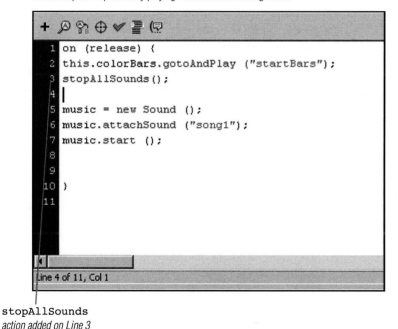

```
1  on (release) {
2  this.colorBars.gotoAndPlay ("startBars");
3  stopAllSounds();
4  |
5  music = new Sound ();
6  music.attachSound ("song1");
7  music.start ();
8
9
10 }
11
```

Line 4 of 11, Col 1

stopAllSounds
action added on Line 3

5. Click the end of Line 2 in the Script pane of the Actions panel, press [Enter] (Win) or [return] (Mac) to create a blank Line 3, then double-click stopAllSounds in the Movie Control folder in the Actions toolbox, as shown in Figure J-34.

   Inserting stopAllSounds ensures that the sound starts at the beginning each time the visitor clicks the button and that multiple copies of the sound file do not play at the same time.

6. Test the scene, click the start button, then click the mute button.

   The music plays when you click start, then stops when you click mute.

7. Close the test window, save your work, then close levels.fla.

You added actions to stop sounds from playing.

Work with sounds.

1. Open flj_4.fla, then save it as **skillsdemoJ.fla**.
2. Move the playhead through the timeline of the movie.
3. Insert a new layer above the buttons layer, rename it **ambient1**.
4. Select the background_loop1 sound from the Sound list in the Property inspector to add it to Frame 1 of the new layer.
5. Set the synchronization for the sound on the ambient1 layer to Event, then set the number of times to loop to **10**.
6. Insert a new layer above the ambient1 layer, rename it **ambient2**.
7. Select the background_loop2 sound from the Sound list in the Property inspector to add it to Frame 1 of the new layer.
8. Set the synchronization for the sound on the ambient2 layer to Event, then set the number of times to loop to **10**.
9. Insert a new layer above the ambient2 layer, rename it **song**, then add an instance of the song1 sound to Frame 15 of the new layer.
   (*Hint*: Insert a keyframe in Frame 15 before you add the sound.)
10. Set the synchronization for the sound on the song layer to Event, then set the number of times to loop to **10**.
11. Save your work.

FIGURE J-35
Completed Skills Review

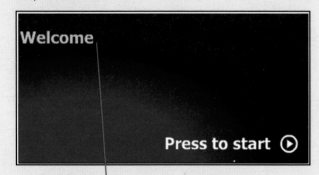

Voice-over and background music begin when page
is displayed; voice-over is synchronized with words

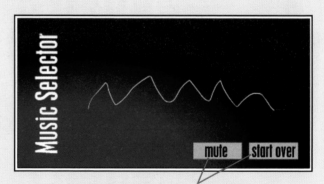

Mute button stops all sounds; start over button
stops currently playing sounds and restarts song
from the beginning

Specify synchronization options.

1. Create a new movie clip symbol named **animated_text**.

2. Rename Layer 1 of the animated_text movie clip symbol **audio**, select the music_selector_audio sound from the Sound list in the Property inspector to Frame 1 of the new layer, then set the synchronization to Stream.

3. Insert a keyframe in Frame 75 on the audio layer, then add a `stop` action to the keyframe. (*Hint*: Adding a keyframe lets you see the full streaming sound. Adding the `stop` action keeps the movie clip from repeating.)

4. Open the Library panel, insert a new layer above the audio layer, rename it **text**, insert a keyframe in Frame 13 of the layer, then drag the Welcome graphic symbol from the Text folder to the stage.

5. Open the Property inspector, double-click the value in the X text box, type **–58.5**, double-click the value in the Y text box, type **–16.7**, then press [Enter] (Win) or [return] (Mac).

6. Insert a keyframe in Frame 17 on the text layer, select the word "Welcome" on the stage, click the Swap button in the Property inspector, click the to graphic symbol, then click OK.

7. Insert a keyframe in Frame 20 on the text layer, select the word "to" on the stage, click the Swap button in the Property inspector, click the the graphic symbol, then click OK.

8. Insert a keyframe in Frame 23 on the text layer, select the word "the" on the stage, click the Swap button in the Property inspector, click the music graphic symbol, then click OK.

9. Insert a keyframe in Frame 27 on the text layer, select the word "Music" on the stage, click the Swap button in the Property inspector, click the selector graphic symbol, then click OK.

10. Test the movie clip symbol, then close the test window. (*Hint*: There is an extra word in the voice-over, "online," which you will edit.)

11. Return to Scene 1, create a new layer above the song layer, rename it **animation**, click Frame 1 on the new layer, then add an instance of the animated_text movie clip symbol to anywhere on the stage from the Library panel.

12. Open the Property inspector for the movie clip symbol instance, double-click the value in the X text box, type **60**, double-click the value in the Y text box, type **40**, then press [Enter] (Win) or [return] (Mac).

13. Insert a keyframe in Frame 15 on the animation layer. (*Hint*: Adding this keyframe keeps the animation from appearing on the second page in the site.)

14. Click Frame 1 on the buttons layer, double-click the right arrow button on the stage to open it, click the Over frame, add an instance of the Plastic Click sound to the frame, then set the synchronization to Start.

15. Click the Up frame, then set the Sync sound to Stop for the Plastic Click sound.

16. Return to Scene 1, then save your work.

Modify sounds.

1. Open the animated_text movie clip, click Frame 1 of the audio layer, open the Property inspector, if necessary, then click the Edit button in the Property inspector.

2. Show units in Frames, then zoom out the view in the Edit Envelope dialog box until you can see the waveform for the entire sound.

3. Drag the Time Out control to approximately Frame 35, then test the sound in the Edit Envelope dialog box to verify that the word "online" does not play.

4. Click OK, then return to Scene 1.

5. Click Frame 1 on the ambient1 layer, click Edit in the Property inspector, drag the enve-lope handles in both channels to just above the bottom of the envelope, then click OK.

6. Click Frame 1 on the ambient2 layer, click Edit in the Property inspector, drag the envelope handles in both channels to just above the bottom of the envelope, then accept changes and close the Edit Envelope dialog box.

7. Save your work.

Specify compression options.

1. Verify that the Library panel is open, then select the Properties for the music_selector_audio sound in the Sounds folder.

2. Select Speech as the Compression option.

3. Test how the compression setting will affect the sound, then close the Sound Properties dialog box.

4. Open the Publish Settings dialog box from the File menu, then click the Flash tab.

5. Open the Sound Settings for Audio Event, set the Bit Rate to 20 kbps, accept the remaining settings, then close the dialog box.

6. Close the Publish Settings dialog box.

7. Save your work.

Use ActionScript with sounds.

1. Click Frame 1 on the buttons layer, click the right arrow button on the stage to select it, open the Actions panel, then click the beginning of Line 2 in the Script pane.

2. Add a `stopAllSounds` action to the beginning of Line 2, before the `gotoAndPlay` action.

3. Move the playhead to Frame 15 on the timeline to display the second page.

4. Select the song1 sound in the Sounds folder in the Library panel, then display the Linkage for the sound symbol.

5. Select the Export for ActionScript check box, then close the Linkage Properties dialog box and the Library panel.

6. Click the mute button on the stage to select it, then in the Actions panel add an `on (release)` action to the button. As the statements for the `on (release)` action, add a `stopAllSounds` action, then a `gotoAndPlay` action that plays the frame named mute in the waveform movie clip symbol.

7. Click the start over button on the stage to select it, then in the Actions panel add an `on (release)` action to the button. As a statement for the `on (release)` action, add a `gotoAndPlay` action that plays the frame named "start" the movie clip symbol named "waveform."

8. In the Actions panel for the start over button, add the following additional statements for the `on (release)` action: a `stopAllSounds` action after the `gotoAndPlay` action to stop all currently playing sounds and actions to start playing the sound with the linkage identifier song1. (*Hint*: You will have to create a sound object, use `attachSound` to attach the song1 sound to the sound object, then use the `start` action to start the sound.)

9. Test the scene, then save your work.

Ultimate Tours would like you to create a banner promoting its "Japan on a Budget" tours. The graphics for the banner are complete; now you need to add music and voice-over. Ultimate Tours would like a musical background to play continuously while the banner is displayed, and they have also provided a voice-over they would like to be synchronized with text on the screen. Finally, Ultimate Tours would like an accent sound to play when a visitor clicks the navigation button on the banner.

1. Open flj_5, then rename the file **ultimatetoursJ.fla**.
2. Test the scene and notice the text banner that appears across the screen against a series of background images.
3. Insert a new layer above the text animation layer, rename it **audio**, add the sound named ultimate_background to Frame 1 of the layer, then set synchronization to Event.
4. Set looping for the sound to **15** to ensure the music plays the entire time the banner is displayed.
5. Open the Edit Envelope dialog box for the ultimate_background sound, then use the envelope handles to decrease the volume at which the background music plays. (*Hint*: You should drag the envelope handles nearly to the bottom of each sound envelope.)

6. Open the Library panel, then open the movie clip symbol named words in the movie clips folder.
7. Insert a new layer above the text layer, name it **voiceover**, add the ultimate_voiceover sound to the layer, then set synchronization to Stream, if necessary.
8. Move the keyframes that control when each word of text appears on the stage to synchronize with when the word is spoken in the voice-over. (*Hint*: Use the playhead to hear the streaming sound, then drag the keyframes on the text layer to create the synchronization effect.)

FIGURE J-36
Completed Project Builder 1

9. Return to Scene 1, then set the green button to play the Switch Small Plastic sound when a visitor clicks the button and stop playing the sound when a visitor moves the mouse off the button. (*Hint*: Be sure to use the Start synchronization option for the Down state and the Stop option for the Up state of the button.)
10. Test the scene.
11. Save your work, then compare your image to Figure J-36.

Voice-over is synchronized with appearance of words

Sound occurs when visitor clicks button

In the previous unit, you created a slide show for your work samples, which displayed a different sample each time the visitor clicked a button. Now add sound to the slide show. If you have access to sound-recording software, you can record your own voice-overs that describe the sample being shown. Alternatively, use the sample files to provide a musical background.

1. Open portfolioI.fla and save it as **portfolioJ.fla**. (*Hint*: If you did not create portfolioI.fla, see your instructor.)
2. Import to the Library panel the voice-overs describing your work, or import the following sound files:
   accent1.mp3
   accent2.mp3
   background.mp3
   portfolio_voiceover.wav
3. Open the samples movie clip symbol, add a new layer named **audio**, and then add a different sound to each frame of the movie clip. You can use either voice-over clips that describe the sample, or the voice introduction and musical backgrounds provided in the sample files.
4. If you used the sample files, set looping for each musical background sound to **50**, to ensure the music plays continuously for the entire time the visitor views the page.

5. If you are using the musical backgrounds, experiment with adding effects to the sounds, such as fades or shifts between channels.
6. Add a `stopAllSounds` action to keep the different sounds from overlapping as the

visitor presses the "Click to view next slide" button. (*Hint*: You should add the action to the button, not the movie clip symbol.)
7. Test the scene.
8. Save your work, then compare your movie to Figure J-37.

FIGURE J-37
Completed Project Builder 2

Voice-over or background music begins
when page is displayed; new voice-over
or music begins when visitor clicks
button to view next slide

Figure J-38 shows a page from a Web site created using Macromedia Flash. Study the figure and complete the following. For each question, indicate how you determined your answer.

1. Connect to the Internet, and go to *www.course.com*. Navigate to the page for this book, click the Student Online Companion, then click the link for this unit.

2. Open a document in a word processor or open a new Macromedia Flash movie, save the file as **dpuUnitJ**, then answer the following questions. (*Hint*: Use the Text Tool in Macromedia Flash.)

   - Do you think sound enhances your experience of this site? Why or why not?
   - Do you think sound increases the usability of this site? Why or why not?
   - Move the mouse pointer around the screen and list the different sounds you hear. Do you think the site uses too many sounds?
   - If you had created this site, how do you think you would organize the different sounds on the timeline?

   - Refresh the page to play it again from the beginning, and this time pay attention to the spoken words. Are there any sound effects being used? How in Macromedia Flash would you go about creating this effect?

   - Navigate around the different pages of the site. Do you notice any other opportunities to use sound to enhance this site?

FIGURE J-38
Design Project

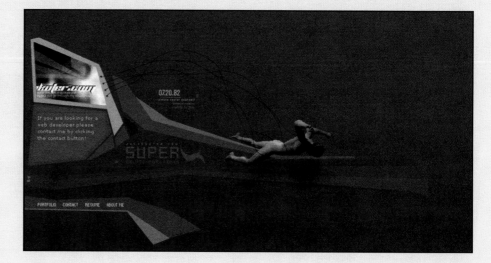

Your group can assign elements of the project to individual members, or work collectively to create the finished product.

Your group works for a software game company. Your newest game, "Match the Shapes," will be developed in Macromedia Flash and marketed to preschoolers. You are working on a prototype of the game to show upper management. You have already completed the visual aspects of the prototype; now you must add sound.

1. Open flj_6.fla, then save it as **game_prototype.fla**.
2. Test the movie to see how the matching game works, then close the test window.
3. Add the ambient_audio sound from the Library panel to the movie as an event sound. Loop the sound 10 times to ensure it plays the entire time the visitor is viewing the page.
4. Add a `stopAllSounds` action that stops the sound from playing when a visitor navigates to the second page of the site. (*Hint*: You can add the action to the Start button or to a frame in the actions layer.)
5. Create a movie clip symbol that synchronizes the welcome_voiceover sound from the Library panel with the words "Welcome to Match the Shapes." Alternatively, create another sort of animation, such as a motion tween from off the stage for the words, and synchronize this animation with the streaming sound. (*Hint*: Be sure to include a `stop` action in the last frame of the movie clip symbol, so the movie clip doesn't play continuously.)

6. Add an instance of the movie clip symbol to the first page of the movie.
7. Create a custom envelope for the ambient_audio sound, so it starts low in volume during the voice-over, then rises to full volume.
8. Add Switch small plastic sound from the Library panel to the Down state of the Start button on the first page of the site.

FIGURE J-39
Completed Group Project

Background music plays low in volume during voice-over/text synchronized animation; button sound plays when the button is clicked

9. On the second page of the movie, attach ActionScript to the square, triangle, and circle in the Start Bin that, when a visitor correctly places the shape on its corresponding shape in the Drop Bin, stops any currently playing sounds, then plays the match sound in the Library panel. (*Hint*: Remember to first create a linkage identifier for the match sound, then create a sound object in the ActionScript for each instance where you want to play the sound.)
10. Test the scene.
11. Save your work and compare your image to Figure J-39.

Voice-over plays when visitor successfully matches the shape

UNIT K

USING ADVANCED ACTIONSCRIPT

1. Creating complex interactivity.

2. Using ActionScript to create external links.

3. Loading new movies.

4. Working with conditional actions.

UNIT K
USING ADVANCED ACTIONSCRIPT

Introduction

In this unit, you will continue to build on your knowledge of ActionScript, with an emphasis on adding actions that encourage user interaction and enhance the user experience. For example, you can replace the mouse cursor with a custom cursor; track user interactions, and offer feedback based on the data you gather; and send information you collect from users to another Web site or program for processing. Breaking down your movies into multiple, smaller movies, then using ActionScript to load these movies when appropriate, can help you better organize a large Web site and provide users relief from lengthy downloads. Conditional actions let you implement complex branching in your movies; looping actions help streamline your ActionScript and provide a way to repeat a set of actions based on a value provided by the user or a task you want the user to perform.

With all the new actions and cool techniques you will see in this unit, remember that you're still just scratching the surface of ActionScript. The more you research and experiment, the more surprised you will be by all you can accomplish with ActionScript, and the more your users will appreciate your efforts.

Tools You'll Use

```
1  onClipEvent (enterFrame) {
2      _root.myCursor._x = _root._xmouse;
3      _root.myCursor._y = _root._ymouse;
4  }
5
```

ActionScript to create
a custom cursor

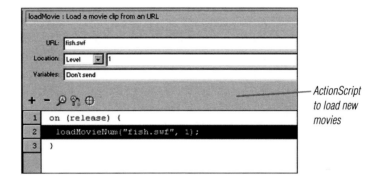

loadMovie : Load a movie clip from an URL

URL: fish.swf

Location: Level ▾ 1

Variables: Don't send

```
1  on (release) {
2      loadMovieNum("fish.swf", 1);
3  }
```

ActionScript
to load new
movies

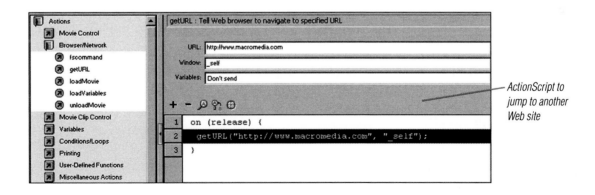

Actions
　Movie Control
　Browser/Network
　　fscommand
　　getURL
　　loadMovie
　　loadVariables
　　unloadMovie
　Movie Clip Control
　Variables
　Conditions/Loops
　Printing
　User-Defined Functions
　Miscellaneous Actions

getURL : Tell Web browser to navigate to specified URL

URL: http://www.macromedia.com

Window: _self

Variables: Don't send

```
1  on (release) {
2      getURL("http://www.macromedia.com", "_self");
3  }
```

ActionScript to
jump to another
Web site

CREATE COMPLEX INTERACTIVITY

What You'll Do

In this lesson, you will use ActionScript to create a custom cursor and count user interactions.

Creating a Custom Cursor

Creating a custom cursor is a fun way to make a Macromedia Flash site distinctive. You might create a cursor with your face on it for a personal site; or you can tie in the cursor with the theme of the site, such as a picture of a yo-yo for an e-business site selling toys. You can also integrate a custom cursor with the purpose of the site: for example, in a game site, the custom cursor might be a cartoon figure the user has to lead through a maze with the mouse. The custom cursor can be a graphic, photograph, or even an animation. The only requirement is that it be a movie clip symbol.

The first step toward implementing a custom cursor is to hide the regular cursor.

You do this with the mouse.hide action. There is a corresponding mouse.show action you can use to redisplay the cursor at any point.

There are two ways to add your own cursor to a movie. In both methods, the custom cursor is an instance of a movie clip symbol. The first method uses the startDrag action. As you add this action to an instance of the movie clip symbol, you should select the Lock mouse to center option. This option centers the hidden mouse pointer beneath the custom cursor, so both the mouse pointer and the custom cursor move when the user drags the mouse. Figure K-1 shows the ActionScript for this method.

Using mouse coordinate information

There are many other ways to use the mouse coordinate information returned by the _xmouse and _ymouse actions to enhance interaction. For example, you might create ActionScript that changes the color of an object or screen area whenever the user passes the mouse over it, or ActionScript that creates a panoramic view of an automobile or other product as the user moves the mouse.

Because only one movie clip symbol at a time can be draggable in a movie, if there are other elements in the movie you want users to be able to drag, startDrag might not be the best method for implementing your custom cursor. A second method uses actions that determine the X and Y coordinates of the hidden mouse pointer, then sets the coordinates of your custom cursor to the same position. As the user moves the mouse, the values constantly update, so the custom cursor tracks where the mouse would be on the screen if it wasn't hidden. The _xmouse and _ymouse actions return the coordinates of the mouse pointer; the _x and _y actions control the coordinates of an instance of a movie clip symbol. Figure K-2 shows the ActionScript for a custom cursor implemented using this method.

Tracking User Interactions

One aspect of interactivity involves responding to user actions, such as jumping to a different point in a movie when a user clicks a button. Another aspect involves providing users with individual feedback based on the actions they take or information they supply. This can be as simple as creating a dynamic text box to display the user's name in a greeting, as you did in Unit I. You can also use ActionScript to gather and display more complex information, such as the number of times a user clicks the mouse or a user's progress in a game or quiz. Collecting such information presents many opportunities to offer users custom feedback. Tracking interactions can also provide you with insight on the way people work with your site.

The increment and decrement actions are useful when tracking user interactions. The **increment action**, ++ (two plus signs), adds 1 to a variable or expression; the **decrement action**, − − (two minus signs), subtracts 1 unit. For example, the ActionScript statement x++ is the equivalent of the expression $x=x+1$. Both add 1 to the variable. You might use the increment operator to keep track of and display the number of correct answers a user has given during an online test.

QUICKTIP

The increment and decrement operators are also useful when setting up the number of times to run a conditional loop. For example, you might want to allow a user to attempt to answer a question a specified number of times before providing the correct answer.

FIGURE K-1

ActionScript to create a custom cursor using startDrag

```
startDrag : Start a drag operation on a movie clip

  Target:
     □ Constrain to rectangle   L:
     ☑ Lock mouse to center     T:

+ -  ⌕ ⌗ ⊕

1  onClipEvent (load) {
2      startDrag("", true);
3  }
```

Centers the hidden cursor
underneath the custom cursor

FIGURE K-2

ActionScript to create a custom cursor by setting X and Y coordinates

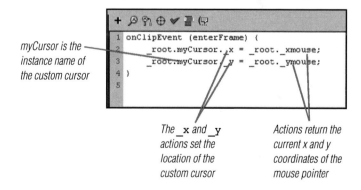

myCursor is the instance name of the custom cursor

```
+ ⌕ ⌗ ⊕ ✔ ☰ ⌑

1  onClipEvent (enterFrame) {
2      _root.myCursor._x = _root._xmouse;
3      _root.myCursor._y = _root._ymouse;
4  }
5
```

The _x and _y actions set the location of the custom cursor

Actions return the current x and y coordinates of the mouse pointer

Hide the cursor

1. Open flk_1.fla, then save it as **interactive.fla**.

2. Click Frame 1 on the actions layer, then open the Actions panel.

3. Click the View Options icon in the Actions panel, then click Normal Mode, if necessary. 🔲

4. Click the View Options icon in the Actions panel, then verify View Line Numbers is selected. 🔲

5. Click the Actions toolbox, click the Objects folder, click the Movie folder, click the Mouse folder, then click the Methods folder.

    | TIP   Scroll down the Actions toolbox until you see the Objects folder.

6. Double-click `hide` in the Methods folder of the Actions toolbox, as shown in Figure K-3.

7. Test the scene.

    The mouse no longer appears in the scene.

8. Close the test window, then save your work

You used ActionScript to hide the mouse cursor.

Create a custom cursor using X and Y coordinates

1. Insert a new layer above the shapes layer, then rename it **cursor**. 🖐️

2. Open the Library panel, drag the cursor movie clip symbol to the center of the stage, as shown in Figure K-4, then close the Library panel.

    | TIP   Collapse or move panels as necessary or convenient.

(continued)

FIGURE K-3
ActionScript to hide the mouse

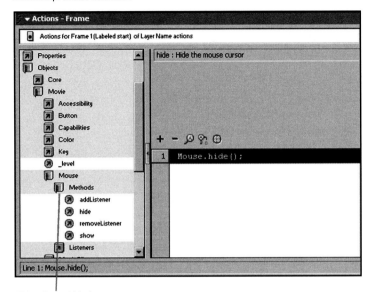

The action to hide the
mouse is located in
the Methods folder

FIGURE K-4
Instance of custom cursor movie clip symbol on the stage

The custom cursor

FIGURE K-5
Naming the movie clip instance

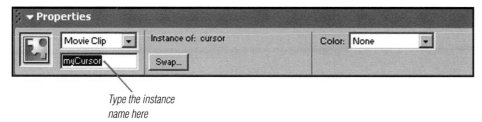

Type the instance
name here

FIGURE K-6
ActionScript to create the custom cursor using X and Y coordinates

```
1  onClipEvent (enterFrame) {
2      _root.myCursor._x = _root._xmouse;
3      _root.myCursor._y = _root._ymouse;
4  }
5
```

*Don't forget to
include the
semicolons*

3. Click the cursor movie clip symbol to select it, open the Property inspector, click the Instance Name text box, type **myCursor**, press [Enter] (Win) or [return] (Mac), compare your image to Figure K-5, then close the Property inspector.

4. Click the View Options icon in the Actions panel, then click Expert Mode.

5. Type **onClipEvent (enterFrame) {** on Line 1 in the Script pane, then press [Enter] (Win) or [return] (Mac).

6. Type **_root.myCursor._x = _root._xmouse;** then press [Enter] (Win) or [return] (Mac) to use the current X coordinate.

7. Type **_root.myCursor._y = _root._ymouse;** then press [Enter] (Win) or [return] (Mac) to use the current Y coordinate.

8. Type **}** then compare your Script pane to Figure K-6.

9. Test the scene.

You can use the custom cursor to click the button on the first screen and to drag and drop the shapes on the second screen.

> TIP The cursor reverts back to the shape for your operating system when you position the mouse pointer on the title bar, menu, or taskbar of the test window.

10. Close the test window, then save your work.

You used ActionScript to designate an instance of a movie clip symbol to act as the mouse cursor using X and Y coordinates.

Using onClipEvent

onClipEvent determines when to run actions associated with an instance of a movie clip. Options include running the actions when the movie clip instance is first loaded onto the timeline, upon a mouse event, upon a key press, or upon receiving data. You can associate different options with the same movie clip instance.

Track user interactions with the increment operator

1. Click Frame 7 on the background layer, click a gray area on the stage to deselect all objects, click the Text Tool on the toolbox, close the Actions panel, then open the Property inspector. A

2. Click the Text type list arrow, click Dynamic Text, click the Font list arrow, drag the slider to **Arial**, click the Font Size list arrow, drag the slider to **14**, click the Text (fill) color box, double-click (Win) or click (Mac) the hexadecimal text box, type **#990000**, verify that Bold is turned off, then click [Enter] (Win) or [return] (Mac).

3. Click the Show Border Around Text icon, then, using Figure K-7 as a guide, draw a text box below the words Mouse clicks. 🔲

   > TIP   If the text box overlaps other elements on the screen, click the Arrow Tool on the toolbox after drawing the text box, then use the mouse or arrow keys to move the box. ⬉

4. Click the Variable text box in the Property inspector, type **myClicks**, press [Enter] (Win) or [return] (Mac), then close the Property inspector.

5. Click Frame 7 on the actions layer, then open the Actions panel.

6. Type **myClicks = 0;** on Line 1 in the Script pane, as shown in Figure K-8.

   This ActionScript resets the value of the `myClicks` variable to 0 each time a user navigates to the page.

   (continued)

FIGURE K-7
Drawing the dynamic text box

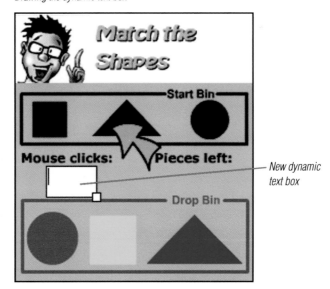

New dynamic text box

FIGURE K-8
ActionScript to set the initial value of the variable to 0

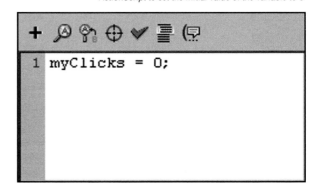

```
1 myClicks = 0;
```

FIGURE K-9

ActionScript to count mouse clicks

```
    + ⊘ ⚲ ⊕ ✔ ≣ ⌨

1   on (press){
2       startDrag ("",false);
3       _root.myClicks++;
4
5   }
6
7   on (release){
8       stopDrag();
9       if (this._droptarget == "/targetSquare")
10      {
11      _root.targetSquare.gotoAndPlay (2);
12
13      setProperty (" root.myBox",  visible, false);
```

*New line of ActionScript;
be sure to include two
plus signs (++)*

7. Click the Arrow Tool on the toolbox, click the black square in the Start Bin to select it, click at the end of Line 2 in the Script pane, then press [Enter] (Win) or [return] (Mac) to create a blank line. ↖

8. Type **_root.myClicks++;** on Line 3 in the Script pane, as shown in Figure K-9.

   This ActionScript increases the value of the myClicks variable by one each time the mouse is clicked. Including _root in the target path ensures that Macromedia Flash looks for the variable at the main timeline level.

9. Test the scene, then click the black square in the Start Bin repeatedly.

   The value in the Mouse clicks dynamic text box updates each time you click the square.

10. Close the test window, then repeat Steps 7 and 8 for the black triangle and black circle in the Start Bin.

11. Test the scene, click each shape, close the test window, then save your work.

You used the increment operator action to maintain a count of the number of times a user clicks a set of objects.

Track user interactions with the decrement operator

1. Click Frame 7 on the background layer.

2. Click the Text Tool on the toolbox, click a gray area on the stage to deselect all other objects, then draw a text box below the words Pieces left:, as shown in Figure K-10. $\boxed{A}$

   The new text box will be a dynamic text box with the same settings you specified for the Mouse clicks: dynamic text box.

3. Open the Property inspector, click the Variable text box in the Property inspector, type **myPieces**, press [Enter] (Win) or [return] (Mac), then close the Property inspector.

4. Click Frame 7 on the actions layer, click at the end of Line 1 in the Script pane, then press [Enter] (Win) or [return] (Mac) to create a blank line.

5. Type **myPieces = 3;** on Line 2 in the Script pane, as shown in Figure K-11.

   This ActionScript resets the value of the myPieces variable to 3 each time a user navigates to the page.

6. Click the Arrow Tool on the toolbox, double-click the yellow square in the Drop Bin to open the movie clip symbol, then click Frame 2 on the movie clip symbol timeline. $\blacktriangleright$

   In this movie clip, Frame 2 appears when a shape from the Start Bin is successfully dropped on a shape in the Drop Bin.

   (continued)

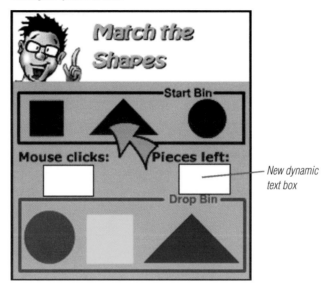

— New dynamic text box

FIGURE K-12

ActionScript to decrement a variable as pieces are successfully matched

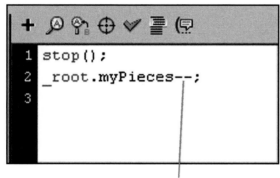

```
1  stop();
2  _root.myPieces--;
3
```

New line of ActionScript;
be sure to include two
minus signs (--)

7. Click at the end of Line 1 in the Script pane, press [Enter] (Win) or [return] (Mac) to create a blank line, then type **_root.myPieces--;** on Line 2 in the Script pane, as shown in Figure K-12.

This ActionScript decreases the value of the myPieces variable by one each time Frame 2 displays, which will count down the number of pieces still left to match.

> TIP You can press the hyphen key on the keyboard to type – (minus sign).

8. Click the Scene identifier icon on the Information bar to return to Scene 1.

   Scene 1

9. Test the scene, click the Start button, then drag the black square to the yellow square.

   The value in the Pieces left: dynamic text box changes to 2 when you match the square, but does not update for the other shapes.

10. Close the test window, then repeat Steps 6 and 7 for the red circle and blue triangle in the Drop Bin.

11. Test the scene, close the test window, save your work, then close interactive.fla.

You used the decrement action to maintain a count of the user's score in the game.

USE ACTIONSCRIPT TO CREATE EXTERNAL LINKS

What You'll Do

 In this lesson, you will create e-mail and Web page links.

Creating a Link to a Web Site

Many Web sites contain links to other sites. You might want to lead the user to a site related to your own, or just another site you want to share. The getURL action lets you jump from a button or movie clip symbol to another Web site or open another file, as shown in Figure K-13. The new site or file can appear in the same browser window as your site, or in a new window Table K-1 displays the target options for Web site and external file links.

> **QUICK**TIP
>
> You can also enter the HTML file name of a specific window or frame as a target. This might be appropriate if you have multiple links on a page and want a separate window to open for the first link the user follows, but not for subsequent links.

When you use getURL to lead to another Web site, you must supply the URL for the file. Make sure to include the entire URL, including the protocol prefix, for example, *http://www.yahoo.com*, which is known as an absolute path. If you are creating a link to a file, you can include an **absolute path**, which specifies the exact location of the file, or a **relative path**, which indicates location based on the current location of your movie file. For example, to jump to a file you will be including in the same

TABLE K-1: Target options for Web site links

option	opens site or link in:
_self	The current frame in the current window
_blank	A new window
_parent	The parent of the current frame
_top	The top-level frame in the current window

server location to which you will be publishing, you can include just the file name, without any path.

Creating a Mailto: Link

You can also use getURL to create a mail link from a button or movie clip symbol. When a user clicks an e-mail link, a new e-mail message window opens, with an address field you have specified already filled in. If you want to create an e-mail link from text, not a button or movie clip symbol, you can use the Property inspector.

To create an e-mail link, include mailto: and then the e-mail address in the URL field of the getURL action. To test an e-mail link, you must display your movie in a browser by clicking File on the main menu, then clicking Publish Preview. The e-mail link is not active in the test window.

Posting Information to a Web Site

The best kind of communication is two-way, and along with displaying a Web site, getURL can send variables to another application or a Common Gateway Interface (CGI) script located on a Web server. The application or script can perform actions using, storing, or responding to the variables—creating instant feedback that can be displayed on a user's site. Forms with

user surveys and shopping carts are examples of posting information. Figure K-14 shows a form to send an e-mail message.

There are two options when sending variables: GET and POST. Both methods collect all the variables defined at the main timeline level of a movie and send them to the URL you specify in the getURL action for processing. GET is best for small amounts of information, as it can send a string of up to 1,024 characters. Information sent using GET is also less secure, as the variables are appended to the URL string, and so appear in the Address field of the browser. POST can accommodate more variables, and is also more secure, because the variables are collected and sent in a file. POST is the recommended way to send data to a script.

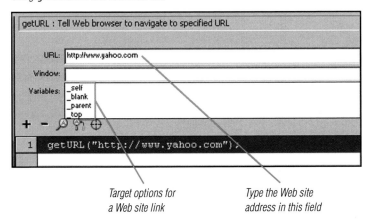

FIGURE K-13
Using getURL to link to a Web site

Target options for a Web site link

Type the Web site address in this field

FIGURE K-14
A form that posts information to a CGI script

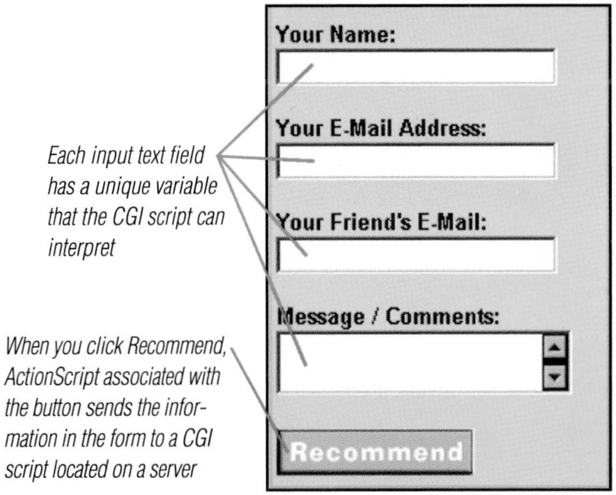

Each input text field has a unique variable that the CGI script can interpret

When you click Recommend, ActionScript associated with the button sends the information in the form to a CGI script located on a server

Create a Web site link

1. Open flk_2.fla, then save it as **links.fla**.

2. Click the Arrow Tool on the toolbox (if necessary), click the Visit our Web site button to select it, then open the Actions panel. ⬉

3. Click the View Options icon in the Actions panel, then click Normal Mode. ▣.

4. Click the Actions toolbox, click the Actions folder, click the Browser/Network folder, then double-click getURL.

5. Click the URL text box, then type **http://www.macromedia.com**.

6. Click the Window list arrow, click _self, then compare your Script pane to Figure K-15.

7. Test the scene, then click the Visit our Web site button.

   The Web site opens in a browser window.

8. Close the browser window, close the test window, then save your work.

You created a button that links to a Web site.

FIGURE K-15
ActionScript to link to a Web site

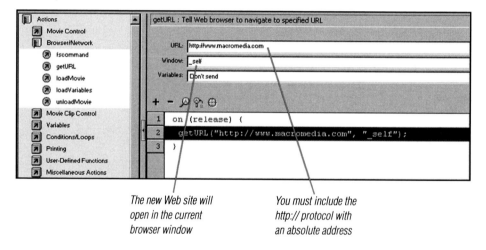

The new Web site will open in the current browser window

You must include the http:// protocol with an absolute address

FIGURE K-16

ActionScript to create an e-mail link

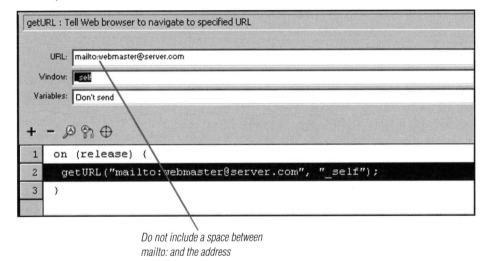

```
getURL : Tell Web browser to navigate to specified URL

    URL:  mailto:webmaster@server.com
  Window:  self
Variables:  Don't send

+  -  🔍 ╬ ⊕

1   on (release) {
2       getURL ("mailto:webmaster@server.com", "_self");
3   }
```

*Do not include a space between
mailto: and the address*

Sending an e-mail through the Web

To send an e-mail completely through the Web, you can collect the recipient and
message information for the e-mail in variable fields, then send the variables to a CGI
(Common Gateway Interface) script for processing. Common mail scripts include
mailform.pl and tellafriend.cgi. See your Webmaster or network administrator for
information about scripts available on your server.

Create an e-mail link

1. Click the E-mail us at
   webmaster@server.com button to select it.

   TIP It's good practice to include the
   e-mail address as part of a mail link, just
   in case your user doesn't have access to an
   e-mail program.

2. Double-click getURL in the Browser/
   Network folder in the Actions toolbox.

3. Click the URL text box, then type
   mailto:webmaster@server.com for the
   e-mail address.

4. Click the Window list arrow, click _self, then
   compare your Script pane to Figure K-16.

5. Click File on the main menu, click Publish
   Preview, then click Default – (HTML).

   The movie opens in a browser window.

6. Click the E-mail us at
   webmaster@server.com button.

   A new e-mail message window opens in
   your default e-mail program, with the To:
   field already filled in.

   TIP If an e-mail message does not
   appear, your current computer may not have
   access to an e-mail program.

7. Close the mail message, click No if
   prompted to save changes, then close the
   browser window.

8. Save your work, then close links.fla.

You created an e-mail link button.

Post information to a Web site

1. Open flk_3.fla, then save it as **search.fla**.

2. Click Frame 1 on Layer 1.

3. Click the Text Tool on the toolbox, then open the Property inspector. [A]

4. Click the Text type list arrow, click Input Text, click the Font list arrow, drag the slider to **Arial**, click the Font Size list arrow, drag the slider to **18**, click the Text (fill) color box, click the first black color swatch (**#000000**), click the Show Border Around Text icon swatch (if necessary), then draw a text box below the Yahoo graphic, as shown in Figure K-17. [icon]

5. Click the Variable text box in the Property inspector, type **p**, press [Enter] (Win) or [return] (Mac), then close the Property inspector.

   p is a variable used in the CGI script to which you will be sending information. The script conducts a search using the information in the p variable.

6. Click the Arrow Tool on the toolbox, click the search button to select it, then open the Actions panel. [arrow icon]

7. Double-click `getURL` in the Browser/ Network folder in the Actions toolbox.

(continued)

FIGURE K-17
Drawing the text box to collect the variable information

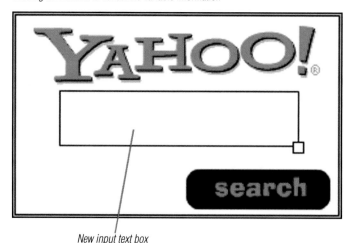

New input text box

8. Click the URL text box, then type **http://search.yahoo.com/bin/search** to enter the CGI script location and name.

"search" is the name of the CGI script to which you will be sending a variable.

9. Click the Window list arrow, then click _self.

10. Click the Variables list arrow, click Send using GET, then compare your Script pane to Figure K-18.

11. Test the scene, type **ActionScript** in the input text box, then click the Search button.

The Yahoo Web site opens, with the Search field already filled in and search results displayed. You can see the format in which the GET option sent the variable by looking in the Address field of the browser.

12. Close the browser window, close the test window, save your work, then close search.fla.

You sent information to a CGI script.

FIGURE K-18

ActionScript to send variable information to a CGI script

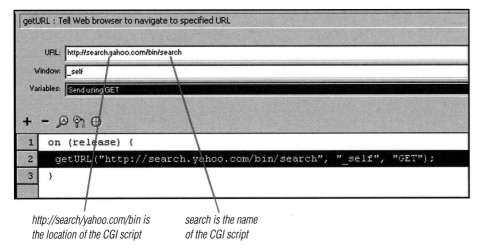

http://search/yahoo.com/bin is the location of the CGI script

search is the name of the CGI script

LOAD NEW MOVIES

What You'll Do

fish   unload   frog

In this lesson, you will load new movies into and unload movies from the Flash Player.

Understanding Multiple Movies

In previous units, you have seen how you can use scenes and movie clip symbols to break large movies up into smaller, more manageable components. Another strategy is to split a single movie into a number of different movies, and then use ActionScript to load the movies as needed. For example, you might have a site with a number of discrete areas, not all of which are of interest to every user. By splitting each area into its own movie, you can save download time for the user, since instead of having to download a large movie for the entire site, the movie for each area will be downloaded only when the user visits it. Multiple movies can create smoother transitions between pages, since the new movies load into the current HTML page. Using multiple movies can also help you keep organized during development of a movie, especially if different people are working on different parts of the movie. Figure K-19 shows an example of a way to use multiple movies.

Loading Movies

You use the loadMovie action to load a movie. You must know the name of the Flash Player movie file you want to load (Flash Player files have a .SWF extension) and also its location. As with the getURL action, you can specify an absolute or relative path for the location.

You can load a new movie either in place of or on top of the current movie, or into a movie clip symbol. If you load a new movie into the current movie, the new movie will inherit the frame rate, dimensions, and background color of the current movie. The new movie will appear starting in the upper-left corner of the current movie, which may cause design issues if your movies are not the same size; make sure to test how the additional movies will load before publishing a site. Loading a new movie into a movie clip gives you more control over the size and placement of the movie. One useful technique is to create a blank movie clip symbol, position it on the stage where you want the new movie to appear, and then load the movie into the blank movie clip symbol. Figure K-20 shows options for loading movies.

Understanding Levels

The concept of levels becomes important when you add new movies to the current movie. Levels are similar to layers on the timeline; they establish a hierarchy that determines what's displayed on the screen. The current movie, also called the base movie, is considered to be at Level 0. You can add the new movie at Level 0, in which case it replaces the current movie; or at Level 1, in which case it appears on top of the current movie. The movie originally at Level 0 continues to control the frame rate, dimensions, and background color of all other movies, even if you replace it.

For example, a new movie could appear on top of the current movie if loaded at Level 1. Parts of the current movie, such as the links or areas of a background image, could remain in view and active. Alternatively, you could load the new movie at Level 0, in which case none of the original movie would remain in view.

As you load additional movies, you can continue to add them in place of an existing movie, or at a higher level. Movies at higher levels appear on top of movies at lower levels. Each level can contain only one movie.

> **QUICK**TIP
>
> The `loadMovie` action becomes `loadMovieNum` when you specify a level at which to load a movie. If you are working in expert mode, use `loadMovieNum` to load a movie at a level.

Unloading Movies

Macromedia Flash also includes `unloadMovie` (for movies loaded into movie clips) and `unloadMovieNum` (for movies loaded at a level) actions to remove a movie from the Flash Player. Including this action when you no longer need a movie loaded can create smoother transitions between movies, ensure there's no visual residue between movies of different sizes, and reduce the memory required by the Flash Player.

> **QUICK**TIP
>
> Loading a new movie into the same level as an existing movie automatically unloads the existing movie from the Flash Player.

FIGURE K-19
A Macromedia Flash site that takes advantage of using multiple movies

FIGURE K-20
Options for loading a new movie

This setting determines whether the new movie opens at a new level or into a movie clip target

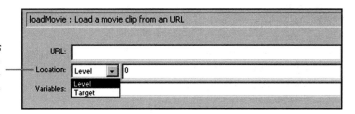

Each of the links on this page could open a separate .SWF file, saving the user download time

Load a movie

1. Open flk_4, then save it as **letterf.fla**.

   TIP The steps in the Objectives use relative paths to load new movies. Make sure to copy the two movies you will load, fish.swf and frog.swf, to the same location where you save the data file, letterf.fla.

2. Click the Arrow Tool on the toolbox (if necessary), click the fish button to select it, then open the Actions panel. ▶

3. Double-click loadMovie in the Browser/Network folder in the Actions toolbox.

4. Click the URL text box, type **fish.swf**, then compare your image to Figure K-21.

5. Test the scene, click the fish button, then compare your image to Figure K-22.

   The fish movie replaces the original movie.

   TIP If an error occurs, make sure that fish.swf is in the same location as letterf.fla.

6. Close the test window, then save your work.

You specified that a new movie replace the currently playing movie in the Flash Player when the user clicks a button.

FIGURE K-21
ActionScript to replace a movie with a new movie

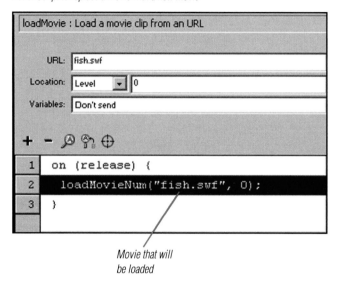

Movie that will
be loaded

FIGURE K-22
The fish movie loaded in place of the original movie

Using Advanced ActionScript

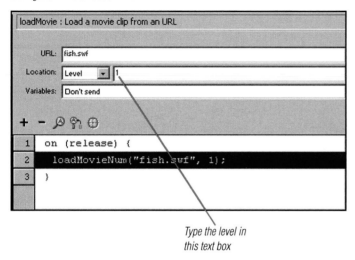

```
loadMovie : Load a movie clip from an URL

    URL:  fish.swf

Location:  Level    ▼  1

Variables:  Don't send

+  −  🔍 🐒 ⊕

1    on (release) {
2        loadMovieNum("fish.swf", 1);
3    }
```

*Type the level in
this text box*

FIGURE K-24

The fish movie loaded on top of the original movie

Set a level for a movie

1. Verify the fish button is still selected, then verify that the `loadMovieNum` action on Line 2 of the Script pane is still selected.

2. Double-click the Level text box, then type **1**, as shown in Figure K-23.

3. Test the scene, click the fish button, then compare your image to Figure K-24.

   The fish movie appears on top of the original movie.

4. Close the test window, then save your work.

You set a level for a movie.

Stack movies

1. Click the frog button to select it.

2. Double-click `loadMovie` in the Browser/Network folder in the Actions toolbox.

3. Click the URL text box, then type **frog.swf**.

4. Double-click the Level text box, then type **2** for the level.

5. Test the scene, click the fish button, click the frog button, then compare your image to Figure K-25.

   Each movie appears on top of the original movie. No matter the order in which you click the buttons, the frog movie will always appear on top.

6. Close the test window, then save your work.

You loaded two movies at different levels.

FIGURE K-25
The fish movie loaded at Level 1 and the frog movie at Level 2

Referencing loaded movies in ActionScript

You can create a reference to the timeline of a loaded movie by including the level number of the movie. For example, to add a `goto` action that goes to Frame 10 of the movie loaded at Level 1, type `_level1.gotoAndStop(10);`

FIGURE K-26

ActionScript to unload movies at Levels 1 and 2

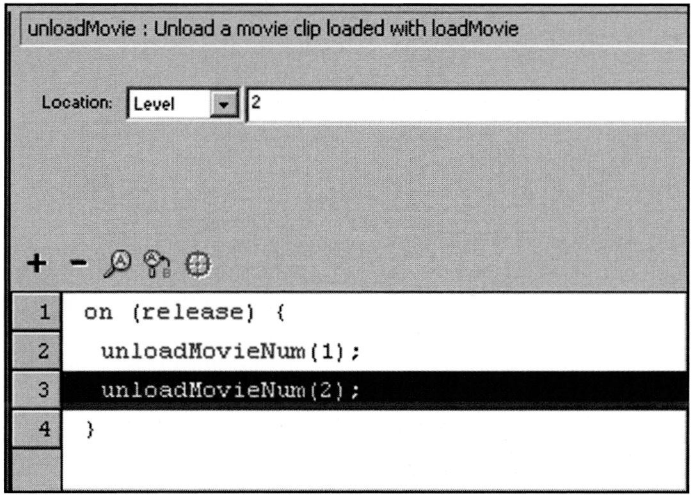

```
unloadMovie : Unload a movie clip loaded with loadMovie

Location:  Level  ▼  2

+  -  🔍 🐍 ⊕

1  on (release) {
2    unloadMovieNum(1);
3    unloadMovieNum(2);
4  }
```

1. Click the unload button to select it.

2. Double-click `unloadMovie` in the Browser/Network folder in the Actions toolbox.

3. Double-click the Level text box, then type **1**.

   This line of ActionScript removes the movie loaded at Level 1, which is fish.swf.

4. Double-click `unloadMovie` in the Browser/Network folder in the Actions toolbox.

5. Double-click the Level text box, type **2**, then compare your Script pane to Figure K-26.

   This line of ActionScript removes the movie loaded at Level 2, which is frog.swf.

6. Test the scene, clicking the fish, frog, and unload buttons in different sequences.

   The fish and frog movies both unload when you click the unload button.

7. Close the test window, save your work, then close the file.

You added actions to unload movies.

WORK WITH CONDITIONAL ACTIONS

What You'll Do

 In this lesson, you will work with conditional actions and use ActionScript to duplicate movie clip symbols.

Using the `else` and `else if` actions

In Unit I, you used the `if` action to test for a condition. If the condition was true, the `if` action ran a series of actions enclosed in braces. Otherwise, it skipped the actions in braces and ran the next set of actions in the Script pane.

ActionScript also includes an `else` action you can use to create more sophisticated branching. An `else` action lets you specify one set of actions to run if a condition is true, and an alternate set to run if the condition is false. If a condition has more than two possible states, you can use `else if` to set up a series of possible branches. For example, if you are creating an online test, there might be four possible answers a student could provide, and you might want to create a different branch for each answer. Figure K-27 shows ActionScript that uses `else if` to create multiple branches.

Creating conditional loops

A loop is an action or set of actions that repeat as long as a condition exists. Creating a loop can be as simple as taking a variable, assigning a value to it, executing a statement, and if the statement is false adding one to the variable and trying again. You can often just use an `if` action to create loops.

ActionScript includes other actions with which you can create more sophisticated conditional loops. `for`, `while`, and `do while` all let you set up conditions for a loop and actions to run repeatedly. `for` takes a series of arguments with which you set up a condition, a series of actions to take if the condition is true, and a counter that keeps track of the number of loops; this counter is often used in conjunction with the condition, for instance, to run the loop a user-specified number of times. `while` and `do while` let you enter a series of actions to run while a condition is true. The difference is that do while runs the actions at least one time, then evaluates if the condition is true, where while evaluates the condition and then runs the actions. Figure K-28 shows some examples of using ActionScript to create loops.

Duplicating movie clip symbol instances

An action frequently used with conditional loops is duplicateMovieClip. This action displays one of the more powerful abilities of ActionScript, which is to add and remove movie clip symbols as a movie

is playing. duplicateMovieClip creates a copy of a movie clip symbol instance; it includes arguments that let you specify a new instance name and a depth level at which to insert the new movie clip symbol (either in place of or on top of existing instances). You can then use the setProperty action or specific Properties actions (such as _x and _y) to change the location and appearance of the new instance of the movie clip symbol.

duplicateMovieClip is often used in games to create multiple copies of an object based on a variable or user interaction—for

example, a juggling game could ask a user how many balls they want to try to keep up in the air. Based on the answer, a looping action determines the number of times to run the duplicateMovieClip action.

QUICKTIP

There must already be an instance of the movie clip symbol on the stage for you to create duplicate instances. The new instance of the movie clip symbol always begins playing at the first frame.

FIGURE K-27
ActionScript to create multiple branches

```
1 on (release) {
2     if (answer == A) {
3         gotoAndStop(2);
4     } else if (answer == B) {
5         gotoAndStop(3);
6     } else if (answer == C) {
7         gotoAndPlay(4);
8     }
9 }
10
```

If the user types the answer A in an input text box, the movie jumps to Frame 2; other answers jump to other frames

FIGURE K-28
ActionScript to create loops

This for loop increments the variable n a number of times specified by a separate variable named counter

```
1 for (counter=0; counter<100; counter++) {
2 n++;}
3
```

```
1 n = 0
2 do {n++;
3 } while (n < 100);
```

This do while loop also increments a variable n, but repeats based on the value of n

Create conditional branching using `if` and `else` actions

1. Open flk_5.fla, then save it as **branching.fla**.

2. Click the Arrow Tool on the toolbox (if necessary), click the login button on the stage to select it, then open the Actions panel.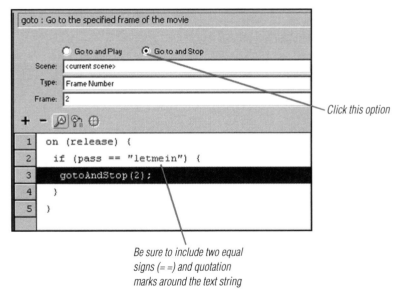

3. Verify that normal mode is selected, then double-click on in the Movie Control folder in the Actions toolbox.

4. Double-click `if` in the Conditions/Loops folder in the Actions toolbox.

   The action appears in the Script pane without a condition set.

5. Type **pass == "letmein"** in the Condition text box.

   "pass" is the variable name for the input text field on the Super Secure Login page.

6. Double-click `goto` in the Movie Control folder in the Actions toolbox.

7. Click the Go to and Stop option, double-click the Frame text box, type **2**, then compare your Script pane to Figure K-29.

8. Double-click `else` in the Conditions/Loops folder in the Actions toolbox.

(continued)

FIGURE K-29

Adding an `if` *action*

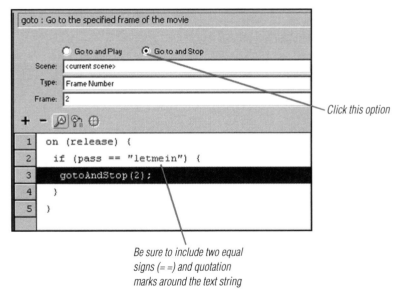

Click this option

```
on (release) {
    if (pass == "letmein") {
        gotoAndStop(2);
    }
}
```

Be sure to include two equal signs (= =) and quotation marks around the text string

FIGURE K-30

Adding an else *action*

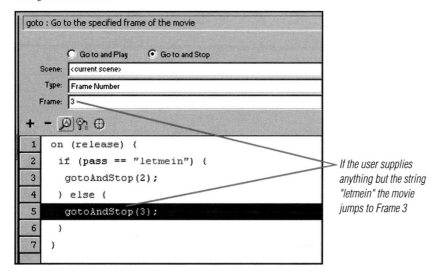

If the user supplies anything but the string "letmein" the movie jumps to Frame 3

9. Double-click goto in the Movie Control folder in the Actions toolbox.

10. Click the Go to and Stop option in the top of the Script pane, double-click the Frame text box, type **3**, then compare your Script pane to Figure K-30.

11. Test the scene, type **xyz** for the password, then click the login button.

 The movie jumps to the "Access Denied" screen.

12. Close the test window, test the scene again, type **letmein** for the password as shown in Figure K-31, then click the login button.

 The movie jumps to the "Access Granted" screen.

13. Close the test window, then save your work.

You used if *and* else *actions to create a conditional branch that takes different actions based on user behavior (correct input of password).*

FIGURE K-31

Entering the password to log in

Create a loop using `if`

1. Click the View Options icon on the Actions panel, then click Expert Mode. 🔄

2. Click Frame 1 on Layer 2, click the beginning of Line 1 in the Script pane, then press [Enter] (Win) or [return] (Mac) to move the `stop();` action to Line 2 and create a blank Line 1.

3. Click Line 1 in the Script pane, then type **n = 0;** on the line.

   This line of ActionScript creates a variable named "n" and sets the value of the variable to 0.

4. Click a gray area on the stage to deselect all objects, click the login button to select it, click at the end of Line 4 in the Script pane of the Actions panel, then press [Enter] (Win) or [return] (Mac) to create a blank Line 5.

5. Type **n++;** on Line 5 in the Script pane, then press [Enter] (Win) or [return] (Mac).

   This line of ActionScript increments the variable n by one each time the `else` statement is processed—that is, each time the user provides the wrong password.

   (continued)

FIGURE K-32

Using the `if` action to create a loop

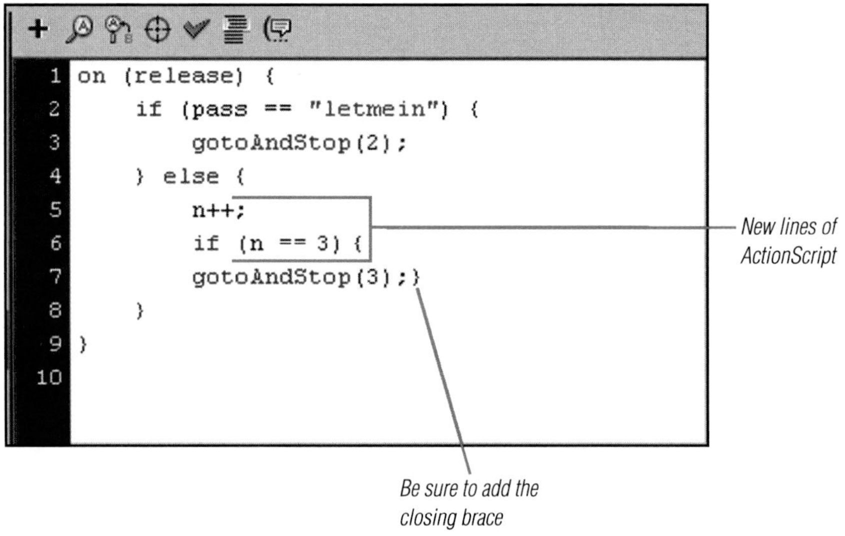

```
1  on (release) {
2      if (pass == "letmein") {
3          gotoAndStop(2);
4      } else {
5          n++;
6          if (n == 3) {
7          gotoAndStop(3);}
8      }
9  }
10
```

— New lines of ActionScript

Be sure to add the closing brace

FIGURE K-33

Logging in with an incorrect password

6. Type **if (n == 3) {** on Line 6 in the Script pane.

   This line of ActionScript creates a condition: the statements that follow the if action will only be processed when the variable n is equal to 3.

7. Click at the end of Line 7 in the Script pane, type **}**, then compare your Script pane to Figure K-32.

   The closing brace is necessary to complete the new if action.

8. Test the scene, type **xyz** for the password as shown in Figure K-33, then click the login button three times.

   The movie jumps to the Access Denied screen only after the third attempt to log in.

9. Close the test window, then save your work.

You used the if action to create a loop that, based on user behavior, repeats three times and then takes another action.

Add user feedback to the loop

1. Click the Text Tool on the toolbox, then open the Property inspector. **A**

2. Click the Text type list arrow, click Dynamic Text on the Property inspector, verify that Arial appears as the Font type, click the Font Size list arrow, drag the slider to **14**, click the Bold icon **B**, click the Show Border Around Text icon to deselect it, then draw a text box below the words "Super Secure Login," as shown in Figure K-34. ▤

3. Click the Variable text box in the Property inspector, type **feedback**, press [Enter] (Win) or [return] (Mac), then close the Property inspector.

4. Click the Arrow Tool on the toolbox, click the login button to select it, click at the end of Line 5 in the Script pane of the Actions panel, then press [Enter] (Win) or [return] (Mac) to create a blank Line 6. ▶

5. Type **feedback = "Sorry. Tries left: "** + **(3-n);** on Line 8 in the Script pane, then press [Enter] (Win) or [return] (Mac).

   This line of ActionScript populates the dynamic text field named feedback with a text string and number. The number is calculated by subtracting 3 (the maximum number of tries) from the variable n, which is incrementally counting the number of attempts the user makes.

   > TIP Be sure to include a blank space after the colon and before the closing quotation mark.

   (continued)

FIGURE K-34
Drawing the input text box

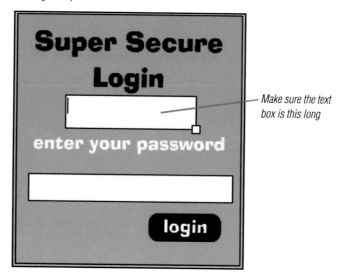

— Make sure the text box is this long

FIGURE K-35

ActionScript to provide user feedback

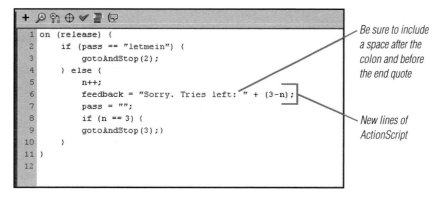

```
1  on (release) {
2      if (pass == "letmein") {
3          gotoAndStop(2);
4      } else {
5          n++;
6          feedback = "Sorry. Tries left: " + (3-n);
7          pass = "";
8          if (n == 3) {
9              gotoAndStop(3);}
10     }
11 }
12
```

Be sure to include a space after the colon and before the end quote

New lines of ActionScript

6. Type **pass = ""**; on Line 7 in the Script pane, then compare your Script pane to Figure K-35.

   This line of ActionScript clears the incorrect password the user has entered.

7. Test the scene, type **xyz** for the password, click the login button as shown in Figure K-36, then repeat twice more.

   The password screen provides feedback, and the movie jumps to the "Access Denied" screen only after the third attempt to enter the password.

8. Close the test window, then save and close branching.fla.

You added actions to provide user feedback as part of a conditional loop.

FIGURE K-36

Logging in with an incorrect password with user feedback

The **feedback = "Sorry. Tries left: " + (3-n);** *ActionScript statement populates the dynamic text box*

The **pass = "";** *ActionScript statement clears the input text box of the incorrect password*

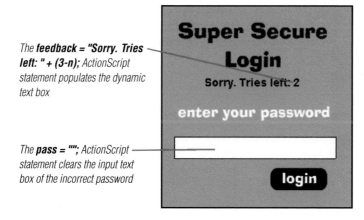

Using the Password line type in an input field

You may not want passwords to be visible onscreen as users enter them. For security, you can set an input text field to display asterisks rather than the actual keystrokes being typed by a user. To do this, display the Property inspector for the text field, click the Line type list arrow, then click Password.

Create a while loop to duplicate movie clip symbols

1. Open flk_6.fla, then save it as **duplicator.fla**.

   This file contains an input text field with the variable name "amount" and the face movie clip symbol.

2. Click the Arrow Tool on the toolbox, then click the duplicate button to select it. ▶

3. Click Line 1 on the Script pane in the Actions panel, type **on (release) {** then press [Enter] (Win) or [return] (Mac).

   > TIP A code hint menu will appear as you type the opening parenthesis of the on action. You can continue typing the release parameter, or double-click to select the parameter from the menu.

4. Type **n = 0;** on Line 2, then press [Enter] (Win) or [return] (Mac).

   This line of ActionScript creates a variable, n, and sets its value to 0.

5. Type **while (n < amount) {** on Line 3, then press [Enter] (Win) or [return] (Mac).

   This line of ActionScript creates a while loop that takes the n variable and checks to see if it is greater than the amount variable.

6. Type **duplicateMovieClip ("_root.face", "face_" + n, n);** on Line 4, then press [Enter] (Win) or [return] (Mac).

   This line of ActionScript runs as long as the while condition is true. It duplicates the face movie clip symbol instance, assigning it a name of the text string "face_" concatenated with the current value of the variable n, and putting it on a level determined by the current value of the variable n.

   (continued)

FIGURE K-37

ActionScript to create a loop to duplicate a movie clip symbol

```
1  on (release) {
2      n = 0;
3      while (n < amount) {
4          duplicateMovieClip ("_root.face", "face_" + n, n);
5          setProperty ("face_" + n, _x, random(250));
6          setProperty ("face_" + n, _y, random(200));
7          n++;
8      }
9  }
```

Be sure to include two parentheses—one to close the random action, and one to close the setProperty action

Using Advanced ActionScript

10 duplicate instances of the movie clip symbol appear on the stage

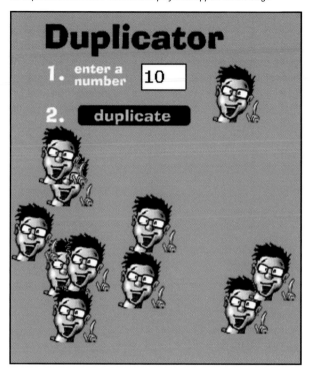

Using the `random` action

The `random` action returns a random integer between 0 and one less than the value specified as an argument for the action. You can use `random` with `setProperty` to create unpredictable behavior for movie clip symbols or to generate random numbers for variables. When using `random` to position movie clip symbols, consider adding an offset value to keep the movie clip symbols from overlapping other objects on the screen. For example, `setProperty("instance_" + n, _y, random(200)+130);` adds 130 units to the random number generated for the Y coordinate of the new movie clip symbols.

7. Type **setProperty ("face_" + n, _x, random(250));** on Line 5, then press [Enter] (Win) or [return] (Mac).

   This line of ActionScript sets the x coordinate of the new instance to a random number between 0 and 249 (1 less than 250, which is the argument value for the `random` action).

8. Type **setProperty ("face_" + n, _y, random(200));** on Line 6, then press [Enter] (Win) or [return] (Mac).

   This line of ActionScript sets the y coordinate of the new instance to a random number between 0 and 199.

9. Type **n++;** on Line 7, then press [Enter] (Win) or [return] (Mac).

   This line of ActionScript increments the value of the n variable by 1.

10. Type } on Line 8, then press [Enter] (Win) or [return] (Mac).

11. Type } on Line 9, then compare your Script pane to Figure K-37.

12. Test the scene, type **10** in the box next to the words "enter a number," click the duplicate button, then compare your image to Figure K-38.

    The ActionScript loops 10 times, creating 10 instances of the movie clip symbol on the screen.

13. Close the test window, then save and close duplicator.fla.

You used a `while` action to create a loop that duplicates a movie clip symbol a number of times specified by a user.

Create complex interactivity.

1. Open flk_7.fla, then save it as **skillsdemoK.fla**.

2. Click Frame 1 on the actions layer, open the Actions panel, switch to expert mode, if necessary, then add a `mouse.hide ();` action on Line 1 in the Script pane to hide the mouse cursor. (*Hint*: Don't forget to include a semicolon at the end of the action.)

3. Select the cross-hairs symbol on the stage, then open the Property inspector.

4. Assign the movie clip an instance name of **aim**, then close the Property inspector.

5. Open the Actions panel, then type `onClipEvent (enterFrame) {` on Line 1 in the Script pane to indicate the next set of actions should happen as soon as the movie clip instance displays, then add a new line.

6. Type `_root.aim._x = _root._xmouse;` on Line 2 in the Script pane to set the x coordinate of the aim movie clip instance equal to the x coordinate of the hidden mouse pointer, then add a new line. (*Hint*: If a code hint menu appears, continue typing to dismiss the menu.)

7. Type `_root.aim._y = _root._ymouse;` on Line 3 in the Script pane to set the y coordinate of the aim movie clip instance equal to the y coordinate of the hidden mouse pointer, then add a new line.

8. Type `}` (a closing brace) on Line 4 in the Script pane.

9. Test the scene. (*Hint*: The game ends when the value in the "shots" box falls below 0.)

10. Save your work.

Use ActionScript to create external links.

1. Click Frame 51 on the actions layer, then select the More Games button.

2. Switch to normal mode in the Actions panel, then double-click `getURL` in the Browser/Network folder in the Actions toolbox.

3. Type **http://www.macromedia.com** for the URL address, then select _self as the Window.

4. Select the Comments? button on the stage, then double-click `getURL` in the Browser/Network folder in the Actions toolbox.

5. Type **mailto:webmaster@server.com** as the URL link, then select _self as the Window.

6. Save your work.

Load new movies.

1. Click Frame 1 on the actions layer, then select the Easy button on the stage.

2. Click Line 3 in the Script pane, then add the `loadMovie` action from the Browser/Network folder in the Actions toolbox.

3. Type **easy_level.swf** for the URL address for the movie to load, then change the Level to **1**. (*Hint*: The two movies you will load, easy_level.swf and hard_level.swf, must be in the same file location where you saved skillsdemoK.fla.)

4. Click the Hard button to select it.

5. Click Line 3 in the Script pane, then add the click `loadMovie` action from the Browser/Network folder in the Actions toolbox.

6. Type **hard_level.swf** as the URL address for the movie to load, then change the Level to **1**.

7. Click Frame 50 on the actions layer, click Line 1 in the Script pane, add the `unloadMovie` action from the Browser/Network folder in the Actions toolbox, then change the Level to **1**.

8. Preview the movie in your default browser from the File menu.

9. Close the browser window, then save your work.

Work with conditional actions.

1. Click Frame 51 on the actions layer, then switch to expert mode in the Actions panel.

2. Click Line 1 in the Script pane, add a new line to move the `stop ();` action to Line 2, then click Line 1 again to begin adding actions.

3. Type `if (hits > 8) {` on Line 1 in the Script pane to set a condition, then press [Enter] (Win) or [return] (Mac).

4. Type `feedback = "You're a winner";}` on Line 2 in the Script pane to specify the actions to perform if the condition is true, then press [Enter] (Win) or [return] (Mac). (*Hint*: "feedback" is the variable name of a dynamic text box on this page.)

5. Type `else {` on Line 3 in the Script pane to perform different actions when the `if` condition is not true, then press [Enter] (Win) or [return] (Mac).

6. Type `feedback = "Better luck next time";}` on Line 4 in the Script pane to specify the alternate actions.

7. Test the scene.

8. Compare your image to Figure K-39, save your work, then close skillsdemoK.fla.

FIGURE K-39
Completed Skills Review

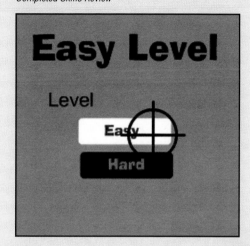

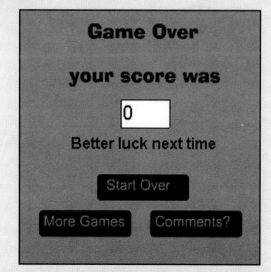

Ultimate Tours would like you to build a banner for their Web site which, when a button on the banner is clicked, will load a new movie containing their latest travel specials. By creating the banner in one SWF file and the specials in another, Ultimate Tours can update the specials at any time, just by replacing one file. As a way to encourage users to look at and interact with the banner, they would also like you to create an input text field in the banner which, when the user types in the name of a city and clicks a button, displays a page from *www.weather.com* with the current weather for that location.

1. Open flk_8, then rename the file **ultimateK.fla**.

2. Select the see specials button, then open the Actions panel in normal mode.

3. Add actions which, upon a click of the button, load a new movie called **specials.swf** at Level 1. (*Hint*: Use the `on (release)` and `loadMovieNum` action to create this effect. The specials.swf movie must be in the same file location where you saved ultimateK.fla.)

4. Click Frame 1 on the content layer, click the Text Tool on the toolbox, then draw an input text box beneath the text that reads, "Traveling? Type a city to check the weather:" Use these settings: color of black, font of Times New Roman, size of 12, Bold, with a border displayed around text. Assign the new input text box a variable name of **where**.

5. Select the get weather button, then in the Script pane of the Actions panel add a `getURL` action which, upon a click of the button, uses the GET method to send variables to a CGI script with a URL of **http://www.weather.com/search/search**. The new Web site should open in the current browser window.

6. Test the scene, click the see specials button to load the new movie, then type a city name and press the get weather button.

7. Save your work, then compare your image to Figure K-40.

FIGURE K-40
Completed Project Builder 1

As the finishing touches to your portfolio, add two new pages: one that contains examples of the Macromedia Flash work you have done throughout this book, and one that creates a password-protected clients-only area. You will create the links to your Macromedia Flash movies by loading new SWF files. You can use your favorites from the files you have developed throughout this book, or any other SWF files you have created on your own.

1. Open portfolioJ.fla and save it as **portfolioK.fla**. (*Hint*: If you did not create portfolioJ.fla, see your instructor.)
2. Create a new page called **Flash Samples**, using a format that fits in visually with the rest of your site. On this page, include at least three buttons, each of which, when clicked, loads a new Flash movie at Level 1. (*Hint*: New movies appear starting in the upper-left corner of the current movie. You may need to reduce the size of your SWF files or change the location of your navigation buttons to achieve the effect you want.)
3. Create a new page called **Clients Only**. On this page, create text that reads "Enter your password," and then create an input text box with the variable name **password**.
4. Create another new page that says, **Welcome to the clients only area.**
5. Create another new page that says, **Sorry, that is not correct. Please contact me to receive or verify your password.** Then add

a button to the page which, when clicked, opens the user's default e-mail program to a new mail message with your e-mail address filled in.

6. On the Clients Only page that prompts for a password, create a button with the text **Submit**. Open the Actions panel, then set up a conditional action which, if the user types the word "password" in the input text box, jumps to the "welcome" page, or, if the user types anything else, jumps to the "sorry" page.

FIGURE K-41
Completed Project Builder 2

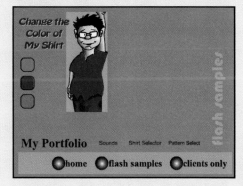

7. Add buttons to your portfolio home page which, when clicked, jump to the new Flash Samples and Clients Only pages.
8. Add an `unloadMovieNum(1)` action to each navigation button on the "Flash Samples page" that jumps to a new page. (*Hint*: If you don't add this action, the movies you load on the Flash Samples page will remain loaded, even when you navigate away from the Flash Samples page.)
9. Test the scene.
10. Save your work, then compare your movie to Figure K-41.

DESIGN PROJECT

Figure K-42 shows a page from a Web site created using Macromedia Flash. Study the figure and complete the following. For each question, indicate how you determined your answer.

1. Connect to the Internet, and go to *www.course.com*. Navigate to the page for this book, click the Student Online Companion, then click the link for this unit.

2. Open a document in a word processor or open a new Macromedia Flash movie, save the file as **dpuUnitK**, then answer the following questions. (*Hint*: Use the Text Tool in Macromedia Flash.)

   ■ What is the purpose of this site? Does the design of the site contribute to its purpose?

   ■ Move the mouse pointer around the screen and note the different effects as you pass over links. Do you think these effects were achieved with ActionScript, or some other way?

   ■ Click the links in the main navigation bar. What changes occur on the screen? Do you think the links are jumping to a different frame in this movie, or loading a new movie? What specific actions could be used to achieve this effect?

   ■ List some of the advantages of loading a new movie for links in the context of this site.

■ Click the Portfolio link, click the link for Internet samples, select a sample, then click the Launch Project button. What happens? What specific actions might be associated with the Launch Project button to achieve this effect?

■ Near the bottom of the page, there is a field to enter an e-mail address and press a Submit button. What do you think happens when you press the Submit button? What specific actions might be involved in the processing of the e-mail information?

FIGURE K-42
Design Project

Your group can assign elements of the project to individual members, or work collectively to create the finished product.

Your group has volunteered to use Macromedia Flash to create an interactive, educational counting game that will get first-graders comfortable with computers. The game will display a random number of cookies spilled from a cookie jar, ask students to count the cookies and type the number, and then give feedback on whether or not the answer is correct.

1. Open flk_9.fla, then save it as **counting_game.fla**.
2. Click Frame 1 on the content layer, then create an input text box with a variable named **check** above the go button that is big enough to accommodate a two-digit number. Settings: Arial, 16pt, border displayed around text.
3. Click Frame 2 on the content layer, then create a dynamic text box with a variable named **score** that fills the area above the cookie jar image. Use these settings: Arial, 24pt, Multiline line type.
4. Copy the dynamic text box named score from Frame 2 of the content layer to the same location in Frame 3 of the content layer.
5. Select the cookie movie clip symbol in Frame 1 on the content layer, open the Property inspector, then assign it an instance name of **cookie**.

6. Select the start button in Frame 1 on the content layer, then add ActionScript which, upon a click of the button, does the following:
   - Creates a variable named value and sets it to a random number between 1 and 5
   - Creates a variable named n, and sets its value to 0
   - Creates a loop using the `while` action, which says that while the variable named n is less than the variable named value, duplicate the cookie movie clip symbol, name the new instance with the word "cookie," an underscore, and the value of the variable n, and set the new instance at a depth of the value of the variable n. The `while` loop should also use two `SetProperty` actions to set the location of the new movie clip instance: the x coordinate should be set to a random number between 1 and 200, with an offset of 10, and the Y coordinate should be set to a random number between 1 and 100, with an offset of 250.
   - Increments the value of the variable n by 1
7. Select the go button in Frame 1 of the content layer, then add ActionScript that, upon a click of the button, does the following:
   - Uses the `if` action to check if the number in the variable named check is equal to the number in the variable named value and, if so, jumps to Frame 2 and populates the dynamic text box named score with the words "Good job, the number of cookies that spilled is" and then the variable named value.
   - Uses the `else` action to perform the following actions when the condition is not true: jump to Frame 3 and populate the dynamic text box named score with the words "No, that's not right, the number of cookies that spilled is" and then the variable named value.
8. Test the scene, save your work, then compare your image to Figure K-43.

FIGURE K-43
Completed Group Project

Read the following information carefully!

Find out from your instructor the location of the Data Files you need and the location where you will store your files.

- To complete many of the units in this book, you need to use Data Files. Your instructor will either provide you with a copy of the Data Files or ask you to make your own copy.

- If you need to make a copy of the Data Files, you will need to copy a set of files from a file server, standalone computer, or the Web to the drive and location where you will be storing your Data Files.

- Your instructor will tell you which computer, drive letter, and folders contain the files you need, and where you will store your files.

- You can also download the files by going to *www.course.com*. See the inside back cover of this book for instructions to download your files.

Copy and organize your Data Files.

- Use the Data Files List to organize your files to a zip drive, network folder, hard drive, or other storage device.

- Create a subfolder for each unit in the location where you are storing your files, and name it according to the unit title (e.g., Unit A).

- For each unit you are assigned, copy the files listed in the **Data File Supplied** column into that unit's folder.

- Store the files you modify or create in each unit in the unit folder.

Find and keep track of your Data Files and completed files.

- Use the **Data File Supplied** column to make sure you have the files you need before starting the unit or exercise indicated in the Unit column.

- Use the **Student Saves File As** column to find out the filename you use when saving your changes to a provided Data File.

- Use the **Student Creates File** column to find out the filename you use when saving your new file for the exercise.

Macromedia Flash MX

Unit	Data File Supplied	Student Saves File As	Student Creates File	Used In
A	none		devenvironment.fla	Lesson 1
	fla_1.fla	demomovie.fla		Lesson 2
	none		tween.fla	Lesson 3
	none		layers.fla	Lesson 4
	none	none		Lesson 5
	fla_2.fla	skillsdemoA.fla		Skills Review
	none		demonstration.fla	Project Builder 1
	fla_3.fla	recycle.fla		Project Builder 2
	none		dpuUnitA	Design Project
	none	none		Group Project
B	none		tools.fla	Lessons 1–4
	flb_1.fla	layersB.fla		Lesson 5
	none		skillsdemoB.fla	Skills Review
	none		ultimatetoursB.fla	Project Builder 1
	none		portfolioB.fla	Project Builder 2
	none		dpuUnitB	Design Project
	none		jazzclub.fla	Group Project
C	flc_1.fla	coolcar.fla		Lesson 1
	flc_2.fla	CarRace.fla		Lessons 2–4
	flc_3.fla	skillsdemoC.fla		Skills Review
	(files continued from Unit B)	ultimatetoursC.fla		Project Builder 1
	(files continued from Unit B)	portfolioC.fla		Project Builder 2
	none		dpuUnitC	Design Project
	none		isa.fla	Group Project
D	fld_1.fla	frameAn.fla		Lesson 1
	fld_2.fla	carAn.fla		Lesson 2
	fld_3.fla	carPath.fla		Lesson 3
	fld_4.fla	carRotate.fla		Lesson 4
		frameAn.fla		Lesson 5

Unit	Data File Supplied	Student Saves File As	Student Creates File	Used In
	fld_5.fla	skillsdemoD.fla		Skills Review
	(files continued from Unit C)	ultimatetoursD.fla		Project Builder 1
	(files continued from Unit C)	portfolioD.fla		Project Builder 2
	none		dpuUnitD	Design Project
	none		summerBB.fla	Group Project
E	fle_1.fla	antiqueCar.fla		Lesson 1
	fle_2.fla	morphCar.fla		Lesson 1
	fle_3.fla	shapeHints.fla		Lesson 1
	fle_4.fla	classicCC.fla		Lesson 2
	fle_5.fla beep.wav CarSnd.wav	rallySnd.fla		Lesson 3
	fle_6.fla	cccHome.fla		Lesson 4
	fle_7.fla	coolCars.fla		Lesson 5
	fle_8.fla	skillsdemoE.fla		Skills Review
	(files continued from Unit D) applause.wav click.wav	ultimatetoursE.fla		Project Builder 1
	portfolioD.fla	portfolioE.fla		Project Builder 2
	none		dpuUnitE	Design Project
	none		zodiac.fla	Group Project
F	flf_1.fla	planeLoop.fla planeLoop.swf planeLoop.html planeLoop.gif planeLoop.jpeg		Lesson 1
	flf_2.fla	planeFun.fla		Lesson 2
		planeFun.swf planeFun.html		Lesson 3
	index.html planeGo.swf planeGo.html planeGo.fla	planeGo.fla		Lesson 4

Unit	Data File Supplied	Student Saves File As	Student Creates File	Used In
	flf_3.fla	skillsdemoF.fla skillsdemoF.swf skillsdemoF.html skillsdemoF.gif skillsdemoF.jpeg		Skills Review
	(files continued from Unit E)	ultimatetoursF.fla ultimatetoursF.gif ultimatetoursF.html ultimatetoursF.jpg ultimatetoursF.swf		Project Builder 1
	(files continued from Unit E)	portfolioF.fla portfolioF.gif portfolioF.html portfolioF.jpg portfolioF.swf		Project Builder 2
			dpuUnitF	Design Project
			[selectedfilename].fla *[selectedfilename]*.swf *[selectedfilename]*.html *[selectedfilename]*.gif *[selectedfilename]*.jpeg	Group Project
G	dragonfly.png grass.jpg tree.ai moon.jpg sky.jpg		gsamples.fla	Lessons 1–4
	logo.fh10 mountain.jpg nightsky.jpg roses.jpg		skillsdemoG.fla	Skills Review
	gtravel1.jpg gtravel2.jpg gtravel3.jpg gtravel4.jpg gtravel5.jpg gtravel6.jpg		ultimatetoursG.fla	Project Builder 1
	(files continued from Unit F)	portfolioG.fla		Project Builder 2
	none		dpuUnitG	Design Project

Unit	Data File Supplied	Student Saves File As	Student Creates File	Used In
	gantho1.jpg gantho2.jpg gantho3.jpg gantho4.jpg gantho5.jpg		anthoartG.fla	Group Project
H	flh_1.fla	animated_leaves.fla		Lesson 1
	flh_2.fla	animated_trees.fla		Lesson 2
	flh_3.fla	dragonfly.fla		Lessons 3 & 4
	flh_4.fla	skillsdemoH.fla		Skills Review
	(files continued from Unit G)	ultimatetoursH.fla		Project Builder 1
	(files continued from Unit G)	portfolioH.fla		Project Builder 2
	none		dpuUnitH	Design Project
	none		ocean_life.fla	Group Project
I	fli_1.fla	sale.fla		Lesson 1
	fli_2.fla	shirt.fla		Lesson 2
	fli_3.fla	shapes.fla		Lesson 3
	fli_4.fla	math.fla		Lesson 4
	fli_5.fla	skillsdemoI.fla		Skills Review
	(files continued from Unit H)	ultimatetoursI.fla		Project Builder 1
	(files continued from Unit H)	portfolioI.fla		Project Builder 2
	none		dpuUnitI	Design Project
	none		test_question.fla	Group Project
J	flj_1.fla	vectors.fla		Lesson 1
	flj_2.fla	supertips.fla		Lesson 2
		nightclub.fla		Lesson 3
	flj_3.fla	levels.fla		Lesson 4
	flj_4.fla	skillsdemoJ.fla		Skills Review
	flj_5.fla	ultimatetoursJ.fla		Project Builder 1

Unit	Data File Supplied	Student Saves File As	Student Creates File	Used In
	(files continued from Unit I) accent1.mp3 accent2.mp3 background.mp3 portfolio_voiceover.wav	portfolioJ.fla		Project Builder 2
	none		dpuUnitJ	Design Project
	flj_6.fla	game_prototype.fla		Group Project
K	flk_1.fla	interactive.fla		Lesson 1
	flk_2.fla flk_3.fla	links.fla search.fla		Lesson 2
	flk_4.fla fish.swf frog.swf	letterf.fla		Lesson 3
	flk_5.fla flk_6.fla	branching.fla duplicator.fla		Lesson 4
	flk_7.fla easy_level.swf hard_level.swf	skillsdemoK.fla		Skills Review
	flk_8.fla specials.swf	ultimatetoursK.fla		Project Builder 1
	(files continued from Unit J) shirt.swf shirt2.swf sounds.swf	portfolioK.fla		Project Builder 2
	none		dpuUnitK	Design Project
	flk_9.fla	counting_game.fla		Group Project

Absolute path
A path that works downward from the top level of a movie.

ActionScript
A scripting language that allows those with programming expertise to create sophisticated actions.

Actions panel
The panel where you create and edit actions for an object or frame.

ADPCM (Adaptive Differential Pulse-Code Modulation)
A sound compression option best used for short sounds, such as those used for buttons or accents. When you select this option, you can also set sound conversion from stereo to mono (which will reduce file size), a sampling rate (a lower sampling rate degrades sound quality but reduces file size), and a number of bits (again, a lower bit rate reduces both sound quality and file size).

Animated graphic symbol
An animation stored as a single, reusable symbol in the Library panel.

Animation
The perception of motion caused by the rapid display of a series of still images.

Balance
In screen design, the distribution of optical weight in the layout. Optical weight is the ability of an object to attract the viewer's eye, as determined by the object's size, shape, color, etc.

Bandwidth profiler
A feature used when testing a Flash movie that allows you to view a graphical representation of the size of each frame.

Bitmap image
An image based on pixels, rather than mathematical formulas. Also referred to as a **raster image**.

Break apart
The process of making each area of color in a bitmap image into a discrete element you can manipulate separately from the rest of the image. Also, the process of breaking apart text to place each character in a separate text block.

Code hints
Hints appearing in a pop-up window that give the syntax or possible parameters for an action as you are entering the action in expert mode in the Actions panel. To see a code hint, type the action statement, then type an opening parenthesis. To dismiss the code hint, type a closing parenthesis or press Esc.

Controller
A window that provides the playback controls for a movie.

Decrement action
An ActionScript operator, indicated by — (two minus signs), that subtracts 1 unit from a variable or expression.

Design notes
A file (.mno) that contains the original source file (.png or .fla) when a Fireworks document or Macromedia Flash file is exported to Dreamweaver.

Dot syntax
A way to refer to the hierarchical nature of the path to a movie clip symbol, variable, function, or other object, similar to the way slashes are used to create a path name to a file in some operating systems.

Dynamic text field
A field created on the stage with the Text Tool that takes information entered by a user and stores it as a variable.

Event sound
A sound that plays independently of the timeline. The sound starts in the keyframe to which it is added, but can continue playing even after a movie ends. An event sound must download completely before it begins playing.

Expert mode
A display option in the Actions panel that allows you to write ActionScript directly in the Script pane.

Expressions
Formulas for manipulating or evaluating the information in variables.

External links
Links from a Macromedia Flash file or movie to another Web site, another file, or an e-mail program.

File Transfer Protocol (FTP)
A standard method for transferring files from a development site to a Web server.

Flash player
A program that needs to be installed on a computer to view a Flash movie.

Frame animation
An animation created by specifying the object that is to appear in each frame of a sequence of frames (also called a frame-by-frame animation).

Frame label
A text name for a keyframe, which can be referenced in actions.

Frames
Individual cells that make up the timeline in Flash.

GET
An option for sending variables from a Macromedia Flash movie to another URL or file for processing. GET is best for small amounts of information, as it can only send a string of up to 1,024 characters. Information sent using GET is appended to the URL string, and so appears in the address field of the browser, which makes this method less secure than the alternate method, POST.

Graphics Interchange Format (GIF)
A graphics file format that creates compressed bitmap images.

Increment action
An ActionScript operator, indicated by ++ (two plus signs), that adds 1 unit to a variable or expression.

Input text field
A field created on the stage with the Text Tool that displays information derived from variables.

Joint Photographic Experts Group (JPEG)
A graphics file format that is especially useful for photographic images.

Keyframe
A frame that signifies a change in an object being animated.

Layers
Rows on the timeline that are used to organize objects and that allow the stacking of objects on the stage.

Level
A hierarchical designation used when loading new movies into the current movie; similar to layers on the timeline.

Linkage identifier string
The name used to identify a sound from the Library panel in an ActionScript statement. You assign a linkage identifier in the Linkage Properties dialog box.

Macromedia Flash MX
An authoring program that allows you to create compelling interactive experiences, primarily by using animation.

Mask layer
A layer used to cover up the objects on another layer(s) and, at the same time, create a window through which you can view various objects on the other layer.

Morphing
The process of changing one object into another, sometimes unrelated, object.

Motion guide layer
A path used to specify how an animated object moves around the stage.

Motion tweening
The process used in Flash to automatically fill in the frames between keyframes in an animation that changes the properties of an object such as the position, size, or color.

Movement
In screen design, the way the viewer's eye moves through the objects on the screen.

Movie clip symbol
An animation stored as a single, reusable symbol in the Library panel. It has its own timeline, independent of the main timeline.

MP3 (MPEG-1 Audio Layer 3)
A sound compression option primarily used for music and longer streaming sounds, but which can also be applied to speech.

Nesting
Including another symbol within a symbol, such as nesting a graphic symbol, button, or another movie clip symbol within a movie clip symbol.

Normal mode
A display option in the Actions panel in which you build ActionScript by selecting actions from the Actions toolbox.

Number variable
In ActionScript, a double-precision floating-point number with which you can use arithmetic operators, such as addition and subtraction.

Panels
Components in Flash used to view, organize, and modify objects and features in a movie.

_parent
In creating target paths with dot syntax, the movie clip in which the current clip is nested.

Parent-child relationship
A description of the hierarchical relationship that develops between nested symbols, especially nested movie clip symbols. When you insert a movie clip inside another movie clip, the inserted clip is considered the child and the original clip is the parent. If you place an instance of a parent clip into a scene and change it, you will also affect the nested child clip; and any time you change the instance of a parent clip, the associated child clip updates automatically.

Playhead
An indicator specifying which frame is playing in the timeline of a Flash movie.

Portable Network Graphics (PNG)
A graphics file format developed specifically for images that are to be used on the Web.

POST
An option for sending variables from a Macromedia Flash movie to another URL or file for processing. POST collects variables and sends them in a file. POST can accommodate more variable information and is more secure than the alternate method of sending variables, GET.

Publish
The process used to generate the files necessary for delivering Flash movies on the Web.

QuickTime
A file format used for movies and animations that requires a QuickTime Player.

Raster image
An image based on pixels, rather than mathematical formulas. Also referred to as a **bitmap** image.

Raw
A sound compression option that exports a sound with no compression. You can still set stereo to mono conversion and a sampling rate.

Relative path
A path for a link or to an object that is based on the location of the file in which the path is entered.

_root
Refers to the main timeline when creating target paths with dot syntax.

Scene
A section of the timeline designated for a specific part of the movie. Scenes are a way to organize long movies.

Shape hints
Indicators used to control the shape of a complex object as it changes appearance during an animation.

Shape tweening
The process of animating an object so that it changes into another object.

Sound object
A built-in object that allows ActionScript to recognize and control a sound. To associate a specific sound with a sound object, use the new Sound action.

Speech compression
A sound compression option best used for voice-overs and other speech. You can also set a sampling rate when you choose this option.

Stage
The area of the Flash workspace that contains the objects that are part of the movie and that will be seen by the viewers.

Stage-level object
A vector object that you draw directly on the stage, unlike a symbol, which you place on the stage from the Library panel.

Start synchronization option
A synchronization option that can be applied to sounds and that act just like event sounds, but will not begin again if an instance of the sound is already playing.

Stop synchronization option
A synchronization option that can be applied to sounds and lets you end an event sound at a specific keyframe.

Streaming sound
A sound that is tied to the timeline. No matter its length, a streaming sound stops at the end of the movie. Streaming sounds can start playing as they download.

String variable
In ActionScript, a sequence of characters including letters, numbers, and punctuation. To indicate a string variable, enclose it in single or double quotation marks.

Target
A reference in an action to a movie clip symbol or other object that includes a path and name.

Time In control, Time Out control
Controls in the Edit Envelope dialog box that let you trim the length of a sound file.

Timeline
The component of Flash used to organize and control the movie's contents over time, by specifying when each object appears on the stage.

Toolbox
The component of Flash that contains a set of tools used to draw, select, and edit graphics and text. It is divided into four sections.

Trace
The process of turning a bitmap image into vector paths for animation and other purposes.

Tweening
The process of filling the in-between frames in an animation.

Unity
In screen design, how the various screen objects relate. Inter-screen unity refers to the design that viewers encounter as they navigate from one screen to another.

Upload
The process of transferring files from a local drive to a Web server.

Vector image
An image calculated and stored according to mathematical formulas rather than pixels, resulting in smaller file size and a robust ability to resize the images without a loss in quality.

Web server
A computer dedicated to hosting Web sites that is connected to the Internet and configured with software to handle requests from browsers.

Financing
State and Local
Governments

Studies of Government Finance